DATE DUE

JA 3 1 '01			

DEMCO 38-296

Policy Making in
ISRAEL

Pitt Series in Policy and Institutional Studies

BERT A. ROCKMAN, *Editor*

Policy Making in
ISRAEL

*Routines for Simple Problems and
Coping with the Complex*

IRA SHARKANSKY

University of Pittsburgh Press

Published by the University of Pittsburgh Press, Pittsburgh, Pa. 15261

Copyright © 1997, University of Pittsburgh Press

Manufactured in the United States of America

Printed on acid-free paper

10 9 8 7 6 5 4 3 2 1

LIBRARY OF CONGRESS CATALOGING-IN-PUBLICATION DATA
Sharkansky, Ira.
    Policy making in Israel : routines for simple problems and coping with the
complex / Ira Sharkansky.
        p.   cm. — (Pitt series in policy and institutional studies)
    Includes bibliographical references and index.
    ISBN 0-8229-3984-3 (cloth : acid-free paper).
— ISBN 0-8229-5633-0 (pbk. : acid-free paper)
        1. Israel—Politics and government—Decision making.
    2. Political planning—Israel—Decision making.   1. Title.
    11. Series.
    JQ1830.A56S53   1997
    320' .6' 095694—dc21   97-4756
                                                                    CIP

A CIP catalog record for this book is available from the British Library.

Contents

Preface

Since coming to Israel from the United States in 1975, I have asked myself, and have been asked by others, why I emigrated. The answer, in part, is that I was fascinated by the country's politics and policy making. At the beginning of my career, I had sought a teaching position in the American South in order to learn at first hand the problems and responses of people in politically difficult circumstances. Then, after a period at the University of Wisconsin–Madison, I was offered a position at the Hebrew University in Jerusalem. This, I thought, would give me the opportunity to observe politics and policy making at their most difficult, and to observe Jews dealing with the experience of building a still new country in the problematic context of the Middle East. I recall a morning newspaper in Madison that featured a debate in the Wisconsin legislature about the length of the deer hunting season. That story did not send me to Israel. Wisconsin's reactions to the war in Vietnam and to the issues of racism, sexism, and environmental pollution provided their own learning experiences. Nonetheless, the momentary preoccupation of Wisconsin with the deer hunting season suggested to me that life in Jerusalem would be more meaningful.

Against this background, it should be no surprise that the nature of policy problems continued to attract my attention. Israeli political science as well as Israeli politics kept me on this track. My colleague Yehezkel Dror is well known for writings that examine the normative side of policy analysis and how governments should structure themselves and approach their problems. Yehezkel noticed my work when I wrote a critical review of his seminal book *Public Policymaking Reexamined.* In helping to bring me to Hebrew University, he sought to introduce to the university an approach to policy analysis distinctly different from his own. Over the years we have had numerous conversations and not a few disagreements, both directly and through the comments of students studying in his classes and mine. Another colleague, David Dery, has sharpened my interests by his repeated queries about how policy makers think about the issues that face them.

More than twenty years of working alongside Yehezkel Dror have not led me to abandon an empirical approach to policy analysis for a normative approach. The questions "What influences policy decisions?" and "How do policy makers behave?" have greater appeal for me than "What should governments do?" or "How should governments make their decisions?" To be sure, the empirical and normative issues intersect. In my work I have concentrated on the utility of coping with difficult or insoluble issues, as opposed to offering solutions for policy makers. Over time, coping becomes a solution.

The thrust of this book is description and analysis directed at the question of how Israeli officials respond to their problems. It returns to and updates detailed analyses of mine published earlier. Here I examine those problems using a scale that arrays policy issues from least to most difficult and links policy issues with styles of policy making. Routines prevail in dealing with simple problems, while coping prevails in dealing with difficult problems. Most of the issues examined here are difficult. Not only do they attract a disproportionate amount of attention from policy makers, they are also the most interesting for political scientists. Difficult problems cause a society's cleavages to present themselves and give politicans opportunities to display their creativity or their lack of suitability.

Although a model that links degrees of difficulty with routines or coping may appear simplistic, it explains much of what occurs in the governments of Israel and other countries. If the model adopted here joins other simplifications that have proved useful in policy analysis, like the weight of incrementalism and economic influences on policy decisions, then this book's message will remain relevant despite the changing details of Israel's problems and policies.

CHAPTER 1

Introduction

The primary purpose of this book is to describe key features of policy making in Israel by examining issues that have troubled the country's officials and citizens for many years. A secondary purpose is to explain the difficulty of problems influences policy makers. Israel provides an excellent setting for describing and explaining this linkage between a problem's difficult and the style of policy making. Israel seems to have a greater incidence of serious problems than the typical democracy. This book does not systematically compare Israel with other countries. However, it does suggest possibilities of cross-national comparative analysis. The present chapter and chapter 2, in particular, offer a discussion of policy problems and policy making that will allow the reader to place the Israeli material in a comparative context.[1]

Israel and Its Problems

Political scientists in Israel and elsewhere identify Israel as a Western-style democracy, in the same category as the countries of Western Europe and North America, Australia, New Zealand, and Japan.[2] These countries all enjoy freedom of political discussion, orderly elections and changes of government, and high levels of economic development. Israel deserves a place in this group, although its placement is problematic for several reasons.

Much of Israel's population is not "Western," or has only recently become Westernized. Jews who migrated only a generation or two ago from North Africa, the Balkans, Yemen, Iran, Iraq, and Central Asia account, with their descendants, for more than one-half of the Jewish population. They are called Oriental (that is, Eastern) Jews or Sephardim, after the Sephardi (Spanish) ritual followed in their synagogues; most Jews of European background (except for those of Greece, Bulgaria, Turkey, and Yugoslavia) are called Ashkenazim. That portion of Israel's population that is not Jewish—18 percent—are mostly of Palestinian or other Middle Eastern background. About 10 percent of the Jewish population is ultra-Orthodox. Their education focuses almost exclusively on religious texts, is strictly segregated by sex, and provides little or no instruction in science, mathematics, secular history, or the other humanities.

In per capita GNP and other economic indicators, Israel ranks either among the poorest of the First World nations or among the wealthiest of the Third World nations. The per capita GNP figures in U.S. dollars for a representative group of countries in 1993 appear in table 1.1.

Israel has the political structure and formal procedures of a parliamentary democracy. Numerous political parties compete in an electoral system based on proportional representation. Transitions of political power take place in an orderly fashion. The political culture features shrill criticism directed at government leaders and policies by members of the Knesset (parliament), journalists, and distinguished individuals. From within the government establishment Israel's Office of the State Comptroller criticizes government policies and the work of government administrators.

The most sensitive questions about Israel's democracy concern the balance of opportunities between the Jewish majority and the non-Jewish minority.[3] No democracy is truly egalitarian, but Israel explicitly departs from the egalitarian standard by proclaiming itself a Jewish state. Israeli intellectuals (Jews and non-Jews) and government reports concede that Jews receive the lion's share of political and policy benefits. Intellectuals argue about whether it is possible to justify Israel's democratic imbalance on the basis of security threats, the small size of the non-Jewish minority, or the disinclination of the Palestinians to recognize the legitimacy of the Israeli regime.

Key ministers and senior technocrats in Israel's government dominate national policy making. As in other national parliaments, the principal work of the Knesset is to support the govenment. It is less a policy maker than a forum for debate, providing opportunities for opposition parties to vent their criticism. Unlike their counterparts in the U.S. Congress, Knesset members and committees can rely on little in the way of staff assistance, and they seldom make major changes to govern-

TABLE I.I Gross National Product per Capita
for Representative Countries, 1993

Switzerland	$35,750
United States	24,780
Sweden	24,740
Singapore	20,130
Italy	19,840
United Kingdom	18,050
Israel	**13,920**
Spain	13,580
Portugal	8,950
South Korea	7,660
Greece	7,480
Mexico	3,730
Chile	3,170
Malaysia	3,140
South Africa	2,910
Colombia	1,390

SOURCE: *World Data 1995* (Washington, D.C.: World Bank,
1995), CD-Rom version.

ment proposals. As for municipal governments, they have virtually no
formal autonomy to determine their own policies. As we will see, however, the style of Israel's democracy rewards aggressive activists, who
know how to maneuver for opportunities outside the framework of formal rules.

To a greater degree than other Western democracies, Israel has suffered severely from war, terrorist attacks, heavy immigration, boundary
disputes, economic uncertainty, ethnic and religious strife, and the
scars of the Holocaust and other persecutions. Since 1948 some 14,000
Israelis have died as a result of military engagements, not counting
civilians killed in terrorist raids.[4] The American equivalent would be
900,000 deaths, but in fact only about 90,000 American military personnel died in the Korean and Vietnam wars.[5] Another 300,000 Americans
died in World War II (0.2 percent of the national population), at a time
when the Nazis and their allies were killing 40 percent of the world's
Jews. A substantial part of the Israeli population comprises Holocaust
survivors or their descendants. Many others have come to Israel as
refugees from persecution in Arab lands.

Family losses add poignancy to discussions of what Israelis are willing to risk in terms of physical security for treaties with enemies who only a short while ago called for the country's destruction. Israel's 1979 peace treaty with Egypt was its first with a neighboring country. The second such agreement was concluded in 1994 with Jordan. There is now an interim accord with the Palestinians, subject to continuing talks with the Palestinian Authority. Still pending are negotiations with Syria and Lebanon.

As a percentage of GNP, Israel's annual financial outlays on security are five to ten times greater than those of other democracies. They distort the economy in the direction of a major role for government ministries in economic management. According to statistics prepared by the International Monetary Fund (IMF), Israel ranks very high among the democracies with respect to the percentage of its national economy accounted for by governmental budgets. In some years the expenditures of governmental and quasi-governmental bodies have exceeded GNP.[6] Overseas purchases of military equipment contribute to a high international debt and a chronic imbalance of imports over exports. Israel's inflation rate reflects the pressures on its economy. Price increases were above 100 percent annually from 1979 through the middle of 1985. Since 1992 they have been considered modest, in the range of 10–15 percent. Inflation in other Western democracies is now generally below 4 percent per annum.

A history of violence against the state and its citizens explains why Israel employs censorship laws and other security-related legal provisions that are more severe than those of other democracies. Israel has arrested, tried, and sentenced terrorists, spies, and other violators of its security laws without revealing details of the cases to the public or to attorneys for the accused. Israeli security forces are allowed under some conditions to use "moderate physical pressure" in interrogations.[7]

Immigration was especially burdensome during the years 1948–1951. The population more than doubled at a time when the economy was small, poor, and recovering from a war more costly in Israeli casualties than any since. Almost all of the immigrants came as refugees from Europe or Arab lands and depended on the state and other public institutions for housing, job assistance, and social services. They have bitter memories of poor housing and meager rations, as well as authorities who were insensitive to personal needs. Immigration peaked again with the collapse of the Soviet Union. The recent wave of immigrants from the former Soviet Union has added more than 15 percent to Israel's population since 1988 and has led to job competition with native Israelis, a sharp increase in the price of housing, the construction of new towns, and concerns about crowding, traffic jams, land use, and environmental protection. In positive terms, immigration from the former Soviet Union has contributed new consumers and skilled workers to the national economy and has increased Israel's skills in the professions and the arts.

Jerusalem presents its own cluster of domestic and international problems. Israel has had control of the city since the 1967 war and claims to be administering a united city that will remain its national capital. In practice, however, the city is divided. Voluntary segregation in housing and schooling is nearly universal. Jews and Palestinians speak their own languages, read their own newspapers, travel in taxis and buses run by separate Jewish and Palestinian companies, and shop in their own sections of the city. In the current political negotiations the Palestinians claim a portion of the city for the capital of their own country. Some major countries formally support United Nations decisions of the 1940s calling for the city's internationalization.

The Jewish majorities in Israel and Jerusalem (82 percent of the national population and 72 percent of the city's population) present their own problems to the Israeli authorities. About one-tenth of the Jews in Israel and one-quarter of those in Jerusalem are ultra-Orthodox. Jews who are religious and those who are secular or antireligious bicker continually about religion. The issues in dispute include Sabbath observance, the availability of nonkosher food, who is a Jew, who may be married to a Jew, who is a rabbi, the burial of non-Jews, the disturbance of ancient graves by construction projects, and the status of non-Orthodox Judaisms. The longevity of these disputes justifies their being labeled insoluble. Controversies triggered by religious issues take on the color of political rituals, which generally pass through several stages: the making of initial demands, recourse to loud demonstrations and nondeadly violence, and then a partial and ambiguous resolution of specific issues that does not resolve the main point of contention underlying the episode in question. The killing of Prime Minister Yitzhak Rabin by a religious Jew in 1995 raised the specter of a religious-secular conflict serious enough to threaten a civil war.

The Question of Israeli Distinctiveness

The concepts of the Chosen People and the Promised Land have served the Jews well. Since biblical times these concepts have been associated with self-esteem in the face of adversity. We can surmise that self-esteem has contributed to Jewish solidarity and survival, as well as to individual success in business, cultural endeavors, and politics. Yet the concepts of the Chosen People and the Promised Land may hinder accurate self-assessment in modern Israel by emphasizing the uniqueness of the nation and its homeland. Israeli social scientists, journalists, and policy analysts make assertions about national traits that differ significantly from the traits revealed by comparative analysis.

There is no denying that Israel, like other countries, has traits that truly are distinctive. For Israeli Jews, however, the temptation to claim distinctiveness may be greater than in other countries. Biblical accounts, of course, mention Jews in the land of Israel and can encourage parochialism even among Israelis who do not think of themselves as religious. The period 1945–1967 saw a change in Jewish status from victim to victor, a mass migration of Jews to Israel that recalled the return from Babylonian exile described in the biblical books of Ezra and Nehemiah, and the uniting of Jerusalem under Jewish rule for the first time in two millennia. Believers saw all of this in the context of Judaic themes of redemption. Nonreligious and antireligious Zionists also saw parallels with the Hebrew Bible.[8]

Flaws in the distinctiveness argument appear when cross-national comparisons indicate that Israel is not significantly different from other countries or is different in ways that contradict conventional wisdom. The dangers of parochialism lie not only in mistaken analyses, but in its influence on the deployment of economic resources. Israeli policy advocates who do not bother to compare their country with others may contribute to an undue allocation of effort to problems that are widely perceived to be extreme, but which in reality are no worse, or are even less grave, than in other countries.

We return to the issue of Israel's distinctiveness in chapter 3, which addresses two perceived social problems that distinguished intellectuals and high-ranking officials in Israel have condemned in very strong terms and have made the subject of special campaigns and government programs, but which comparative analysis shows are no more severe, and in some cases less severe, than in other countries. These problems are, first, the "social gap" associated with family income inequality, and second, the allegedly high incidence of traffic deaths. Chapter 7 draws the same conclusions with respect to the power of religious activists to dominate policy making in Israel. In contrast to the claims made by many observers about the power of religious Jews, the fact is that religious Jews do not dominate policy making in Israel any more than religious Christians dominate policy making in the United States or other Western countries.

There are, however, several distinctive national traits that affect Israeli policy making. The stress on security concerns and the high rates of public expenditure make the state and its bureaucracy prominent in many fields which in other countries are dominated by the private sector. The socialism that is associated with Zionism and with the older Jewish tradition of communal aid reinforces the weight of a modern defense budget in providing power to the state. In contrast to the American tradition of looking to government aid as a last resort, Israeli political activists tend to call on state assistance at the first sign of a problem, whether it has to do with health care, housing, education, or the stock market. When Israeli share indices fell by more than 6 percent in one month in 1996, for example, some people called for taxes on alternative forms of investment to encourage the public to funnel more of its money into the stock market.[9]

Israel's small size and compact population are also distinctive and important in policy making. Israel is a bit larger than New Jersey and a bit smaller than Massachusetts. It is geographically smaller than any Western European country except for the mini-states of Luxemborg, Monaco, San Marino, Andorra, and Vatican City. Among Western European countries, only the Netherlands and Belgium are more densely populated. Ninety percent of Israel's population lives in settlements of more than 2,000 people, and 81 percent in settlements of more than 10,000.[10] Of twenty-two developed countries, only the United Kingdom has a higher proportion of its population in urban centers.[11] California is the only American state to have a more urbanized population than Israel's.[12]

Israel's population and economic base are concentrated in a triangular megalopolis that extends along the coast from Ashkelon in the south to Nahariya in the north, with a center bulge eastward toward Jerusalem. This area contains 81 percent of the national population and almost all major institutions of government decision making, private industry, education, science, culture, and mass communications. The result is that national government, local government, and metropolitan coordination are largely coterminous. As we shall see in chapter 3, this allows Israelis to avoid some of the problems that other countries suffer, but also produces its own distinctive complications.

Policy Problems, Politics, and Policy Making

Before we turn to the nature of Israel's problems and its policy making, it will be useful to consider some issues related to policy making that appear continually in country after country. But first, it is necessary to define two essential terms. *Policy* refers to the important things that governments do. The term includes actions or proposals that affect large sums of money, large numbers of people, or values that people hold dear. Policy also includes the actions that governments pointedly choose not to engage in. The second term, *politics*, has been defined as collective decision making, or a determination of who gets what in a polity.[13] Politics is a civilized way of dealing in a nonviolent manner with conflict over difficult issues. The analysis and assessment of policy and the politics of policy making are major concerns of political scientists. The questions political scientists seek to answer include: Who participates in policy making? How do they make key decisions? What economic, social, and political conditions influence their actions? Who benefits from the policies that are created? To what extent are policies actually implemented in the ways indicated by formal laws and regulations? What problems remain unsolved by public policies?

In both the description of policy making and the assessment of its failure or success it is often possible to see the perspective of the analyst. Where you sit determines what you see.[14] What one person sees as an intolerable condition that must be changed at all costs is, in another's eyes, the best situation attainable. During the fighting in Lebanon, an Israeli television crew interviewed Lebanese who seemed to be enjoying their holiday at a beach north of Beirut. "How can you relax like this in the midst of a war?" was the obvious question for an outsider. But for the Lebanese, who had learned the art of survival, the answer was, "Here it is quiet. The fighting is sixteen kilometers [ten miles] away."

Where the participants in policy making sit often determines what they report. A cardinal rule is to make yourself look good. Let antagonists look after their own reputations. As Ronald Reagan's budget director, David Stockman failed in his effort to restrain spending and thus satisfy the president's desire for a significant reduction in taxes. Stockman's book, *The Triumph of Politics: The Inside Story of the Reagan Administration*, provides numerous vignettes of a chief executive who seemed too old for the job and did not grasp the contradictions in his decisions.[15] Yet Stockman's reports of folly are marked by a one-sided attempt to justify his own actions. There is more to government than tidy budgets, but Stockman seemed unable to look at the issues through the president's eyes and thus understand the importance of other considerations.[16]

Occasionally the behavior of senior officials seems to reflect their own interests regardless of the official rules. Seymour Hersh describes the behavior of two of the most overtly power-hungry and distrustful of the high-ranking figures in the Nixon administration, the president himself and Henry Kissinger, as well as the behavior of others in the administration who were looking after their own interests. Bomber pilots were instructed to lie about the targets they were sent to destroy, in order to make it look as if the government was complying with its own policy against broadening the war in Vietnam to Cambodia. The Pentagon planted spies in the White House to report on the policy options being considered by the presidential staff. Junior staffers distorted the information they supplied to senior officials, who punished their juniors for reporting bad news.[17] Israeli parallels to these stories appear in reports on the war in Lebanon that describe how Defense Minister Ariel Sharon provided Prime Minister Menachem Begin with incomplete plans and distorted reports on the military's accomplishments and casualties.[18]

Perspectives on Policy Failure

The issues that attract the attention of policy makers and political scientists are those where problems are prominent and policies have proved inadequate. Many answers are offered to the question, "Why do policies fail?"[19] A brief review of the answers amounts to a summary of the political science that deals with issues of public policy.

The rationalist explanation of policy failure focuses on the errors made by those who define the policies. Perhaps, it is argued, they did not follow every step in the procedures urged on them by rationalists, or made errors in carrying out a step. According to the rationalist formula, policy makers should identify the problem they wish to solve, specify and prioritize all of their goals, measure the costs and benefits associated with each policy option available for achieving their goals, and select the package of policy options that offers the greatest benefits at the least cost.[20]

Rationality is widely supported as the right way to make policy, but it is also widely discredited. Several factors complicate an issue beyond the capacity of rational calculations to identify and measure all of the relevant options and their costs and benefits: the many ways of defining a problem, the many possible assessments of a problem's causes, the many ways of handling a problem, and the many factors that interfere with the policy process. As one commentator remarks, rational policy making is unlikely to overcome "long, unconscious growth deriving from the unhampered creativity of individuals."[21]

Various explanations of policy failure testify to the limits on the rationalist explanation. They make the point that policy failure is not simply a shortcoming of rational calculation, but is likely to reflect other influences on poliy making.

The psychological explanation holds that policy making is less than rational because participants have perceptions or commitments of long standing that limit their capacity to make objective calculations. In their interpretations of events policy makers are conditioned by previous experiences.[22] Some policy makers approach their tasks with some options ruled out and others highly favored. Groupthink occurs when members of a policy body reinforce one another's perceptions and isolate themselves from outside influences.[23] Israeli policy makers were so convinced in 1973 that the Arabs would not attack that they delayed interpreting the signs of Egyptian and Syrian preparations for the war that began on Yom Kippur. In 1987 Israeli and Jordanian officials and the leadership of the Palestine Liberation Organization (PLO) were so accustomed to the passivity of the Palestinians in the occupied territories that they misinterpreted the signs of a popular uprising.[24] In the aftermath of the assassination of Prime Minister Yitzhak Rabin in 1995, it appeared that Israel's security services had discounted the possibility that a religious Jew would kill another Jew, and had not responded adequately to information about plans for the assassination.

We can divide political explanations for policy failure into a number of subtypes, whose boundaries are blurred and overlapping. They include the psychological explanation insofar as policy makers are led to some postures by prior political beliefs and alliances. The personal explanation puts the emphasis on individuals—the chief executive or key legislators, advisors, or administrators—whose distinctive interests and talents influence policy design or implementation. The partisan explanation describes the commitments that appear in party platforms and political rivalries and have the effect of hindering compromise with party principles. The organizational explanation focuses on the predispositions of government agencies, which are likely to consider their own interests as top priority and to oppose policy options that allow rival agencies to be given responsibility for a program.

A variant on the organizational explanation of policy failure, the bureaucratic explanation, focuses on the capacity of individual administrators to frustrate the goals of policy makers. The key individuals in this instance may be entrepreneurial managers with huge budgets and work forces[25] or middle managers who can promote projects aggressively or delay them endlessly if their own preferences are not satisfied.[26] "There is always some son-of-a-bitch who doesn't get the word" was John F. Kennedy's way of describing civil servants who do not comply with instructions.[27] Policy influences can also come from the very lowest levels of government. Anonymous police officers, building inspectors, schoolteachers, and welfare workers define the quality of public services received by individual clients and the actual meaning of equality and justice.[28] Another variant on the organizational explanation is the interest group explanation. In this view, policy failure results from a group's pursuit of its own goals to the extent that it is oblivious to any overriding national interest. (A different view is that there is no such thing as a national interest, just varieties of group interests, with each group likely to assert that its interest is important enough to be considered the national interest.)

The organizational, bureaucratic, and interest group explanations of policy failure overlap when there are alliances between government agencies and interest groups. One example appears in alliances between government regulatory agencies and interest groups representing the regulated industries. The interest groups try to have industry-friendly personnel appointed to the regulatory agencies. They also provide a constant stream of documentation to justify their demands for weak implementation of regulations.[29] On the other hand, a committed and skillful administrator can change policy despite the demands of seemingly powerful industries. Such an administrator may benefit from the support of a high-ranking politician[30] who views industrial regulation as an issue of special importance and can mobilize groups of supporters to frustrate other interest groups wanting to keep things as they are.[31]

The structural explanation of policy failure puts the emphasis on the structure of government. It is common to fault the U.S. government for having too many parts. Policy gridlock is one way of describing the problems that arise in attempting to arrange agreements between the White House, the two houses of Congress (with their committees and subcommittees), self-interested federal administrative departments, and state and local authorities that must be persuaded to support major departures in domestic policy.[32] Policy gridlock favors supporters of the status quo, who need to control only one key body in order to stop a proposal. Advocates of change, on the other hand, must win the support of all the bodies that have a say in the policy process. The Israeli version of gridlock arises from the perennial need to form coalition governments. Voters select members of the Knesset on the basis of proportional representation. The government that is created must have the support of the majority of the Knesset. No political party has ever won a majority in a Knesset election, with the result that every Cabinet has been a multiparty body in which Cabinet ministers of opposing parties and perspectives agree to work together but also thwart each other's programs.

The management explanation is yet another political explanation for policy failure. The management explanation can also be termed a failure of implementation, insofar as it is at the stage of implementing a policy that a management failure is likely to appear.[33] What is called a management failure may also involve a failure of rational calculation. Program managers make errors in budgeting, in choosing the personnel for a program, or in defining the details of a program and its standard operating procedures. Political opposition may limit the resources that can be budgeted for a program, or lead to the appointment of administrators who give the program a low priority. Occasionally, program administrators are chosen for their known opposition to a program and the skill they can apply to keeping the program small or killing it.[34]

Some explanations of failed implementation range much further than issues of management. Events in the economic, political, and social environments, including those that occur outside the country trying to implement a program, can limit government resources or political support for a program.

It is said that individuals who do not know history are fated to repeat it. However, the lessons of history are seldom clear. Richard Neustadt and Ernest May describe many cases of policy makers who followed their sense of history on the way to policy failures.[35] Neustadt and May point out that it is possible to view historical episodes in different ways. Some episodes have been turned into folk memories that distort what really happened. Policy makers may have only the barest sense of analogies between the great events of the past and the problems they face. History that is not well analyzed for differences as well as similarities with the present may become an enemy of creative vision and a recipe for failure.

Barbara Tuchman's *The March of Folly* explores several great failures of history to make the point that governments have pursued activities counter to their own best interests. She describes cases where self-destructive policies have continued despite strong warnings about the dangers of those policies and the availability of more sensible courses of action. Her message is that the stubbornness of willful politicians may contribute to the fatal flaws in a project's planning or execution.[36]

Tuchman's judgments on flawed activities, however, are influenced by her own strong feelings. In this respect, her book makes an important point, albeit unwittingly: policy evaluation is affected by the politics of the evaluator. Tuchman clearly disapproves of decisions taken, or not taken, by governments on their way to the follies she describes. Her own feelings are clearest in the case of American policy in Vietnam. Surprisingly for a historian, Tuchman forgets the advantage of hindsight. She places too much reliance on early warnings against activities that led to disaster and skips over the problem that leaders receive many warnings and must distinguish between what is wise and what is inappropriate. If policy makers were to heed all warnings of failure, there would be no departures from existing programs, and regimes would not respond to new conditions.[37]

The image of policy failure or success may overcome the reality. Activists do what they can to put a bad or a good face, as the case may be, on what they oppose or support. Programs and leaders acquire reputations that can dominate the mass media and intellectual opinion.[38]

The Politics of Policy Analysis

The pervasive character of politics may render trivial the question of why policies fail. With a little creativity a political activist can find perspectives and information to argue that a program has done well or poorly. The criticism of existing policy that is endemic in political competition makes it likely that a project will be termed a failure with respect to some of its goals by at least some commentators. In a situation of special complexity, where a project is innovative, involves many parts, or requires the cooperation of various organizations or various national governments, it is even less likely to achieve anything close to widely acknowledged success.[39] If the declared goals seem to have been met, an entrenched opponent can argue that the goals themselves were flawed and were related to only a small portion of the real problem.

Program supporters also play their games at the evaluation stage. Even if a program has not met its declared goals, supporters can read the outcome as success rather than failure. They can argue that the goals were intentionally defined in extreme terms to boost the aspirations of administrators. What critics view as abject failure can be viewed as a success by program advocates, who can claim that conditions would have been even worse without the program.

For some people, Israel's adventure in Lebanon that began with the invasion of June 1982 was doomed from the beginning. After two and a half years of fighting and 650 deaths Israel had accomplished none of its stated goals. The PLO had been mauled but not eliminated. The Lebanese government had not become the second Arab state after Egypt to establish normal relations with Jerusalem. The Syrian army had not left Lebanon. Israel's forces had tarnished their international reputation by the televised shelling of Beirut and by being nearby while Lebanese Christians slaughtered the Palestinian residents of Sabra and Shatila. Newly emerged Lebanese terrorist groups lobbed rockets into Israel's northern settlements and tried to penetrate the border. Within Israel itself Arab youths attacked Jews with kitchen knives, stones, and Molotov cocktails. The 1982 Israeli promise to end the threat of Arab terrorism was mocked by the wave of violence in the occupied territories that began in December 1987 and became known as the intifada.

No simple, final evaluations of Israel's Lebanon war or of the intifada are available. Judgment in both cases is often colored by preconceptions. Neither side in the Israeli-Palestinian conflict has been able to defeat the other. The suffering of both communities may have led more and more Israelis and Palestinians to lessen their aspirations and begin negotiations.

The Importance of a Problem's Difficulty

The close connections between politics and policy appear not just in the influence of political competition on public policy and the assessment of policy results. It is also the case that the nature of a policy problem influences the politics of policy making. Proposals to redistribute resources from haves to have-nots are likely to generate opposition from the haves. The acronym NIMBY (not in my backyard) describes the neighborhood reaction to such projects as prisons, waste disposal sites, and halfway houses. A program to create or expand benefits is more likely to attract the cooperation of the target populations than a program designed to regulate and limit the activities of firms or individuals.[40]

A theme pursued throughout this book is that the difficulty of a problem is prominent among the elements that shape the activities of policy makers. The essence of the argument is that simple problems call forth administrative and political routines, whereas difficult problems evoke coping mechanisms that are politically complex.

The next chapter presents a schema that situates problem types along a spectrum from simple (lowest level of difficulty) to insoluble (highest level of difficulty) and links them to policy makers' responses. At one end of the spectrum (lowest level of difficulty) is the problem presented by a client with conventional characteristics that fit the definition of who is eligible to take advantage of a program. An administrator using established routines or standard operating procedures, most likely detailed in an agency manual, can assess the client's traits and authorize the award of benefits. Further along the spectrum are client demands that require the use of discretion, perhaps by a clerk in consultation with a supervisor or through deliberation by a committee.

At the higher levels of difficulty are issues that involve multiple clients and the political processes of negotiation and coalition formation. One example might involve a group of residents concerned about the location of a public facility. Routine procedures are well established, although they are of a type that is more complex than what is used for dealing with an individual client. These procedures include advertising the project to be built and holding a public hearing before a committee, with opportunities for opponents to appeal to a higher administrative authority and a court of law. Modest levels of political involvement, together with a bit of persuasion or compromise, resolve most project-centered disputes. More complicated are projects that affect entire communities and raise the issue of economic development versus the preservation of historic buildings or the environment. The treatment of complex problems involves combining coping mechanisms such as extensive negotiation and goal redefinition.

Problems requiring investment in science, engineering, or technology present conditions for routines or coping mechanisms. Designing a bridge to overcome a geographical obstacle appears at the low end of the spectrum of difficulty. The controversies involved in decisions to invest heavily in AIDS research or to use fetal tissue for research appear at the high end of the spectrum of difficulty.

Some problems are insoluble, at least in current circumstances. Officials may find some solution or treatment for individual incidents, but the same basic problem returns sooner or later, perhaps with other personalities demanding a solution to a different set of circumstances. The components of an insoluble problem are many and likely to be ambiguous. They lend themselves to competing views on how to define the basic problem and to conflicting claims about the costs and benefits of proposed solutions. When a problem generates intense feelings, activists may cross the boundary that separates peaceful from violent politics.

The concept of an insoluble problem is itself problematic. An issue can remain unsolved for years, then change its character as a result of shifts in political constellations and norms. At one time the Arab-Israeli conflict seemed insoluble either by political or military means. Each side postured before international audiences of supporters and prepared for another round of war, terror, and retaliation. More recently the Arab-Israeli struggle has become a difficult but possibly soluble multidimensional political conflict, characterized by maneuvering in both camps, ongoing negotiations, and the resolution of what had been significant elements in the overall problem.

What is meant by *problem* is also problematic. What one person describes as a problem may be merely a phenomenon or a condition to someone who is not troubled by it. A problem may be personal and not public. At one time, being physically disabled was only a personal problem. Now it has the status of a public problem. Governments invest substantial resources in the care of disabled people and require that public buildings and transportation be accessible to them. Moreover, what some observers describe as a single problem is to others a cluster of problems that may or may not be related to one another. The Arab-Israeli problem is a loosely related cluster of problems involving Israelis and Palestinians, Jews and Moslems, the governments of Israel and several Arab states, and rival groups within the Israeli and Arab populations. No problem has an objective existence. Each reflects the views of observers and policy makers who combine many pieces of reality into their descriptions of a "problem."[41]

Most policy problems that attract the attention of the public and of political scientists are of middling complexity—neither simple nor insoluble. What can make them interesting are their implications for the interests of numerous groups, their high financial costs, or their relevance for widely held values like justice, morality, or religious beliefs. A government's budget causes is likely to cause its moments of public controversy, but negotiators succeed in finding a compromise that wins the support of those with the power to decide. Disputes about proposals relating to major construction projects, tax reform, or the content of public education move on and off the agenda with the approval of some proposals and the rejection of others. More difficult are issues such as abortion, the legality of recreational drugs that many people find attractive, the role of economic development versus environmental protection, and the relationship between secular government and citizens who hold intense religious beliefs.

Chapter 2, which sets forth a schema of policy problems, expands on the present discussion of policy problems and the nature of policy making and serves as a guide to the material presented in subsequent chapters. Chapter 3 describes Israel's government and politics, with an emphasis on how various institutions and behaviors come together to shape public policies and their implementation. Chapters 4–7 discuss prominent issues in Israel's recent history and and the responses to them by Israeli officials and citizens. The cases discussed in chapters 4–7 are meant to illustrate how Israeli officials make policy rather than to provide a comprehensive survey of policy making in all areas of Israeli life. For this reason, some important issues are left out or treated only in passing, for example those related to economic development, water, housing, and health. The issues selected for discussion, however, appear again and again on the national agenda: the drama and routines of immigration; the once insoluble problem of the Arab-Israeli conflict, which combines issues of national defense and international relations; the difficult and perhaps insoluble problems that Jerusalem presents for intercommunal and intracommunal relations; and what seem to be the insoluble problems of religious conflict among Jews. Chapter 8 assesses the utility of routines and coping in policy making, considers their implications for widely held political values, and examines the significance of the Israeli case for understanding policy making in other countries.

CHAPTER 2

Simple Problems, Complex Problems, and Insoluble Problems

Policy makers do many things. For those who are elected to legislative or executive positions, policy making may be less important than electoral politics. Such officials attend to the activities of political parties, recruit financial contributors, and handle complaints or requests from constituents. Some of the constituents may be important to an official's political future, and some may be people with problems that speak to the official's sense of justice or inclination to do a favor.

Senior civil servants are likely to have managerial responsibilities relating to departmental budgets or personnel decisions, and to shoulder the policy-making functions of chairing panels of experts, overseeing the drafting of proposals, and seeing to the implementation of projects. Advisors to government officials are among the key actors in defining policy options and clarifying the implications of policy for the electoral interests of the officials they advise.

This book is concerned with public problems and policy making more than with electoral politics. It examines the policy making of elected officials, civil servants, advisors, and citizen activists. The focus is Israel, but the lessons have wider significance.

The larger relevance of this book derives from the vantage point that it selects as a guide to policy making in Israel. It emphasizes the difficulty of policy problems as a factor that influences how policy making operates. The argument is that a similar process operates elsewhere as well. The present chapter looks at policy making in general terms in order to emphasize the relevance for our analysis to other countries.

The point is that the character of public problems affects the way policy making operates.

Our guide is a schema that lays out problem types along a scale from the simple to the complex and includes the policy making responses to each type of problem (see table 2.1). Implicit in the schema are propositions that link the degree of difficulty to the use of administrative routines or coping mechanisms. At the extreme are problems that, at least for the time being, appear to be insoluble.

The scale of policy problems and responses provides the link between the analysis of Israel and the implications of that analysis for policy making more generally. The purpose of this book, and chapters 4–7 in particular, is to illustrate how the severity of a problem affects the way that Israeli policy makers respond. The lessons of table 2.1 explain Israelis' treatment of immigration, the Arab-Israeli conflict, the complex issues of Jerusalem, and religion. The lessons should also help Americans and people in other democracies comprehend why their officials respond the way they do to simple issues as well as to the more complex problems of health care, drug abuse, and budget deficits.

Simple and Complex Problems

Like an exercise in arithmetic, a simple problem has only one solution. An example in government is a client who seeks to take advantage of a program that offers fixed benefits according to the traits of each applicant as defined by laws or regulations. A clerk can determine a client's characteristics and authorize a financial grant or program of services.

Further along the scale (but still within level 1) are client requests in the context of a program that requires the use of discretion. Demands of this kind are likely to reach officials with professional training or pass through the hands of several individuals who must consult one another and reach agreement on the appropriate response. This more complex procedure appears in disability payment programs. The granting of a benefit may require an initial assessment of the applicant by medical personnel or review by a committee with discretionary powers.

A full step along the scale toward complexity are issues that involve more than one client and are likely to present opportunities for engaging in the political processes of coalition formation and negotiation. The more simple issues are unidimensional and appear in level 2. One example is a project whose location a group of residents wants to alter, such as a road of prison. They are given opportunities to express their

TABLE 2.1 Problem Types and Responses

Type of Problem	Response	Examples	Implications
Simple			
1. Client application for benefits	Administrative routines or standard operating procedures	Match client traits with those demanded by law administrative rules, as in the case of immigrants	Problem resolution with limited implications for continued political action
2. Political but unidimensional problem	Routine hearings, with opportunities for appeals and negotiations	Group opposes proposed project	Problem solution generally found with modest incidence of political involvement
3. Political problem with both unidimensional and multidimensional elements	Application of political routines, with politicking at the micro level	Incremental budgeting; ticket balancing; proportional appointments according to ascriptive traits	Macro predictability; micro variability
4. Political and multidimensional problem	Cope: Search for acceptable opportunities among the large number of options	Illicit drug use; reform of health care; Arab-Israeli dispute during a period when negotiations offer promising alternatives to violence; Israeli organ transplants	Extensive politicking among groups with different perception of problem and proposed solution
5. Insoluble problem but of low immediate threat	Cope: Temporize	Religious versus antireligious activists	Chronic tension; no resolution
6. Insoluble and high-threat problem	Cope: Be alert to danger and opportunity	Arab-Israeli conflict during periods of intransigence and violence	Uneven cycles of increased and reduced threat of violence
?. Predicament or dilemma	Cope: Search for different formulation	Formulations of demands that defy solution but may change in significance with a change in wording	—
Complex			

views before an administrative body and to appeal that body's decision to higher-ranking administrators or a court of law. Projects with extensive economic and environmental implications, or that excite the concerns of a community, may provide long-term work for interest groups and administrative, judicial, and political personnel. Such projects are appropriate to levels 3 or 4 of table 2.1.

Level 3 includes political issues with multidimensional elements. That is, they are issues likely to involve many individuals or groups presenting numerous sets of demands, rather than one individual or group presenting one set of demands. The political implications are wider than at level 2, but there are routines for dealing with some of the controversies. Budgeting illustrates a mixture of routines and coping mechanisms. The routines of incrementalism accommodate most of the decisions in each budget cycle. Officials accept the level of spending that was authorized in previous years and authorize increments that take account of inflation or increases in client population. Incrementalism makes the size of the budget predictable, although intense public controversy and opportunities for negotiation influence allocations for individual programs. In other words, there is likely to be more predictability at the macro level than at the micro level.

In another arena, personnel use the routine of ticket balancing to satisfy multiple interests in a political organization. With this routine, an organization distributes its jobs and other benefits in proportion to the various traits of its members, such as sex, occupation, area of residence, or whatever other trait the members use to distinguish themselves from one another. The routine of representing traits that have been made politically relevant appears either formally or informally in appointments to administrative positions or the acceptance of students into universities. It may be possible to predict the size of each group's benefits even when individuals' appointments are determined by competition, negotiation, or the dispensing of personal favors at the micro level.

As we move up the levels of table 2.1 in the direction of greater complexity, problems lend themselves more often to creative proposals and coalition building rather than to the use of simple routines. The Arab-Israeli dispute during a period when negotiations offer an alternative to violence is placed in level 4. It remains multidimensional with numerous parties, each having some claims against the other that may get in the way of the primary Arab-Israeli dispute. At times, Syria and Jordan, Syria and the Palestinians, and Syria and Lebanon have preferred to score points against one another at the expense of progress in resolving their disputes with Israel. Many kinds of antagonism affect the pace of bargaining. Negotiators must be patient in waiting for opportunities. The situation is similar to the American dispute over national health insurance, which creates competition between reformers on the one hand and hospitals, insurance companies, and organizations representing health care professionals on the other, and within each group of reformers and care providers.

Problems that require considerable investment in science, engineering, or technology can appear at various levels of table 2.1 depending on the weight of politics in key decisions. Building a road through a swamp or mountains is a problem that appears at the lower end of the scale. The politics involved in decisions to invest heavily in AIDS research move that issue higher up the scale. Problems associated with organ transplants are higher up the scale in Israel than elsewhere in the West. Many religious Jews, including some rabbis, have been reluctant to accept modern secular definitions of death or to violate the body of a dead person to obtain organs for transplant. Israeli organ transplants belong in level 4, whereas elsewhere they may be an issue of public policy only because of their expense and questions of public health insurance coverage.

Politics are dynamic. Policy makers find solutions that remove issues from the public agenda. Popular attitudes change and render issues less pressing. Creative leaders can bring a population to see an issue in a different light and facilitate agreements where none had been possible. Events occur in the nation or the world to change economic or political realities. In 1989 the collapse of the Soviet Union produced a migration to Israel and facilitated dramatic moves toward peace in the Middle East. Both migration and the peace process continue eight years later.

The Arab-Israeli conflict appears twice in table 2.1. One of its locations reflects earlier conditions when it seemed insoluble. Policy makers were locked into fixed postures, Arab terrorists and their allies killed Israeli civilians and overseas Jews, Israeli security forces retaliated, and the governments of Israel and its neighbors issued routine condemnations of their adversaries and prepared for another round of fighting. Anwar Sadat changed the picture, at least partly, when he visited Jerusalem in 1977 and declared "No more war" in a speech to the Knesset. At that point, Egypt and Israel ceased being enemies and began negotiations. Violence continued on other fronts before representatives of Israel, Jordan, Syria, Lebanon, and the Palestinians met in Madrid in 1991. That meeting reflected two dramatic events outside the immediate Arab-Israeli arena: first, the collapse of the Soviet Union and the end of its backing for an Arab front that had rejected Israel's existence, and second, the cooperation of a broad Arab alliance with the United States in the Gulf War earlier that year. Since then, Israel has signed an accord with the PLO and a peace treaty with Jordan.

The Arab-Israeli conflict is complex, even at the best of times. Israel has its doves and hawks, including some with religious convictions so strong that they are determined to hold onto every square inch of the ancient Land of Israel. Arab governments and Palestinian organizations have their separate interests with respect to Israel, for instance in the matters of boundaries, water, and refugees. Problems not related to Israel have on occasion led Arab political entities to thwart each other in their efforts at accommodation with Israel. Palestinians who reject peace with Israel have launched campaigns of violence that threaten the capacity of Palestinian and Israeli officials to keep the conflict in level 4.

Illicit drug use appears in level 4. It shows the effects of value conflicts in which disciplined lifestyles oppose hedonism. There are medical controversies about particular substances, as well as disputes about which substances should be the targets of serious law enforcement, which laws should be enforced lightly if at all, and which techniques of education may work against drug use. The case of illicit drugs also demonstrates how problems vary in their severity over time and from one country to another. American researchers describe a public antidrug panic in the 1980s fueled by high rates of drug use, postures adopted by key figures in the Reagan and Bush administrations, strenuous efforts to interdict the foreign and domestic drug supply, and considerable controversy over such efforts. Public concern may have reached its peak in 1989, when 64 percent of poll respondents said that drug abuse was the nation's number one problem. The figure declined to 30 percent in surveys taken in April 1990 and was in the range of 8–12 percent by late 1991. Drug use also declined, although not as much, and the decline was primarily among middle-class, recreational, and occasional users. In the inner cities drugs were consumed at a stable or increased rate.[1] Drug use also troubles Israeli policy makers, but it has not been as prominent a concern as in the United States. In American surveys, up to 50 percent of the young people questioned admit to using drugs, but Israeli figures are less than 10 percent.[2]

Complex problems lend themselves to slow, piecemeal solutions. The problems of disease or adult illiteracy may involve components that can be solved one by one in the hope that the larger problem will be eliminated or its incidence significantly reduced. Getting an astronaut to the moon was a classic problem of science and engineering. The task was complex, but lent itself to being broken down into a series of manageable tasks that could be completed in sequence.

A problem may be rendered complex by political opposition. Choosing a location for an undesirable facility such as a prison or a waste storage site may require a lengthy sequence of hearings and negotiations to accommodate the objections of local interests.

Experts with different perspectives may argue about which of several strategies is appropriate. Policy makers can pursue the economic development of a depressed region by programs of training, constructing roads, power grids, and other infrastructure resources, or adjusting taxes to make the region more attractive to private investment.

An issue may begin in level 1 with an action by a client whose characteristics lie on the borderline between qualification and disqualification for a program. An entrepreneurial official may exploit such a case in arenas where rules or laws are made in order to expand the definition of who is eligible for services. The result may push the case to a higher level, perhaps 3 or 4, depending on its political implications.

There is much ambiguity at the higher levels of table 2.1. Analysts argue about whether Israel's massive entry into Lebanon starting in 1982 was a misguided adventure that wasted human and material resources and caused a loss of international goodwill, or an initiative that weakened the Palestinians to the point where more of the Palestinian leadership was willing to negotiate terms of coexistence with Israel. Another dispute concerns the intifada that began in 1987. Did it have a winner and a loser, or was it an event that convinced both Israeli and Palestinian leaders that they could not impose their will on the other side by force alone?

As is the case with other models that portray the essential elements of complex processes, the stages laid out in table 2.1 can be expanded or compressed. The addition of intermediate stages would enable more of the subtleties in policy making to become clear. In its present form, however, table 2.1 emphasizes the simple but useful lessons that link the difficulties of problems with policy making routines or coping.

Predicaments and Dilemmas

A predicament is a problem with no attractive solutions, or that presents hard and unwelcome choices. A dilemma is a subset of a predicament and involves alternatives that are equally unpleasant. Citizens face a dilemma when they object strongly to all the candidates for elective office but their commitment to good citizenship and political activism does not allow them to abstain from voting. The need to be precise in establishing policy makers' feelings about alternatives (that is, knowing whether policy makers perceive the alternatives to be equally unpleasant) renders it difficult, even impossible, to know for sure when a problem is a dilemma or only a predicament.

Predicaments or dilemmas occur in health policy when the available resources for treating certain conditions are not sufficient to meet the needs of the patients who could be treated. It is possible to keep some patients alive with transplanted hearts, kidneys, and livers. However, the demand for donated organs exceeds the number available. Policy makers would face the predicament of allocating organs if they sought to legislate guidelines. Meanwhile, physicians face agonizing choices when they are required to determine who will receive donor organs.

Predicaments also occur when a prized development, like a new university, is sought by several jurisdictions but cannot be made available to all. Decisions on road building present predicaments when it becomes clear that one region is likely to prosper by having a new road built through it or near it while other regions will suffer on account of being bypassed.

Predicaments result from government programs that are likely to harm as well as help a community. The strict enforcement of environmental rules may force the closing of industries that are economically marginal and cannot afford the equipment needed to comply with air or water standards. Some residents are prepared to risk their health for the sake of keeping their jobs, while others demand the application of new regulations no matter what the economic implications.

Predicaments are also found in foreign policy. Israel has resisted acting against Iran even though it accuses the Iranian government of supporting anti-Israel and anti-Jewish actions such as attacks on Israeli patrols in southern Lebanon and the bombing of the Israeli embassy and a Jewish community center in Buenos Aires. The several thousand Jews living in Iran would be vulnerable to reprisal if Israel moved directly against Iranian targets. When the Chinese government crushed student and worker protests in June 1989, the White House faced pressure to severely condemn China and curtail American economic activities there. At the same time, there was pressure to maintain economic and political ties with China, especially in view of the problems that occurred when the United States had no diplomatic relations with China for many years after the Communist revolution. The Bush administration sought to accommodate these conflicting pressures by releasing statements that were strong enough to satisfy American critics of China but not so strong as to offend the Chinese government. The administration also indicated that it would maintain American economic assistance to and commercial relations with China.

The category of "predicament or dilemma" is preceded by a question mark in table 2.1. Predicaments and dilemmas belong in levels 4, 5, or 6, depending on their severity. Also, predicaments and dilemmas appear to be fragile and alterable by a change in rhetoric. Inidividuals can reduce a predicament to a dilemma, or even remove it from their agenda of problems, if they expand the time frame in which they are willing to have their demands satisfied or if they tone down their demands. Activists who demand the removal of all contaminants from an industrial smokestack present a predicament or dilemma to policy makers concerned with industrial development and environmental protection. If activists moderate their demand by asking for less than 100 percent removal they can reduce the level of problem difficulty.

Conundrums

The ultimate test of table 2.1 is whether certain problems truly are insoluble. The short answer is that it depends on the definition of the problem in question or the solution achieved. Policy makers may "solve" a problem created by traffic accidents or terrorist attacks by reducing the number or severity of such incidents, even if they cannot be eliminated altogether. The "solution" to a problem also depends on the willingness of politicians to accept options that hold out the promise of fixing a problem to some extent, even if it entails a high financial cost or a moral cost in coercing people to do unpleasant things. Policy makers may succeed in regulating prostitution or drug use without being able to bring about the changes in society necessary for abolishing those activities. The term "solution" may be applied to a particular episode but not to the basic problem of which that episode is a part. Israelis are able to resolve particular controversies about the use of a road on the Sabbath or the sale of pork by a butcher shop, but religious activists will find another road that they want closed on the Sabbath or another shop that sells pork.

The label used for insoluble problems—conundrums—also raises some difficulties. The *Oxford English Dictionary* indicates that the term appeared as early as 1645, perhaps as part of a university joke.[3] Such a beginning justifies academic concern for insoluble problems. It also implies that conundrums should be examined skeptically. *Webster's New Collegiate Dictionary* indicates that a conundrum is "a question or a problem having only a conjectural answer."[4] Perhaps the frustrations associated with a conundrum lead policy makers to guess at possible solutions. Solutions based on conjecture seem likely to be defective and to continue the insoluble nature of the problem.

The word *conundrum* can also be used in association with an intellectual game, as in a puzzle that ends in a pun.[5] This suggests a problem that lends itself to contemplation more than to action. In addressing conundrums, analysts may not get to the point where they agree on what caused the problem, what should be done, or what can be done.

The concept of an insoluble problem is problematic. A conundrum exists as long as no solution appears on the horizon. If conditions change and one or more solutions appear, the issue can become a predicament, a complex problem, a simple problem, or no problem at all.

There are times when different analysts will hold different views on a phenomenon, variously calling it a complex problem, a predicament, a dilemma, or a conundrum. Writers may not be sensitive to the nuances involved, or disagree in their analyses of a situation. Both *dilemma* and *conundrum* are used as synonyms for problems that are perplexing and elude solution.[6]

One type of conundrum is present in all governments. However, it depends on an especially demanding conception of problem solving. An example appears in the field of budgeting. The political scientist V. O. Key provided one version of a conundrum more than fifty years ago: "On what basis shall it be decided to allocate x dollars to activity A instead of activity B?"[7] Although budgeting has become one of the most thoroughly documented fields of political science, Key's question still awaits an answer. His complaint about budgeting is actually part of a more general conundrum: "On what basis shall it be decided to make one policy decision rather than another (e.g., a budget allocation, personnel decision, organizational design, or program detail) when the number of potential influences on the outcomes desired are so great as to foil any attempt to predict the effects of any particular influence?"

Key's problem frustrates policy makers the world over. Policy makers cannot know for sure what the effect will be of spending x dollars on activity A or activity B. Beyond the several influences on programs that respond to the decisions of policy makers (money, the number and quality of personnel to be recruited, and program details), there are economic and social influences from outside the government, or even from outside the country in which the government operates. The attitudes and behaviors of parents affect the success of children in elementary and secondary school. Changes in the international economy can affect a nation's well-being and change the demands for its social programs.[8] Some influences on the quality of government programs may change in unpredictable ways over the course of the year in which the relevant budget allocations are spent. It is not possible to know for sure what will be the result of taking a sum and adding it to or subtracting it from the program's budget.

Policy makers seek "solutions" whenever they encounter a problem like that described by V. O. Key. There are routines or standard operating procedures that one generation after another learns from textbooks on policy making. These routines ignore the insoluble components of a problem and direct the attention of policy makers to aspects of the problem that can be solved. Budget makers parcel out resources to claimants according to the criteria of political formulas. They assume that established programs will continue, more or less, and consider only incremental increases or decreases in existing budgets. Analysts assume stability in existing economic and social trends and calculate the likely effect on program quality of proposed changes in the budget. Activists concentrate their politicking in order to achieve increased allocations for favored programs. Policy makers do not pause over the insoluble problem of knowing with certainty what the effects of their decisions will be.[9] Critics harp on the imperfections, but government proceeds nevertheless.

Insoluble problems that develop within a particular context do not lend themselves to the learning of routine procedures. Problems specific to situations are more pernicious than the universal insoluble problems such as Key's budget puzzle. Where the problems are unique, there is little chance of finding a simple and satisfying solution. Policy makers who confront these problems must learn the details of their history and the perspectives of the adversaries. Coping rather than routine is appropriate for these problems. As we shall see, coping requires judgment and subtlety. At times ambiguity rather than clarity is an appropriate response to a difficult problem. Keeping promises vague may broaden support without having to resolve all the difficult issues. The coping of policy makers is context specific. It seems more likely to be learned through a long apprenticeship and intimate knowledge of a problem than from textbooks in a university course. As we have already seen, conditions may change. Creative policy makers may find a solution, sooner or later, for part or all of what had been insoluble.

Several aspects of a problem can signal its insolubility. First, the problem is persistent. The same or a similar problem crop up again and again, perhaps in different formulations or with different personalities playing the major roles. Second, a high emotional charge is associated with prominent policy options. Many of the participants express themselves in absolute terms and view compromise as a betrayal of cherished principles. Third, important elements of the problem are ambiguous. Participants and observers disagree on how to define it or how to distinguish symptoms from underlying problem. An insoluble problem may be multifaceted. It is made up of different components and thus there is difficulty in reaching agreement on how key elements of the problem should be defined.

Chapter 7 will show how the insoluble problem of religion in Israel illustrates most of these traits. Episodes of conflict over Sabbath observance or over the disturbance of ancient graves by building projects flare up, find their solution, and pass from the scene. But then similar problems appear with respect to another Sabbath or another building site. The high emotion of religious Jews and antireligious Jews appears in the stereotypes that both use to describe the other and in the extreme ways they express their demands. Ambiguity appears in the complexity of Jewish doctrines and in the variety of ways in which rabbis and other scholars interpret points of doctrine. Part of the insolubility derives from the unwillingness of intense adversaries to accept the other side's doctrinal views and from the insults that they direct at the leaders of the opposing camp.

One set of American problems that appears to be insoluble concerns forbidden pleasures, or what are called victimless crimes. Legislation forbidding recourse to commercial sex or illicit drugs reflects different conceptions of what is perverse and what freedoms and dangers should be subject to individual choice. Emotions are strong and derive from religious conceptions of sin. Like Israeli disputes about the Sabbath, kosher food, or ancient graves, disputes among Americans about sex and drugs draw on contentious readings of what are described by the faithful as holy doctrines. Beliefs about absolute goods and bads hinder alliances among individuals who might otherwise agree to some limited form of regulation of commercial sex or drug use rather than their absolute prohibition.

The idea of a conundrum encompasses opportunities for serious analysis or pedantic excess. Those definitions of conundrums that describe puzzles, intellectual games, or university jokes are best left out of the analysis.

In this spirit, we should try to avoid paradoxes. These are problems that are made self-contradictory by their wording.[10] Yet some paradoxes are subtle and invite inspection. Readers with a feel for politics should recognize the paradoxes embedded in searches for "optimal solutions" or for solutions that are defined, without consideration of politics, as being in the national interest. Searches for optimal solutions and the national interest are made, in apparent seriousness, by reputable policy makers and commentators. However, searches for optimal solutions to social problems are likely to be endless and without positive results. The "national interest" is a term that politicians use to describe the programs they favor.

Yet another condition that resembles a paradox is the search for how to improve the quality of services without increasing expenditures. Realists know that improved services are likely to require more or better staff, improved working conditions, or other things that cost money.

Some writers loosely use the term *paradox* for conditions that defy their understanding or their capacity to produce a solution.[11] The term is also used by sophisticated analysts for problems that appear puzzling but can be reduced to a finite number of players and variables and analyzed with the tools of game theory.[12]

What Is a Problem of Government?

Related to the designation of a conundrum is the designation of what is a problem of government.[13] A problem in one jurisdiction may merely be a condition in another when it is not recognized as something that should trouble policy makers. Conditions can become problems when there are changes in attitude. Israelis and the residents of other Western democracies have increased their concern for ethnic minorities, women, disabled people, and homosexuals. With changes in attitude, the conditions of discrimination experienced by these groups become problems for policy makers.[14]

No problem exists as an objective fact. Peoples' conceptions of a problem depend on how observers and policy makers perceive and describe discrete bits of reality. The wording of a description can make a problem into a conundrum or something else. Policy makers can describe problems in ways that enable them to make decisions, allocate resources, and implement programs. They can settle a problem through negotiations or by voting on the question of how much to allocate to a specific program. This treatment is politically manageable, even though it evades underlying issues such as the question of how a budgetary allocation will affect the character of government programs. This question about the influence of a budget allocation remains insoluble.

Crime is another issue that, depending on definitions, can be a conundrum or something else. Generations of policy makers have frustrated their own efforts by defining crime as a problem of criminals who are to be either punished or given treatment to deflect them from antisocial attitudes and behaviors. Perhaps it is best to define the problem of crime as a problem of victims and to concentrate resources on their care and compensation.[15] In this way, crime is redefined from the unsolved problem of what to do about violators of the law to a problem of compensation for victims. Officials can solve the problems of compensation by establishing criteria (such as how much compensation will apply in the case of a murdered spouse) and giving an appeals committee responsibility for cases where the established criteria appear to be unsatisfactory.

Traffic safety becomes an insoluble problem if defined as a question of how to eliminate all the death and destruction caused by motor vehicles. It becomes merely a complex technical problem, amenable to experimentation, if defined as a question of how to reduce the level of death and destruction. It becomes a problem manageable by administrative criteria and an appeals process if defined as a question of compensating accident survivors and the estates of those who do not survive.[16]

Other problems also become insoluble if an absolute solution is pursued. It is beyond the capacity of society to set a zero-tolerance standard for oil spills, the presence of carcinogens in food, prostitution, or illicit drug use. Setting an unattainable official target may do more harm than good, for it can lead a regulatory agency to abandon a serious inquiry into what level of control is attainable.

Scholars use the term "zero-sum" for disputes where the goods to be divided cannot be increased and where one side wins all and the other side loses all. However, defining something as a win-lose problem rather than as a problem fit for compromise may reflect the notions of the definers rather than objective reality. In the abortion debate, prolife and prochoice advocates may both lose if they think only about all-or-nothing options,[17] as opposed to thinking about a compromise that defines the circumstances in which abortion should be forbidden, permitted only on the agreement of a committee of doctors, or entirely the mother's choice. In the Middle East, those who have advocated a Palestinian state in all of the land between the Jordan River and the Mediterranean Sea, and those who have advocated Israeli absorption of the same area, have both lost, for the Israeli state has been strong enough to protect itself, but the Palestinians have been capable of exercising enough violence to limit Israel's enjoyment of the territories occupied in 1967.

How an issue is defined explains why some observers and participants can believe a fight has been won when others believe it has been lost. Israelis and Palestinians who make regional peace a priority can both believe they have won when they agree to divide the Promised Land, while rejectionist members of the same communities who are intent on achieving what they view as justice believe they lose by any compromise. The campaign to pass the Equal Rights Amendment (ERA) in the United States seemed headed for success but ended in failure. It easily received Congressional approval in 1972. Within a year it won ratification, often by sizable majorities, in thirty state legislatures. Perhaps it came to be perceived as an issue of new values and lifestyles rather than as an issue of equality, and for this reason was not ratified by the required thirty-eight states. Even while ERA supporters were losing their fight, however, the principle of sexual equality was winning the support of Congress, state legislatures, and the courts.[18] In other words, those who insisted on a constitutional amendment lost, but those who sought sexual equality by other means made impressive progress.

"Goal substitution" is a term used in situations where aspirations are reduced. Using this term puts the emphasis on replacing an unattainable goal with one that is within reach. The problem is that the original aspirations may remain even when the easier goal is achieved. Despite the fact that some policy makers are satisfied that they are coping with crime in a realistic fashion, crime remains a symbol of an imperfect society as well as a threat to those who fear being its victims. What makes religious issues especially resistant to solution is the absolute way in which the devout hold to their beliefs. Compromise is impossible if Sabbath observance is seen as one of the most important commandments.[19]

The Impact of Change

Things change. Occasionally they change drastically. Sometimes many things change at about the same time. War, economic change, or population movement allow some problems to be solved but create others. The international conditions that followed World War II seem to have solved the chronic problem of warfare among the countries of Western Europe. They also allowed the Jews to create their own state and to end two thousand years of being without a homeland. At the same time, politicians and commentators accustomed themselves to the new problem of rivalry between the United States and the Soviet Union and to the Arab-Israeli problem. The late 1980s–early 1990s was another period when a number of events that began at different times reached a crescendo together. Each event was discrete, but there were linkages between them. They permitted the solution of problems that had seemed insoluble. Protagonists changed their minds and signaled their readiness to accept solutions they had not been ready to accept earlier.

Especially important were changes that had begun some years previously in the Soviet Union. Mikhail Gorbachev led his country through a series of economic and political reforms. Along the way the Soviet Union changed its approach toward the satellite nations of Eastern Europe and revolutionary movements around the globe. With a relaxation of pressure from Moscow, nationalist movements gained the upper hand in Poland, Hungary, Czechoslovakia, East Germany, Romania, and Bulgaria. Defense planners in the United States and its NATO allies calculated the implications of events in the Soviet Union for problems that had seemed permanent for forty years.

Reform in the Soviet Union did not proceed smoothly. Economic conditions worsened, ethnic tensions led to fighting in a number of Soviet republics, and a coup attempt seized world attention in August 1991. One republic after another declared its independence. Relaxed emigration controls led several hundred thousand ethnic Germans to emigrate to Germany and several hundred thousand Jews to emigrate to Israel. The Soviet Union, now reduced in size by the secession of some of its republics, indicated that it could no longer guarantee that Syria would receive the military hardware to offset Israeli power. The prospect of a strengthened Israel, whose new immigrants would gobble up even more of the land in the occupied territories, gave the Palestinians more incentive to negotiate. Meanwhile, political scientists concerned with the nature of state power, and with the nature of political support and legitimacy, were obligated to explain what had happened to allow the once powerful Soviet empire to crumble.

Developments in South Africa were also affected by changes in the Soviet Union and Eastern Europe, although the primary causes of change in South Africa lay elsewhere. When the Pretoria government ended apartheid, released the leaders of the African National Congress from prison, and announced negotiations to determine the country's future, South Africa began the process of moving off the list of the world's insoluble political problems. The primary causes of this change, however, may have been white South Africa's pain in the face of economic sanctions and fatigue from being the focus of global censure. On the other hand, it is possible that the end of the cold war and white

South Africa's consequent inability to any longer gain international support by claiming to be a bulwark against communism also played a role.

Optimists see signs for hope in the once insoluble Arab-Israeli problem. The accord signed by Israel and the PLO has survived several delays in fulfilling its provisions as well as attacks by Arab terrorists that killed scores of Israeli civilians. Jordan's King Hussein has become so popular in Israel, according to some wits, that he could win election as king of the Jews.

Routines and Coping

In analyzing the work of policy makers it is useful to divide it into routines and coping. In terms of the scale of problems set forth in table 2.1, routines prevail in levels 1–3 and coping in levels 4 and above. Policy making in the real world appears as a mixture of the two rather than as wholly one or the other. Routines range from the simplest of administrative procedures to more complicated procedures for preparing budgets and handling citizen complaints. Incremental budgeting and procedures for hearing complaints take account of multiple demands, but do so in ways that are regularized, taught to newcomers by established policy makers, and described in political science textbooks.

Coping is a word used often in the literature on public sector problems and policy making, but typically without much specificity. Coping indicates something less than permanently solving problems to the complete satisfaction of all concerned.[20] It deals with stresses associated with contrasting demands when no simple solutions are apparent.[21] It involves adapting, managing, dealing with, and satisficing.[22] These terms imply decisions that are "good enough" even if they are not what any of the participants really want. One kind of coping, which psychologists label as hardiness or positive coping, suggests a concept that is useful in describing the behaviors of many policy makers who operate under the stress of difficult problems.

Positive coping resembles what we will label "engagement coping" by policy makers. Engagement coping responds to stress in several ways: with efforts to salvage something from a difficult situation; by keeping a process going in the expectation of greater opportunities or of preventing substantial losses; by surveying options and recruiting support; by maintaining one's own integrity and political assets and the integrity and political assets of one's organization; by altering expectations in the face of conditions that are not likely to change in the short term; and by ranking priorities in order to achieve goals that are more important at the expense of those that are less important.

"Avoidance coping" also occurs in policy making and resembles what psychologists call negative coping. It responds to stress with hopelessness, confusion, rigidity, distortion, disorganization, randomness, disorder, distress, depression, anxiety, submission, and lack of control. It exhibits pointless emoting that involves loss of control and direction for oneself and potential allies; a quixotic choosing of options in an effort to do something, anything, without taking account of likely costs and benefits; and a frittering away of resources in efforts that do not produce significant accomplishments.[23]

The essential element of policy makers' coping appears to lie in responding to stresses that take the form of crisis, turbulence, ambiguous power relationships, or other disturbances in the policy environment. These conditions do not repeat themselves exactly from one setting to another and may be fluid within individual settings. The importance of elements unique to each situation resists the routinization and teaching of coping techniques. Coping appears to be more art than craft, and an art not to be learned from textbooks but in the field by sensitive individuals willing to devote a great deal of effort to mastering the details of particular issues.

Policy makers use ambiguity as one of their coping devices. Ambiguity thus serves, first, as a way of confronting problems that otherwise might be insoluble, and second, as a source of stress that adds to the problems of policy making.

There is ambiguity in all political settings. The most enlightened of democratic polities posit values of individual freedom against those of communal order. The exact boundaries between individual rights and community are unclear and shift in response to political choices about which proposals should be enacted into law and how those laws should be enforced.[24] The boundaries between formal policy and the informal rules of the game offer opportunities for individuals to expand their rights, but without knowing for certain when the authorities will intervene and enforce the strict letter of the law. How much faster than the posted speed limit can we drive without encountering the highway patrol? How loud can we party without the police charging us for disturbing the peace? What claims can we make in a tax return without triggering an audit? Such cases present temptations and potential embarrassments that add a bit of spice to conventional citizenship. Flexibility is an attraction, but ambiguous limits to acceptable behavior

invite irresponsible exploitation of flexibility. The situation is especially problematic in situations where there is a history of violence. If good
fences make good neighbors, a situation of undefined boundaries between hostile communities raises the possibility of bloodshed.

Ambiguity serves politicians who make promises with far-reaching
implications but do not specify just what the government will deliver.
Voters choose their leaders on the basis of generalized affection for a
campaign. In office, the successful politician is free to pick and choose
only those commitments that can be reconciled with circumstances.
This reinforces chronic public cynicism about politicians but generally
does not threaten a regime.

The appeal of ambiguity for a policy maker lies in the opportunity to
skip over especially contentious issues in the hope that an "understanding" will facilitate accommodation. Adversaries can reach agreement
on the main outline of a program without becoming bogged down in all
the messy details. Legislators enact laws that describe general lines of
action and leave rule making and implementation to administrative
bodies. Legislators should know from experience that they will not see
the implementation of all that might fit within the frameworks they
endorse. They can return to an issue at a later time if they are not satisfied with what administrators actually deliver, or they can remain satisfied with what is achieved.

Policy makers' "mandates" are not precise. The fog of ambiguity may
cover some of the emperor's nakedness. Fudging is a lubricant of political agreement. If one or another constituency eventually loses something in the implementation, the loss may be acceptable in light of
other gains. Even where a written agreement appears to be comprehensive, fuzziness about which provisions will actually be enforced creates
flexibility to deal with evolving realities, limited resources, and unex-
pected crises. The test of ambiguity is its workability. If a program sur-
vives the charge that it is not exactly what all of its architects intended,
we are likely seeing a case of reasonable deviation from expectations.

The problems of ambiguity are well known. Participants do not
know exactly where they stand. It is not clear what they or their antagonists may do. There are no fixed boundaries or guidelines to behavior
that can be described as legitimate, reasonable, or acceptable. At the
very least, ambiguity produces the stress of not knowing one's own limits or those of one's adversaries.

Israel is a country of intense stresses. Heavy immigration, as we will
see in more detail in chapter 4, was a major stress from 1948 through
the mid-1950s, a time when the population more than doubled. High

levels of immigration were seen again in the late 1980s with the collapse of the Soviet Union and a change of regime in Ethiopia. Between 1989 and the middle of 1996 this spurt of immigration increased the Israeli population by 700,000 or 15 percent. Although these waves of immigration created stresses for Israeli policy making, their repetitive nature produced routines that policy makers called on when faced with a new wave. Immigration also places stresses on the immigrants. Israel's routinized programs of counseling, training, and financial aid seem to help most of them cope, however. Of the cases considered in this book, immigration is the policy problem in which the responses are most completely routinized.

The Arab-Israeli conflict, treated in chapter 5, illustrates the change in a problem's status from insoluble to something else. It also shows a continuing tension between, on the one hand, problem elements that may be insoluble, and on the other, those that seem likely to find a solution. Israel has reached peace treaties with Egypt and Jordan, is moving through the stages of an interim agreement with the Palestinians, and is negotiating with Syria and Lebanon, yet Arab and Israeli rejectionists still use violence in an effort to derail the peace process. Each act of violence causes Arabs and Israelis to question the value of the peace that appears on the horizon and leads some of them to add to the violence by joining the rejectionists.

Chapter 6 looks at the problems raised by Jerusalem as a result of the Arab-Israeli conflict. Chapter 7 examines religious disputes among Israel's Jews. There is considerable overlap between the problems addressed in chapters 5–7. Jerusalem figures prominently in the Arab-Israeli conflict, and many of Israel's religious problems arise in Jerusalem. Jerusalem's difficulties generate Israeli policy-making responses that incorporate both routines and coping mechanisms. These responses are routinized in the sense that policy makers use them repeatedly from one crisis to another. They are coping mechanisms in the sense that they seek to implement only partial or temporary solutions to long-standing religious and ethnic conflicts.

The problems examined in chapters 6 and 7 most closely resemble insoluble problems. Israeli policy makers cope by employing tactics that have been less than thoroughgoing. It is possible to see these tactics as coping routines. Activists also behave in a routinized manner when they repeat demands and behaviors from one occasion to another in a ritual fashion. Policy makers treat details and avoid basic conflicts. They engage in prolonged discussions, offer concessions, and delay rather cancel projects. In some circumstances delay provides time for splits to develop within groups of activists, or wears down the activists. If an issue involving religious and secular Jews becomes sufficiently intense to produce mass demonstrations, both religious and secular leaders are likely to urge a peaceful settlement. The leaders usually point to the ancient Jewish civil wars that exposed the nation to conquest, as well as to modern enemies who might exploit communal conflict within Israel. Like other elements of religious conflict, the leaders' actions are usually ritualized and predictable. Religious disputes produce an occasional flare-up marked by shrill rhetoric, mass demonstrations, the use of nondeadly weapons, and bruises. More typically there is chronic tension marked by complaints from religious and antireligious activists. Both camps express dissatisfaction with the status quo and what they see as their opponents' successes.

CHAPTER 3

Israeli Government and Politics

Israel resembles other parliamentary democracies in the formal structure of its government. The 120-member Knesset is the national parliament. The prime minister and other members of the Cabinet govern as long as they maintain the confidence of a majority in the Knesset. The presidency is largely symbolic and ceremonial. National government ministries are key actors in policy making. The Finance Ministry is especially powerful because of its influence on the budget. Municipalities and other local authorities operate within guidelines defined by national ministries and have limited formal power to set their own policies. A number of government-owned companies and statutory authorities operate business enterprises. There is a hierarchy of courts for adjudicating cases and hearing appeals. The State Comptroller audits the operations of other public bodies and reports to the Knesset.

Several aspects of Israel's formal government structure are distinctive and important for policy making. The Knesset is a single house elected on the basis of proportional representation from one nationwide electoral district. This method of election allows a number of political parties to gain seats in the Knesset and reinforces the tendency in Israeli politics toward divisiveness and factionalism. Israelis vote not for specific individuals but for a party's ranked list of 120 candidates. The major parties select candidates in primaries open to all dues-paying members. Other parties rely on committees to nominate their candidates. The ultra-Orthodox religious parties, for instance, are governed by councils of distinguished rabbis, who are given the power of selection. Winning a seat in the Knesset depends on the overall fortunes of one's party. Thus, if a party obtains one-quarter of the votes cast, roughly thirty of the party's list of 120 candidates will enter the Knesset (slight deviations from strict proportional representation may result from the apportionment formula). More than twenty parties have competed in recent national elections, and ten or so have won seats in the Knesset. No political party has even won a majority in a national election, and every Israeli government has been a coalition. Cabinet ministers associated with different parties in the coalitions argue about major policy decisions and sometimes fail to implement government policy.

Until the national election of 1996, Israel's president was given the task of interviewing the leaders of all the parties that won seats in a Knesset election and choosing as prime minister designate the leader with the best chance of forming a government. The selected individual than had a set time in which to assemble a coalition of parties that could win the support of a Knesset majority. But as a result of a reform in election procedures, Israeli voters cast two ballots in 1996, one for the prime minister and another for the party of their choice. Benyamin Netanyahu won a bare majority (50.4 percent) of the prime ministerial vote, and then faced the challenge of bargaining with the eleven parties that had won seats in the Knesset in order to assemble a Cabinet that could win a vote of confidence.

To date, Israel has not produced a written constitution, although the Knesset has enacted a series of Basic Laws that can be altered only by an extraordinary majority. These are described as the components of a constitution that is being drafted piece by piece. Regular laws that violate the Basic Laws can be struck down by the Supreme Court.

The dominant role of Israel's public authorities in managing the national economy makes Israel distinctive. The IMF identifies Israel as one of the democracies where the central government is very heavily involved in economic management.[1]

The formal structure of Israel's government emphasizes rule from the center. Centralization is made easy because of the country's small size. Israel's 5.5 million people live in an area of 8,300 square miles (not counting the occupied territories), which is a little smaller than Massachusetts. Among Israelis national identity is stronger than any local identity. Most Jewish families arrived in the 1930s or later and have no deep local or regional loyalties. The structure of the Knesset strengthens national as opposed to local identity, because no legislator formally represents a city or region.[2]

The dominant Zionist ideology also reinforces the strength of Israel's central government. The country's founders wanted to build a strong state to protect a people who had suffered from nearly two thousand years of statelessness. The fact that most of the country's founders came from Eastern and Central Europe, where centralized states were the norm, also affected Israel's development. David Ben-Gurion, Israel's first prime minister, pursued a policy of statism that sought to transfer to the new government functions such as education and welfare, which had been provided to the Jewish population of Palestine by the Labor Federation (Histadrut) or the Jewish Agency under the British Mandate from the end of World War I until Israel became independent in 1948.

Economic conditions added to the power of national authorities during the period of state building. Most citizens were poor. Only national institutions had sufficient capacity to develop agriculture, industry, housing, transportation, telecommunications, and social services by drawing on taxes, loans, and overseas grants to build a financial base. In this respect, Israel resembled many other new states that came on the scene after World War II. And like them, Israel gave the state a large role in economic management.

Israel suffered more than other new states, however, from the animosity of its neighbors and the strains of massive immigration. These burdens also added to the power of the central government, which had to organize and finance a large army and integrate into Israeli society immigrants who more than doubled the national population less than ten years after independence.

Parties, Politics, and Policy Making

Political parties are the prominent actors in Israeli politics. Individual candidates who win a place in the Knesset commit themselves to party discipline. With few exceptions, party leaders define the postures to be taken by their legislators, and bloc voting is highly predictable.

Prime Minister Netanyahu leads the Likud Party, which won 25 percent of the vote for the Knesset in 1996 and received thirty-two seats. Likud's most prominent posture is nationalism. Its 1996 campaign criticized the Labor Party (whose prime ministers Yitzhak Rabin and Shimon Peres had governed the country in 1992–1996) for being unduly generous in negotiating with the Palestinians and exposing Israelis to increased casualties from terrorist attacks.

Likud has also identified itself with a posture of free enterprise, in opposition to Labor's tradition of socialism. In reality, however, Likud has made populist appeals to the residents of working-class urban neighborhoods and small towns, who constitute the solid core of its voters. Likud's support of social programs during much of the period when it was in power (1977–1992) was hardly distinguishable from that of the Labor Party during its ascendancy (1948–1977 and 1992–1996).

The dimming of Labor's socialism in recent years has contributed to the similarity of the major parties' views on social issues. In truth, Labor never moved far from its support for the mixture of socialism and capitalism promoted by social democratic parties in Western Europe.[3] Labor is the party of Israel's broad middle and upper-middle classes. Its campaigns in 1992 and 1996 focused more on the importance of peace than on social or economic issues. Shimon Peres, Labor's candidate for prime minister in 1996, received 49.5 percent of the vote; his party won 27 percent of the vote and thirty-four seats in the Knesset.

Before Rabin came to power in 1992, the National Religious Party (NRP) had served in every governing coalition since 1948. At present it is a member of the Likud coalition. The NRP represents religious Zionists, that is, Orthodox Jews who support the Israeli state. Its founding rabbis saw the country's emergence as a harbinger of the messianic age. In their view the role of religious Jews was to seek redemption by building a Jewish state in the land given to Israel by the Almighty. Young men from NRP families usually serve in the Israeli army rather than taking advantage of the exemption given to students in Jewish religious academies (yeshivot). Many volunteer for units that combine military service with religious studies. Young women from NRP families take advantage of the military exemption available to religious women, but unlike most other ultra-Orthodox women they volunteer for national service in poor urban neighborhoods and in hospitals and other social institutions.

The Six Day War of 1967 created immediate opportunities and, eventually, problems, for the NRP. On the one hand, stunning victories gave control of the West Bank and all of Jerusalem to Israel. The heart of the biblical Land of Israel was in Jewish hands for the first time in two millennia. This seemed further proof that the Lord was on Israel's side. NRP members created the organization known as Gush Emunim (the Bloc of the Faithful) and took as their cause the promotion of Jewish settlement throughout the newly occupied territories. Their settlement program began modestly under the Labor governments that served until 1977, and then thrived under the Likud governments of 1977–1992.

The problems faced by Gush Emunim and the NRP developed in tandem with the increased prospects for Arab-Israeli peace. The Jewish settlements established by earlier governments became stumbling blocks in negotiations with the Palestinians. The NRP responded to the peace initiatives of the 1990s by moving to the right and taking a position in support of continued settlement and opposition to territorial compromise. The party became politically isolated after other events weakened its hold among the electorate. For some years, the moderate religious orthodoxy that underpinned the NRP had been losing ground to a resurgent ultra-orthodoxy. And when the rise of the Sephardi Torah Observants party (SHAS) provided a Sephardi religious alternative to the Ashkenazi-dominated NRP, many religious Jews of Sephardi background who had supported the NRP defected to SHAS. The NRP's share of the Israeli vote fell from 10 percent in 1969 to 5 percent in 1992; in the same period, the ultra-Orthodox parties increased their share of the vote from 6 percent to 8 percent. For the first time in Israeli history, the government formed after the 1992 election included no NRP Cabinet ministers. In 1996, however, the NRP joined the Netanyahu government after gaining 8 percent of the vote and nine seats in the Knesset.

SHAS is a relatively new player in the ultra-Orthodox sector long dominated by Agudat Israel. SHAS emerged as a protest against what its founders believed was anti-Sephardi discrimination by leaders of Agudat Israel. SHAS also appealed to Sephardi voters who had supported the NRP. In the first national election in which it campaigned (1984), SHAS won four seats in the Knesset; Agudat Israel's representation dropped from four seats to two and the NRP's from six to four. In 1996 SHAS won 9 percent of the vote and ten seats.

SHAS has developed a school system that extends from nursery school through through religious academies for adults. A 1993 report indicated that there were 10,000 children in the party's kindergartens and 6,000 in the higher grades. The system appeals to parents by offering a long school day, a daily hot meal, and transportation to and from school. One source estimates that a third of the families sending their children to SHAS schools are not overtly religious.[4]

SHAS is not known for the subtlety of its political tactics. It used its swing position in coalition politics to acquire government money for its school system; its leaders justified their tactics as making up for years of deprivation at the hands of the Ashkenazim who dominate the Israeli establishment. SHAS stands for the Israeli version of affirmative action or corrective discrimination.[5] One former parliamentarian has served a prison term, another is on trial, and a third is in danger of having his parliamentary immunity lifted so that he can stand trial. SHAS's patronage tactics resemble those used in the past by other Israeli parties. In one view, it was the party's bad luck to come on the scene after a change in the rules of the Israeli political game. Forms of patronage in allocating public resources that had once been routine are now grounds for prosecution and imprisonment. But in the eyes of SHAS supporters, the norms have been changed in order to attack the party. They see the prosecution of party leaders as reflecting jealousy over the movement's success.

SHAS's willingness to compete for resources in state forums has served to bring other ultra-Orthodox bodies into a closer relationship with Israeli government institutions. The ultra-Orthodox, represented by Agudat Israel and a variety of independent congregations, traditionally have sought to distance themselves from the Zionist enterprise. Many of their rabbis opposed the Zionist movement in pre-Holocaust Europe, and some of them continue to oppose the existence of the Israeli state. An exotic few declare the state unholy insofar as it has come into existence without the clear blessing of the Lord or the arrival of the messiah. Others are less fervent in their opposition to state policies that they see as violating Jewish law (halakah). They still believe, however, that the Israeli state has failed to enforce proper religious standards with respect to Sabbath observance, education, food regulation, the enforcement of modesty in dress and public entertainment, marriage and divorce law, the legal question of who is a Jew, and abortion and other medical practices.

Agudat Israel is now a part of United Torah Judaism, a party that won four Knesset seats in the 1992 and 1996 elections. United Torah Judaism is a tense coalition of ultra-Orthodox communities whose animosities toward one another have European roots. Its principal components are Agudat Israel and Degel Hatorah. The congregations that support Degel Hatorah are called either Mitnagdim (a name that distinguishes them from the Hasidim) or Lithuanian (reflecting the location of their pre-Holocaust religious centers in Europe). United Torah Judaism has had some success in attracting support from members of the Lubavitcher (Chabad) movement and among ultra-Orthodox Sephardim who oppose the SHAS leadership.

Meretz formed in the run-up to the 1992 election as a combination of three left-wing parties. Its name is both an acronym formed from the names of its constituent parties and a Hebrew word meaning energy or vigor. Meretz won twelve seats in the Knesset in 1992 and became the second most important party in the coalition formed by Yitzhak Rabin. In 1996 Meretz won 7 percent of the vote and nine seats.

On the extreme right of the Israeli polity is Moledet (Homeland), which has advocated the expulsion of the Arabs from Israel. Moledet won 2 percent of the vote and two seats in 1996. On the extreme left are parties with communist roots or that appeal to Arab nationalist sentiment (some combine both traits). In 1996 Hadash (the New Party) won 4 percent of the vote and five seats, while the United Arab List won 3 percent and four seats.

Two new parties won representation in the Knesset in 1996. A party of Russian immigrants headed by Natan (Anatoli) Sharansky won 6 percent of the vote and seven seats, and a party calling itself the Third Way and seeking to position itself ideologically between Labor and Likud won 3 percent of the vote and four seats. Both of these parties, with SHAS, the NRP, and United Torah Judaism, joined Likud in forming the government headed by Prime Minister Netanyahu.

As well as having a multiplicity of political parties, Israel has a multiplicity of interest groups, which, however, aspire to join the dominant public sector rather than remain as independent sources of pressure on government. Gush Emunim pursued its program of continued Israeli control of the West Bank by winning substantial government aid for its settlement projects.[6] As well as being the leading voice of the Israeli conservation movement, the Society for Nature Preservation has acquired quasi-governmental status as a sponsor of school trips, summer camps, and other nature-related programs. The Manufacturers Association enjoys a formal role as the representative of Israeli employers in economic negotiations with the Labor Federation and the Finance Ministry. The Labor Federation itself not only represents workers but is a prominent part of the Israeli establishment. It either owns or has links to Israel's largest health service, Israel's largest bank, various industrial enterprises, pension funds, and bus cooperatives, and the kibbutzim and moshavim (cooperative farming settlements) that dominate the country's agriculture.

Israel's Distinctive Traits: Claims and Realities

As the world's only Jewish country, Israel reflects the impact on its politics of Jewish beliefs and traditions developed over the course of more than two millennia. Prominent among these is the notion of the Chosen People and the belief that Israel is the land promised to the Jews by God. These are heady ideas, which lead some Israelis to think of their country as unique and themselves as being at the center of God's plan. Schoolchildren have told me that their teacher has proclaimed Israel the most beautiful of the world's countries. Television commentators report that Israel has the world's worst drivers and the world's highest rate of traffic fatalities. Learned university colleagues and distinguished journalists write about the country's deplorable social gap separating rich and poor, which they claim is strikingly large in international terms.

While the relative beauty of the Israeli landscape is a matter that should not concern us here, claims about excessive traffic deaths and income differentials have policy implications that should. Both sets of claims fail to stand up to international comparisons, and thus can be seen as threats to intelligent policy making. Ignorance about the true nature of Israeli conditions can lead to distortions in the allocation of national resources.

Income Inequality

The importance placed on income inequality by Israeli commentators reflects the influence of socialist elements in Zionist ideology, norms of social righteousness rooted in ancient Judaic doctrines, and the fallout from claims of religious and ethnic discrimination that have set Arabs against Jews and Jews of Asian and African background against those of European background.

Claims for the existence of a substantial social gap or high levels of economic inequality are sufficiently widespread to have acquired the status of conventional wisdom. A recent book by Hebrew University political theorist Ze'ev Sternhell argues that Israeli egalitarianism has been an ideological symbol, a rhetorical device, and a rallying cry for a Labor Party that failed to take it seriously.[7] Yosef Goell, a senior columnist with the *Jerusalem Post*, writes, "Recent studies have shown that among developed countries, Israel is second only to the United States in income inequality."[8] According to Hebrew University political sociologist Michael Shalev, Israel falls short of other welfare states in the seriousness and success of its egalitarian policies.[9] Several Israeli intellectuals have written about increasing degrees of inequality between the country's income groups.[10]

It is no easy task to define economic inequality or to measure it, and there are no universally accepted comparisons for judging inequality in Israel versus other countries. No claims about empirical findings can be taken as the final word. However, some comparative analyses indicate that Israel is substantially more egalitarian than Sternhell, Shalev, or Goell say.

Concepts of socioeconomic inequality sometimes encompass justice and fairness in the division of opportunities and outcomes in education, work, housing, and health. It is common, however, for scholars to confine themselves to the more narrow and measurable issue of income inequality. But problems abound even with respect to the most precise definitions, which concern income distribution between the wealthier and poorer segments of a population. Experts quarrel about the strengths and weaknesses of the widely used GINI coefficient for measuring income inequality, about national definitions of a "poverty line," and about distinctions between income and wealth (important for studies of the aged, who tend to score low on monthly income but higher on accumulated wealth). It is no simple task to distinguish between gross and net income; assign monetary values to the public services received by families at different income levels; trace the flow of transfer payments; factor in the amount families in each income group pay to government in the form of sales taxes, value-added taxes, property taxes, and customs duties; take account of the wealth represented by housing, land, savings accounts, government and private pension funds, and similar items; and assess the impact of the murky but potentially important phenomenon of unreported income. In addition to having to confront problems inherent in assessing the impact of formal legislation concerned with taxes and services, scholars also need to assess how taxes are actually levied and collected and how services are distributed. Most research proceeds only part of the way along the chain of increasing precision. Few analyses struggle with the problems of differential policy implementation from one population sector to another, or with questions about such things as uneven tax assessments, discretionary tax discounts in hardship cases, and the value of a public education received in a slum school versus that in a school located in an upper-income neighborhood.

These analytical problems multiply when the subject is comparisons across national borders. Countries do not have identical public services, transfer payments, and tax rates. They also differ on how they record the exclusion of certain kinds of income and expenditure from taxation, as well as in their reputations with respect to the implementation of declared policies and the quality of their economic statistics.[11]

What emerges from this collection of problems is a severely limited corpus of international data. The information we have applies only to some countries and is not always available in consistent time series. It has been assembled and partly refined by individual scholars or teams interested in international comparison.

TABLE 3.1 Coefficients of Simple Correlation Between per Capita GNP and Measures of Income Inequality in Forty-five Countries

Measure of Income Inequality	Coefficient
Percentage of income received by:	
Families in the group with lowest 20% of income	.48
Families in the group with the highest 20% of income	−.70
Families in the group with the highest 10% of income	−.69
Household GINI coefficient	−.67

SOURCE: Adapted from Denny Braun, *The Rich Get Richer: The Rise of Income Inequality in the United States and the World* (Chicago: Nelson-Hall, 1991), 55–57, 75–76.

Inequality and Economic Development

One of the lessons that emerges from international comparisons is a link between a country's status with respect to income inequality and its level of economic development. A mid-1980s analysis of data from forty-five countries, reported in table 3.1, shows sizable coefficients of simple correlation between per capita GNP and measures of income equality. Countries with higher levels of per capita GNP tend to have a more equal income distribution. The findings make sense. Equality is expensive. It depends on a national treasury sufficiently wealthy to afford such things as substantial educational programs and other social services; transfer payments to aid the unemployed, the incapacitated, the elderly, and large families; and an administrative structure sophisticated enough to assess and collect taxes with progressive rates. A wealthy economy also provides more opportunities for personal advancement in the private sector by providing higher wages, better opportunities for savings, and access to nongovernmental bank loans, educational scholarships, and charitable funds.

The data considered here show that Israel is not one of the world's most egalitarian societies, but neither is it one of the wealthiest. Israel's level of income inequality more or less reflects its level of economic development. To the extent that measures of Israel's income inequality depart from levels generally associated with countries at the same stage of economic development, they show that Israel is more egalitarian than a number of other countries at or above its level of wealth. Regression analyses and a consideration of residuals show that Israel's GINI coefficient is lower than one would expect given the country's per capita GNP, which means that the country's level of equality is greater than one would expect. Moreover, the proportions of total incomes received by low-income and high-income families are, respectively, higher and lower than Israel's per capita GNP would lead one to expect, which also indicates a greater than expected level of income equality.[12]

Israel's top earners received a lower percentage of total national income in relation to per capita GNP than comparable groups in Italy, the United Kingdom, France, Australia, West Germany, Sweden, Canada, Norway, the United States, and Switzerland. The picture is similar with respect to other measures of income equality. Israel's poorest families (that is, those in the bottom 20 percent of income earners) received a higher percentage of total national income than comparable groups in New Zealand, France, Australia, Denmark, Canada, and the United States. When the GINI coefficient test is applied, Israel is more egalitarian than the wealthier countries of New Zealand, Italy, France, Australia, Canada, and the United States.

The Luxembourg Income Study is an effort to carefully assemble and reconcile international income data. As its participants admit, however, the final data are not free of national peculiarities. At present information is available for only a small number of countries and a span of a few years. One set of reports draws on data from Israel and some wealthier countries, namely Canada, West Germany, Norway, Sweden, the United Kingdom, and the United States. The findings show that Israel does not differ greatly from the group norm on measures of income inequality and in some respects is more egalitarian than other countries in the group.[13]

The importance of economic development for issues of inequality adds to the criticism that should be directed at Sternhell's analysis. His censure of the Labor party's founders for departing from an ideology of egalitarianism is inappropriate when one considers the primitive and impoverished condition of the Israeli economy before 1948 and during the early years of the state. He writes as if party leaders were free to pursue nationalist goals at the expense of pursuing social equality. What he does not consider is the cost of each option or its likelihood of being achieved in the context when decisions were made. In addition to general poverty and an incomplete administrative infrastructure, the prestate period that occupies much of Sternhell's analysis was, of course, a period in which there was no state sovereignty for the Jews. Until Israel's independence, the Labor party's founders did no more than head Jewish communal organizations within the framework of the

British Mandate (the name given to the British occupying authority in Palestine). They had to rely on voluntary mechanisms and social pressure to collect funds with respect to resource allocation and providing services.

A regime's investment in egalitarian policies can also be viewed within the context of demands on its resources from other policy fields. Israel's unusually high expenditures on security make its efforts with respect to income equality even more impressive. While a group of Western-style democracies was spending an average of U.S.$508 per capita and 2.7 percent of GNP on defense in 1989, Israel was spending U.S.$1,323 per capita and 12.8 percent of GNP.[14]

The Issue of Rising Inequality

Those critics who charge that Israel's economy has become less egalitarian in recent years are essentially correct. However, the same point is also true for many other national economies. There are several indications that the heyday of the welfare state has passed and that welfare policies have retreated in the face of political victories by right-wing parties.[15] Western democracies have accepted the fashions of government downsizing and privatization. Foreign aid budgets have also suffered. Even before the end of cold war competition, elites in Western countries tired of providing charity to the world's poor. The homeless appear to be more prevalent on the city streets of Europe and North America than in Israel.

Data on changes in inequality levels in various countries over time are even more scarce and less easily comparable than data on inequality levels at fixed points in time. National governments alter their tax distribution schemes, program benefits, transfer payments, and statistical concepts without reference to what the changes mean for social scientists who require stable data sets. The GINI coefficient for the United States increased, in the direction of inequality, from .376 in 1947 to .392 in 1986.[16] The proportion of American families below the poverty line increased from 24 percent in 1969 to 36 percent in 1991.[17] In Israel, income inequality increased from 1985 to 1993. However, the changes have not been consistently in the direction of greater inequality. In 1992–1993 there was a narrower gap between the lowest and the highest income groups than in any year since 1986–1987.[18] A spurt of rising inequality from 1988 to 1991 may have reflected not the effects of government policy but the fact that those years were marked by sizable immigration and high levels of unemployment among the new arrivals.

Whatever the state of Israeli inequality, it is ameliorated by progressive taxation rates, which substantially narrow income gaps. In the United States, by contrast, income gaps are widened by a tax system that is, in the aggregate, regressive.[19]

Traffic Safety

In Israel it is common to find the media condemning the "eleventh plague"—the "carnage" and "bloody outrage" on the highways.[20] Policy makers devote special resources to their war against the "slaughter on the roads." A permanent government commission, the National Council for the Prevention of Road Accidents (formerly headed by a justice of the Supreme Court), is charged with improving traffic safety by coordinating police efforts, road construction, and driver education activities. The Knesset has considered proposals to require all new automobiles to include air conditioning, on the assumption that hot and sticky drivers are more likely to cause accidents. Legislators have also looked at the idea of requiring all applicants for a driver's license to tour the hospital wards where the most serious accident cases are treated. The *Jerusalem Post* reported in a front-page story that the Sephardi chief rabbi, Eliahu Bakshi-Doron, had urged Prime Minister Yitzhak Rabin to declare an "emergency situation" on the nation's roads and do everything possible to stop accidents.[21] Another *Jerusalem Post* article reported that "As bad as highway safety has been, it has gotten worse in recent years."[22]

But how accurate are these perceptions? Comparative research on road safety in a number of countries shows that the incidence of traffic deaths in relation to the total number of motor vehicles has a strong negative correlation (-.82) with per capita GNP. Greater economic resources work to lower accidents by promoting better-quality vehicles and roads and higher standards of driver education, and by increasing the amount of driving experience accumulated by a nation's citizens. Israel has a higher incidence of traffic deaths in relation to the total number of motor vehicles than is found in the wealthier countries of Western Europe and North America. When the incidence of traffic deaths in relation to the total number of motor vehicles is plotted against per capita GNP, Israel has a lower incidence of traffic deaths than expected for its level of economic development. With respect to traffic deaths in relation to total population, Israel has a lower death rate than Germany, Belgium, the United States, France, Austria, Canada, Australia, Italy, Finland, Switzerland, Denmark, and Japan. Israel's vehicular death rate has also declined substantially since 1974, when it stood at 21 deaths per 100,000 population. In 1991 the rate was only 9 per 100,000.[23]

At least some Israeli officials realize that the traffic situation is not all that bad. The head of the Transportation Ministry's Road Safety Administration told a Cabinet meeting that Israelis may be among the world's worst drivers, but not among the most dangerous. In this official's list of traffic death rates in twenty-three developed countries, Israel had a better record than all but five countries. It scored better than Switzerland (which many Israelis see as a bastion of law and order), the United States (for Israelis a symbol of all that is modern and desirable), France, Germany, and Italy.[24] However, when the domestic security minister said at the end of 1995 that the year had witnessed a decrease in traffic deaths, a Transportation Ministry official accused him of exaggerating and said that "the situation was far from satisfactory."[25] When one official with responsibility for road safety went before the finance minister with a request for funding, he admitted that Israel scored relatively well among developed countries with respect to its traffic death rate and had seen a decrease in the rate. Nonetheless, he felt obliged to press for an emotional campaign of media advertisements.[26]

There are no simple conclusions or final answers concerning economic inequality and road safety in Israel. For a social critic, it may be enough to proclaim that there is not enough economic equality or that too many people die as a result of road accidents. A social scientist, however, should take account of the conceptual and operational complexities associated with these issues, and, insofar as international comparisons are possible, show how each country performs in relation to others with which it can reasonably be compared.

Comparative analysis indicates results that are reasonable to expect. If, with respect to a particular trait, a country's statistical performance is similar to that of the other countries in the comparison group, it is fair to conclude that its performance is acceptable within the level of resources that states generally are inclined to allocate to the issue. For those who assert that cross-national comparison is not an appropriate standard of judgment, the only solution may be access to a paradise where resources and opportunities are unlimited.

When considered comparatively, income inequality and traffic safety in Israel resemble the conditions in Western democracies generally, perhaps to the dismay of those Israelis who see themselves as the Chosen People of the Promised Land. In some respects, in fact, the picture belies the conventional wisdom: Israel is a little more egalitarian than nations with which it might fairly be compared, and its roads are safer.

The parochialism of Israeli policy makers and policy critics can have serious implications. For those who are not satisfied with a reasonable level of national achievement, as defined by the achievements of countries that resemble Israel in important ways, an insistence on ever greater achievements in a favored policy area can distort resource allocation. The result may be a reduction in the accomplishments of public policies that are less favored, or damage to the private sector caused by the imposition of taxes that are higher in Israel than in countries that are its competitors in international markets.

Israeli parochialism has an additional danger. The centrality of the Promised Land for religious and nationalist Jews produces an intensity and rigidity with respect to national issues. The assassination of Prime Minister Yitzhak Rabin, and his vilification by religious and nationalist Israelis for bargaining away parts of the Promised Land, were extreme examples of emotions whose incidence in the population cannot be accurately gauged. Such emotions represent a threat not only to the flexibility that is important in international negotiations but also to the sanity of the political culture and the democratic character of Israel's regime.

A Metropolitan Nation-State

Israel's character as a metropolitan nation-state is a case in which some Israeli intellectuals would change existing patterns of policy making because they believe that the country is like others, but in reality it is different. Like reformers in other countries, these Israelis complain about the excessive power of national government officials, support greater autonomy for local government, and argue that the efforts of local authorities in metropolitan areas should be guided by the principles of integration, coordination, and cooperation.

These assertions require examination, given the conditions that make Israel an anomaly on the international scene. Israel is not so much a country with cities as one metropolitan area within the structure of a country. Rather than join the chorus of reformers from other countries who complain about insufficient local autonomy or inadequate coordination in metropolitan regions, Israelis with an interest in municipal government should recognize that they have what reformers elsewhere generally cannot achieve—a substantial degree of metropolitan integration that is the result of a convergence of local and national politics.

At first glance, claims on behalf of Israel's local authorities seem warranted. Israel has a highly centralized national government that exercises considerable formal control over local authorities. Over the years a number of prestigious government commissions and reform-oriented individuals in the public service and academia have document-ed the extensive dependence of local officials on decisions taken by na-tional ministries.[27] The Interior Ministry, for instance, approves each local authority's taxes and expenditures and sets the amount of the gen-eral grant to be given to the local authority. The Finance Ministry must approve the Interior Ministry's budget and may take an interest in the finances of individual localities. The Education and Culture Ministry exercises substantial powers over local school curricula and may ap-prove or reject local proposals for the enrollment boundaries of each pri-mary school. Transportation Ministry approval is required for munici-pal council decisions on whether streets should be one-way or two-way, on the placement of traffic signs, and on parking regulations and the placement of parking areas. The Housing and Construction Ministry exercises a great deal of influence in the design and construction of new neighborhoods and the refurbishing of older ones.[28]

Israeli reformers offer conventional arguments about insufficient local autonomy. They focus on the need for democracy in government and on the themes of government responsiveness, accountability, and efficiency.[29] According to the accepted wisdom, a lack of local autono-my lessens the effectiveness of municipal officials, who are the best informed people when it comes to local needs and resources; adds to the costs and delays of government by requiring local authorities to apply substantial effort toward persuading national officials to approve required changes; reduces the responsiveness of government generally; and lessens the quality of democracy by frustrating political involve-ment in local arenas close to the people and their problems.

Israelis have truth on their side when they relate one example after another of central government bureaucrats who are unresponsive to legitimate local demands. However, the critics do not make a convinc-ing case that a radical shift to local autonomy would improve govern-ment responsiveness in a measurable way. There are many stories of arrogant and unresponsive bureaucrats at the local level and of local educational and social agencies that make people's lives miserable.

The current management of Israel's smaller local authorities, in par-ticular, is hardly a model of professional administration or orderly democracy. In the event of greater municipal autonomy, locally domi-nant ethnic groups, powerful extended families, and political machines will undoubtedly take up some of the slack left by weakened central authority. Far-reaching local autonomy may also lessen the weight of national finance in municipal administration and thus increase the gaps in service quality between wealthier and poorer communities. Local officials in smaller and poorer communities may demand local autonomy in programming and spending but also substantial investment from the national government. However, Israel's national officials are unlikely to be more generous than those in other countries when it comes to performing the thankless job of collecting taxes while at the same time allowing officials of local jurisdictions to decide how the money will be spent. If Israel's local authorities are given more authority over taxation and expenditures, the principal losers will be the smaller and poorer towns outside of the metropolitan core. And as we shall see below, the strict formal centralization that allows national ministries to govern Israeli localities is significantly looser in practice.

National government policy makers in Israel display mixed emotions about the prospect of reform. On the one hand, they often express displeasure at excessive central control, and on several occasions have appointed distinguished panels to look into the matter. On the other hand, when faced with concrete proposals for reform their actions have been modest. For instance, when a national commission submitted recommendations in favor of local autonomy in 1981, the Cabinet accepted the report in principle, but neither it nor subsequent Cabinets implemented the major recommendations.

What Israeli reformers overlook in their enthusiasm for local autonomy is that the values of responsiveness, accountability, democracy, and metropolitan coordination are reasonably well achieved in a situation where there is an overlap between national and local regimes. "Metropolitan Israel" does not exist in any formal sense, but appears in the concentration of population, politics, and policy-making activity encompassed by the triangular megalopolis that extends along the coast for about one hundred miles from Ashkelon in the south to Nahariya in the north, with a center bulge thirty-five miles inland to Jerusalem. This area dominates a country that is one of the world's smallest, most congested, and most urban. As was mentioned above, the metropolitan triangle contains 81 percent of the national population.[30] Its approximately 1,800 square miles constitute 23 percent of Israel's land area, not counting the occupied territories. Yet it is smaller than the metropolitan areas of Houston, Los Angeles, and Seattle.

Israeli academics and technocrats have long been aware of the highly concentrated nature of the population. They are also alert to changing fashions in metropolitan reform and skeptical about simple demands for metropolitan integration.[31] The expression "Gadera to Hadera" refers to the coastal area in the middle of the country that is thought of as the urban core, but it is substantially smaller than the single metropolitan region considered here. Experts quarrel about the best way to define the country's urban regions and to judge the relative amount of intercourse within and between each component. Tel Aviv, Jerusalem, and Haifa are the centers of their own commuting and shopping areas. Some experts would count the Beersheba region in the south of the country as part of the Israeli megalopolis. If so, this would add a southeastern bulge to the triangular area and increase the megalopolis's share of the country's population to 86 percent and its share of the land mass to 25 percent. However, Beersheba and its surroundings appear to be more peripheral than Jerusalem, Tel Aviv, or Haifa to the concerns of Israel and its political elite.

There is considerable daily commuting throughout metropolitan Israel. Most frequent are trips between the Tel Aviv area and Jerusalem to the east, Ashdod and Ashkelon to the south, and Natania and Haifa to the north. There is also some daily traffic on the longer route (one hundred miles) between Jerusalem and Haifa.

Israelis loudly proclaim in international forums that Jerusalem is their national capital. In practice, however, important centers of Israeli life are distributed more broadly within the national metropolis. Tel Aviv is the financial and commercial hub and perhaps the cultural capital. Haifa and Ashdod are the major ports. National ministries have important offices in Tel Aviv, where key officials typically spend at least one day a week. The Defense Ministry retains its sprawling headquarters in Tel Aviv, although its key personnel come to Jerusalem to make presentations to the Knesset and to meet with other national figures.

The argument for a convergence between local and national politics and policy making rests on two points: first, on the concentration of the population in one extended megalopolis, and second, on the fact that political culture and the policy-making agenda are focused on issues of concern to the megalopolis's residents. Metropolitan Israel is at the heart of a political culture that is national in character. Most Israeli families arrived in the country only during this century. Despite the claims of some experts that regional loyalties are developing, there are as yet no strong indications of subnational attachments.[32]

The intention of the Zionist pioneers was to build a nation of farmers and thereby correct what they saw as a historical distortion, namely the evolution of the Jews into an urban bourgeois people. According to an Israeli sociologist, however, they succeeded only in ignoring the fact that most immigrants settled in urban areas. This, in turn, meant that city planning was denied the talent it needed during the period of nation building.[33] Moreover, the Zionist myth failed to acknowledge the urban roots of the ancient Judeans. In ancient times the city of Jerusalem was the center of the faith and the locale of many events described in the Hebrew Bible.[34] The Zionist myth also overlooked the urban patterns of Jewish settlement in the diaspora before the creation of modern Israel.

As noted above, the Knesset is elected on the basis of proportional representation from a single national constituency. Although the major parties make some effort to put representatives of key localities and regions on their lists of Knesset candidates, most national figures identify with Jerusalem or Tel Aviv. The mayors of Jerusalem and Tel Aviv have been leading figures in the two major political parties and crucial in bringing local needs to the attention of national policy makers. Israel's daily newspapers and the electronic media are national in character and based mainly in Tel Aviv and Jerusalem.

Arguably the dominant issues in Israeli policy making are those that demand a national perspective. Defense, international relations, and economic viability are perennially at the top of the agenda. These issues are related, insofar as defense makes unduly heavy demands on the national economy and helps to make the economy fragile and dependent on government. The cost of maintaining the military and other security forces, as well as the dependence of Israel's small economy on international trade, produces constant worry over inflation and the imbalance of payments. Immigration is another issue with a national focus. The costs of transportation, housing, job creation, and social services for immigrants fall largely on national ministries and quasi-governmental agencies.

Compared to Mexico City, Cairo, Tokyo, London, New York, and Los Angeles, Israel's megalopolis is decidedly modest. Nonetheless, its prominence in the country and its substantial impact on Israeli policy making suggest reasons why repeated calls for reforming local government have had little success. Metropolitan Israel is virtually synonymous with Israel. The concerns of Israel's residents and local authorities are shared by policy makers who live in the national metropolis and know its various segments, even if they do not formally represent a specific locale. The national capital(s)—Jerusalem and Tel Aviv—are not distant cities but located within the metropolis. Only the most far-flung points of the metropolitan region are separated from one another by a drive of more than two and a half hours.

It is also the case that Israel's small size and the compact nature of its population manages, more or less, the problem of metropolitan integration. The issue of metropolitan integration surfaces in Israel, especially in the Tel Aviv area, which includes the Tel Aviv–Yafo central city with its 350,000 residents, six municipalities in the 100,000–200,000 range, four in the 50,000–100,000 range, and a number of smaller municipalities. The Israeli megalopolis is not without inequalities of resources and social problems, or government activities poorly coordinated across municipal boundaries. However, the police force is national. National ministries play a dominant role in education, public transportation, traffic control, housing, welfare, and the financing of local government. National government bodies have a crucial say about issues relating to water supply and town planning. Reformers criticize the Environment Ministry for being weak by Western European and North American standards, but it is the strongest player in its field. In the Israeli context, problems of metropolitan governance are less pressing than in situations where strong local roles in education, policing, road construction, traffic control, taxation, environmental control, and water supply frustrate policy integration or equity across urban areas.

The Importance of Bureaucracy in Policy Making and Implementation

Israel is distinctive by virtue of its heavy security burden, high levels of government expenditure, and extensive central government involvement in economic matters. These traits are linked; security concerns dominate the national budget, and economic management is important for the monies raised for defense. According to social critics, Israel is not a state with an army as much as it is an army financed by a state.

The combination of extensive social programs and a heavy defense burden creates a state that is heavily bureaucratized. High-ranking ministry officials do much of the work involved in formulating policy. The Knesset's governing parties routinely endorse the bureaucracy's proposals with few if any modifications. Unlike members of the U.S. Congress, members of Israel's Knesset have virtually no staff assistance to help them challenge the government's proposals or formulate alternatives.

By law, all Israelis are members of one the nationwide health maintenance organizations, whose physicians parcel out health care according to the regulations set by the HMO and the Health Ministry. There are no truly private schools for Jews to compete with the elementary and secondary schools supervised and funded by the Education and Culture Ministry or with the government-financed schools administered by the ultra-Orthodox yeshivot. We have already seen the importance of the Interior and Finance ministries in the operation of local authorities. Israeli building contractors and householders are bound by planning regulations that affect structural design and even regulate such details as the color an apartment dweller can paint on the outside of his or her apartment door (if it is not the same color as the other apartment doors in the building, he or she must formally obtain the approval of every other resident).

In practice, however, the strongly centralized and bureaucratic regime does not operate quite as the rules suggest. The nature of Israeli politics produces a set of informal rules and a loose, somewhat chaotic administration.[35] Rules governing the color of apartment doors are overlooked with the same frequency as rules governing structural additions to apartments and houses. Among the ugly charms of Israeli cities are the wild structures that appear on balconies and rooftops. Almost none of them have been erected with the permissions required by law, and in almost no cases do the municipal authorities use their power to remove them.

Part of the explanation for loose administration relates to the tensions of coalition government. No party has ever won a majority in a Knesset election, and leading parties have thus had to create temporary political partnerships, in which Cabinet ministries are handed out to the partners according to the number of Knesset seats each controls. Prime ministers have been unable to impose their will on their partners, except in a few key matters governed by the coalition agreement. Israel's primary concerns have been national security and economic stability. Education, transportation, housing, social welfare, health, and local government have always been lower on the list of priorities. Most ministers have therefore been free to operate as they wish in these less-valued areas of government without having to consider the need for integrated national policies.

The rules that govern appointments in the Israeli bureaucracy are casually administered. Although they prescribe competitive procedures, there is a tradition of evading the rules to facilitate the appointment of people who are politically allied with the responsible minister. Reports prepared by the Civil Service Commission show that 20–40 percent of appointments are not made competitively. Appointments to positions in local authorities and in companies owned by national ministries or local authorities are not closely supervised by the Civil Service Commission and are thought to be even more open to political influence.[36]

The freedom of local authorities to operate outside the rules laid down for them by the central government begins with the inability of the Interior Ministry to learn the intricacies of local government finance and operations. According to a political scientist who also served as a senior official in the Office of the State Comptroller, "The local authority invariably inflates its proposed budget prior to negotiations with the Ministry of Interior, so that even after cutbacks it is left with a budget which may be larger than strictly necessary."[37] A report from the State Comptroller found that most local authorities did not comply when the Interior Ministry ordered them to reduce their personnel as part of a governmentwide economy measure.[38]

Also working in favor of clever municipal officials are the separate relations between local authorities and ministries that implement their own programs in the local communities. Ministries also provide funds to local authorities for specific programs in ways that are not coordinated by the Interior and Finance ministries. The Housing and Construction Ministry pays for the construction of housing and roads. The Religions Ministry supports synagogues, ritual baths, churches, and mosques. The Defense Ministry pays part of the costs of local civil defense. The Health Ministry supports local clinics. Through its grants to schools and control over principals and local educational offices in matters concerning curriculum, school boundaries, and enrichment programs, the Education and Culture Ministry can make a neighborhood or a whole city more or less attractive as a place for families to live. With the onset of massive immigration from the Soviet Union in 1989, the Immigration and Absorption Ministry became an important source of funds for social services.

Ministries operate under a large number of national laws, ministry regulations, and precedents. Some of these are holdovers from the British Mandate, while others reflect the considered judgment of prestigious commissions of inquiry or the actions of the Supreme Court in response to suits brought by municipalities or private citizens. Academic and government commentators have remarked on the problems that arise in sorting through many years' worth of legislation, committee recommendations, judicial decisions, administrative rules, ministerial rulings, and financial records in order to identify the major lines of policy pursued by national authorities.[39] The ministries may not move together in response to the same policy themes. Municipal officials have offered national politicians the opportunity to be the patrons of local projects. Ministers seek to advance their own reputations by favoring certain local projects, whether or not those projects have the blessing of the Finance or Interior ministries.

The Interior Ministry has evaded its own formal rules. Its minister was the subject of a severe report by the State Comptroller for the manner in which he provided special allocations for municipalities to use in supporting programs sponsored by his political party.[40]

National and local officials are aggressive players in an intergovernmental game that is something of a free-for-all among contending authorities wanting to safeguard their powers or expand the resources at their disposal.[41] Ministers and senior civil servants withhold payments or approvals for local projects in order to force a municipality's compliance with a ministry ruling or to punish a municipality for overstepping its discretion. National ministries send inspectors to schools, welfare offices, and other institutions they support, but there are not enough inspectors to keep watch on local authorities. Local politicians and administrators seek money where they can find it and do not always follow the rules governing the transfer of funds between budget categories or the discretion they may exercise in program implementation.[42] Much occurs behind the scenes, with only the occasional story made available by insiders or through the media. School principals may try to preserve smaller-than-average class sizes by telling newcomers to the neighborhood that there is no room for their children, and such tricks may work with timid parents. Other citizens have learned that they must know their legal rights and insist on them against officials who would serve their own organization's interests rather than the public's. From time to time one hears of frustrated citizens who, in dealing with local authorities, resort to shouting and upsetting office furniture.

Quasi-governmental bodies also moderate the formal centralization of Israel's government. The Jewish Agency finances its own social service programs and supplements the budgets of other organizations using contributions received from Jewish communities in the diaspora. The mayors of Jerusalem and Tel Aviv have the support of foundations that use donated money to support programs in their cities. The Jerusalem Foundation, for instance, has contributed to over one thousand projects. While Teddy Kollek was mayor of Jerusalem from 1966 to 1993 he was also president of the Jerusalem Foundation. Kollek approached potential donors with the argument that he could supple-

ment their contributions with funds recruited from municipal and national government budgets. He also approached municipal and national
government officials with the argument that he could supplement their
allocations to Jerusalem projects with funds collected from overseas
donors.[43]

The Nature and Sources of Israeli Democracy

Political scientists describe Israel as a democracy,[44] but its asserted
status as a Jewish state sets it apart from other democracies. Although a
number of democracies have an established church, include a cross in
their national flag,[45] or adopt religious holidays as national holidays, the
tendency during the past century has been to associate democracy with
norms that are secular and egalitarian and do not favor members of one
religious community over another.

Israel earns its place on the list of democratic regimes because of its
free and open elections, use of proportional representation in the Knesset and local councils, and peaceful transfers of power after elections.
The ideological spectrum represented in the Knesset has ranged from
communist and Arab-dominated parties on the left to free-enterprise,
Jewish religious, and Jewish nationalist parties on the right. Candidates
representing Islamic religious parties have won places on local councils.
Both Jewish and non-Jewish Israelis turn out to vote in impressive
numbers—about 80 percent in national elections. The largest parties
now nominate candidates for major offices using primaries open to all
dues-paying members. The multiplicity of political parties and an electoral system based on proportional representation are phenomena that
both reflect and reinforce a tendency toward the proliferation of a diversity of options but without clear choices among them.

One of the most delicate questions concerning Israel's democracy
relates to the balance of opportunities between the Jewish majority (82
percent of the population)[46] and non-Jews. The 1948 Declaration of
Independence proclaimed Israel a Jewish state even as it promised
equality of rights regardless of religion, ethnicity, or sex. Jews receive
most of the political opportunities and policy benefits available to
Israelis. Whether this state of affairs is justified by the threats to Israel's
security or the Arab disinclination to recognize the legitimacy of the
Israeli regime is a question that Israelis have argued about for a long
time. The voter turnout rate for Israeli Arabs is about the same as that
for Israeli Jews, except in Jerusalem. However, Israel's Arabs have mini-

mized their political influence by voting for communist and other anti-establishment parties, which remain outside the circle of politicians who trade support for the government for constituent benefits. As we shall see in chapter 6, few East Jerusalem Arabs have accepted Israel's offer of citizenship, and only a limited number take advantage of opportunities to vote in municipal elections. They thereby forgo the influence that they, as a substantial portion of the local population, could gain through skillful political maneuvering.

An approach of Palestinians to Israeli politics is one of the conditions that have been changing in recent years, and has added its weight to the peace process. In 1992–1996 the Arab-dominated parties lent their support to the Rabin-Peres government, which until then had had the formal endorsement of fewer than half the Knesset's members. The collapse of the Soviet Union contributed to the Jewish-Arab political rapprochement in Israel, as once stridently communist parties softened their ideology and spoke in the language of social democracy for poor Jews and Arabs. At the same time, Palestinian leaders in East Jerusalem increased their rapport with the Israeli public by speaking in Hebrew about peaceful coexistence.

Israel's capacity for self-criticism is prominent among the traits that make it a democracy. The late Yehoshafat Harkabi, head of military intelligence and later professor of international relations at Hebrew University, was among the first prominent Israelis to urge the government to deal openly with the PLO, at a time when it was conventional to view the PLO as a terrorist organization beyond the pale of political discourse. He was especially critical of Israelis who revered the heroic religiosity and nationalism of the Bar Kokhba rebellion against the Romans in 131–135 C.E. According to Harkabi, Bar Kokhba was guilty of conducting irrational warfare that was bound to end in disaster. Harkabi compared Bar Kokhba to modern extremists who insisted that the West Bank should be Israel's eternal possession. Harkabi predicted disaster, perhaps even the destruction of the Jewish people, if the zealots did not stop of their own accord or if they were not stopped by more reasonable Israelis.[47]

Meron Benvenisti was active in Jerusalem politics during the late 1960s and early 1970s, serving as a member of the municipal council and as deputy mayor. He worked unsuccessfully to create a borough system to give political expression to the city's ethnic and religious communities. After earning a doctorate at Harvard, he returned to Israel, and for several years investigated Jewish settlements in the occupied territories. He has referred to the Israelis as conquerors and parasites and has compared them to medieval autocrats who plundered the lands they occupied.[48]

The late Yeshayahu Leibowitz was a religious Jew and emeritus professor of chemistry at Hebrew University. He appeared frequently on Israeli television, usually in rumpled clothes with his eyeglasses and skullcap askew. Soon after the end of the Six Day War in June 1967, Leibowitz began to warn Israelis about the moral costs of military occupation. In his opinion, it was impossible to realize Jewish values in a binational state. He projected a scenario of brutalization carried out by Israelis who would achieve the upper hand by force and put people like him in concentration camps.[49]

Harkabi and Leibowitz were both awarded the Education and Culture Ministry's prestigious Israel Prize in 1993. The public accepted Harkabi's award without protest, but Leibowitz's evoked both condemnation and praise. Much of the censure was directed at his use of the term *Nazi* to describe Israel's actions. For a society built on the ashes of the Holocaust, that was criticism beyond public honor. After a controversy that lasted a few days, Leibowitz resolved the issue by declining the award.

Israel's Office of the State Comptroller is a prominent source of moral reflection. The laws empowering this body are unusually broad in comparison with those written for government auditors in other countries. Israel's auditor is authorized to review government activities for their moral integrity as well as with regard to the usual standards of legality, economy, efficiency, and effectiveness. The Office of the State Comptroller has gone beyond the auditing of program implementation to criticize major policies, high-ranking politicians, and citizen activists. Its reports have targeted sensitive issues such as the handling of Arabs suspected by the police of terrorism, the allocation of government resources to Arab education, and citizens' financial contributions to both of the country's major political parties.[50]

Israeli politics are contentious. Israelis are more likely than residents of other Western democracies to resort to mass demonstrations rather than letters of complaint to express their political dissatisfaction.[51] Activists all along the political spectrum criticize their adversaries in shrill terms. Yet a study of political killings in Israel before the Rabin assassination in 1995 concluded that their incidence was low in comparison with other nations.[52]

Explaining Israel's Democracy

Criticisms and explanations of Israel's shortfalls from democratic ideals are well known. It has been accused of the illegal occupation of territory, the repression of a conquered population, illegal detentions, torture, media censorship, and piracy.[53] Israeli officials counter that their actions are legitimate forms of self-defense justified by Israeli or international law. They admit that the behavior of some officers exceeds Israeli norms, but assert that such actions are subject to investigation and discipline according to Israeli law.[54]

Less attention has been devoted to the tantalizing question of why Israel is as democratic as it is. Most of its settlers came from places in Central and Eastern Europe or the Middle East where democracy was weakly established, if it existed at all. The first years of the state's existence were marked by war and mass immigration. Almost all of the immigrants were desperately poor and in need of housing and social services. The economy was so short of resources that it could barely provide basic foodstuffs for the population. Such conditions are typically cited as explanations for coups d'état or other abrogations of democratic rights elsewhere. Nevertheless, few of the countries that were created in the decade after World War II came close to Israel's achievements in fulfilling their promises of democracy.

That democracy in Israel survived despite the circumstances surrounding the country's birth is a fact that should prompt us to look deeper into the country's political culture. Factionalism and severe self-criticism have been pointed to as hallmarks of Jewish culture. A high level of literacy has characterized Jewish life for millennia and as a result Jewish communities have not relied for guidance on small groups of learned elites. Factionalism may have given Jews the ability to tolerate the coexistence of many perspectives, and thus seems to explain, at least in part, why democracy has persisted in Israel.[55]

Israeli factionalism may also be tied to the fact that the country's settlers came from many lands, where they experienced different ways of confronting public issues, including the fundamental question of how Jews should relate to gentiles. The European Jews of the nineteenth century, from which many among the founding generations of Israeli leaders were descended, were exposed to new intellectual and political options when they left the isolation of their closed religious communities. Organizations advocating various ways of dealing with the new opportunities available to European Jews, and with the residual problems those Jews faced, sprang up. These opportunities and problems included the need to learn gentile languages and integrate into the surrounding national society and culture; to learn Hebrew and prepare for emigration to Palestine; and to promote Yiddish and keep the Jews where they were, but as a distinct community that would pursue its interests within the framework of a European nation. Many Jews became enthusiastic socialists, and some became supporters of humanistic, agnostic, atheistic, or anticlerical ideas. Some were attracted to liberalism, while others remained religious and aloof from secular issues. For the religious there were Hasidic and anti-Hasidic congregations to choose from. In Western Europe and North America especially, religious congregations developed several liberal variations from orthodoxy.

The first generation of Israeli politicians was not made up of immigrants from democratic societies, but these leaders did emigrate from countries where numerous prodemocracy and other political movements seethed on or beneath the surface. Israel's first prime minister, David Ben-Gurion, was typical of the Eastern European Jewish settlers who, during the late Ottoman and British Mandate periods in Palestine, joined a Jewish youth movement before emigrating, entered a kibbutz on arriving in Palestine, and then joined the Labor Federation and the Jewish Agency. Like many others of his generation, Ben-Gurion had limited formal academic training. Nonetheless, he engaged Israel's leading scientists and scholars in disputes about philosophy, science, and biblical interpretation. Many of the controversies he provoked dealt with issues surrounding state building: the appropriate limits of government authority, the nature of democracy, and the contributions to be expected from intellectuals in creating a new country. He also encouraged and participated in biblical scholarship and polemics. One of Ben-Gurion's biographers describes an argument in which the prime minister saw a parallel with his own style of political vision in the biblical books of the prophets. A distinguished biblical scholar responded that the prophets were noted for their criticism of political elites no less than for being visionaries.[56]

Biblical Politics and Israeli Democracy

The shrill criticism of political elites expressed by the biblical prophets suggests that we look to the Hebrew Bible for some of the roots of Israel's political style. This does not introduce a messianic vision of a God-ordained Israel, nor is it an effort to judge politics in modern Israel along biblical lines. It is not an attempt to describe clear lines of development between ancient and modern polities. Yet there are some fascinating parallels between elements of the political culture apparent in the Bible and that of modern Israel.[57]

Israeli politicians and opinion leaders often turn to the Bible, not only as a source of inspiration but also for its description of the nation's ancient history in the same place and with some of the same conditions that influence the modern country. Two kinds of material in the Hebrew Bible contribute to this argument. The first kind includes episodes that describe attempts to limit the power of rulers. Another is the very diversity of politically relevant themes in the Bible. The compilers of the Bible were open to numerous perspectives.

Analyzing Israeli politics by drawing on biblical perspectives is a contentious issue in several fields of scholarship. The Bible's style itself contributes to the disputes. Stories, proclamations, allusions, metaphors, hyperbole, and contradictions ensure a continuing supply of creative commentators. Unlike the ancient Greeks and the modern academics who trace their intellectual lineage to Greece, the people called Hebrews, then Israelites, and then Jews were not preoccupied with supplying a clear enunciation of general principles and specifying the implications logically subordinate to those principles.[58] What one modern reader sees as dominant themes in the Bible another may overlook or call insignificant. Some political scientists have found signs of republicanism and federalism in the Bible.[59] Although the meanings of politically relevant episodes in the Bible are too ambiguous to substantiate claims of such specificity and certainty, the very diversity of themes reinforces other signs that the ancient regimes were not harshly authoritarian. The Bible includes episodes that provide support for skepticism toward authority figures, for legitimizing criticism of elites, and for a pragmatic acceptance of what can be achieved, even if results fall short of aspirations.

There is much that is political in the Bible. Moses was a student of God's way and a revolutionary who freed the slaves in Egypt, founded the Israelite nation, and became its principal lawgiver and administrator. He was a politician who sought to find a path between the demands of God, the power of Pharaoh, and the obstinacy of the Israelites he sought to lead. The Exodus story illustrates numerous problems created by difficult conditions. It describes laws of high moral content, the challenge of revolt, and the postponement of a major goal (the return to the Promised Land) in a pragmatic recognition of problems that seemed insurmountable.[60] The Books of Genesis through Kings describe the building of a nation by Moses, Joshua, and the Judges, and then a state by Saul, David, and Solomon. Also described are the splitting of the nation into two parts and the problems of each in handling foreign and domestic issues. The Books of Ezra and Nehemiah relate the story of national and state reconstruction after the Babylonian exile.

Deuteronomy calls on the Israelites to appoint as king the man chosen by God.[61] However, the final passage of Judges is a classic expression of individual freedom unfettered by monarchical rule: "In those days there was no king in Israel, and every man did what was right in his own eyes."[62] The prophet Samuel acceded to the people's demand for a king, but warned that a king would take for himself their sons, daughters, and fields.[63]

The candid telling of heroes' stories suggests that the Bible's writers were not purists in maintaining strict ideas about acceptable behavior. David offers several political and psychological puzzles. He was an adulterer, killer, and penitent; a musician, composer of pious poetry, and military leader; a man of lascivious greed and cruelty; a provider of care for a mentally ill king; a bandit chief who ran a protection racket[64] and offered to fight on the side of a foreign king against his own people;[65] a rural innocent raised to prominence in a story to rival that of Cinderella; a love object (perhaps bisexual) who seemed to become senile and impotent; a cunning plotter who became a venerated king but could not keep his own family from fratricide and civil war.

The Bible says that political regimes should be just and responsive to the needs of the people, but may have to be cruel and arbitrary. A political scientist looking for a clear ordering of principles will find no indication of when a government should be one or the other. According to one opinion, the ultimate message is that people must ponder the circumstances and judge wisely.[66]

In the Bible not even the Almighty is beyond reproach. Both Abraham and Moses question his justice and persuade him to moderate punishments decreed against sinners. God's reputation for omnipotence and omniscience does not protect him from an unreliable people. And none of the leaders he chooses for his people are without blemish. "Dissonance" is an appropriate description for a biblical characteristic that is especially prominent in the Book of Job, where God appears as insecure and unjust.[67]

The Bible also concedes that government is imperfect. It describes regimes that oppress the poor[68] and priests who are scoundrels,[69] and curses corrupt judges.[70] The biting skepticism of Ecclesiastes is directed against government: "If you witness in some province the oppression of the poor and the denial of right and justice, do not be surprised at what goes on."[71]

The Bible's regard for the prophets shows the respect given to critics of the monarchical regime. The list includes Samuel against Saul, Nathan against David, Elijah and Micaiah against Ahab, and Elisha against Jehoram, and reaches a culmination in the stories of Jeremiah's encounters with Jehoiakim and Zedekiah. Especially telling is an episode that describes a prophet's greater freedom to criticize a regime than has been allowed by modern democracies to their citizens under similar conditions of national emergency. Jeremiah had urged the soldiers of Jerusalem to abandon their posts during what the prophet believed was an improper defense against the Babylonians. Although Zedekiah's courtiers urged that Jeremiah be executed for treason, Zedekiah himself gave the prophet a hearing and ultimately refuge.[72]

It is important to emphasize that the present argument does not claim that the Hebrew Bible is primarily a political book or that the politics revealed in the Bible and practiced in Jewish communities from ancient to modern times were democratic. The concepts of monarchy, theocracy, oligarchy, and plutocracy are more applicable than democracy in summarizing what is known about Jewish governance throughout much of history. However, the Bible does describe beliefs and behaviors focused on limiting the power of rulers. There is a multiplicity of perspectives in the Bible, skepticism about the legitimacy of authority, an acceptance of sharp criticism directed at elites, and a sense that lofty goals may not be achievable. Viewed from the perspective of political life in modern Israel, these features of the Bible may be seen as the building blocks of a democratic culture, even though they developed in undemocratic ancient polities.

As noted above, modern Israel qualifies as a democracy whose imperfections are no worse than the imperfections of many other democracies. Several features of Israel's democracy affect the character of policy making. The contrast between formal centralization and the rules of the game places considerable authority in the hands of individual ministries, administrative departments, and local authorities. This leads to a great deal of conflict between authorities whose powers and responsibilities are not clear-cut but are subject to political pressure and negotiations. The mixture of rigid centralization in the formal rules and flexibility in practice has produced conflicting official decisions and confusion over what policy really is, which programs will be implemented, and how they will be implemented. Israel's tolerance of shrill criticism adds an element of hyperbole to political language. Hyperbole may combine with the confusions of informal rules to add more noise than action to policy making. This is especially evident in religious conflict among Jews, where there is a great deal of sound and fury. As we shall see, however, the results seldom change anything in a fundamental or lasting manner.

Chapters 4–7 illustrate Israeli policy making in operation. Administrative routines are most prominent in the response to immigration. Although the current influx has been dramatic, lessons learned from the country's previous experience with immigration have been evident in the activities of officials at all levels of the government and in quasi-governmental bodies concerned with immigration. The Arab-Israeli dispute exemplifies an issue in a period of profound change. What had been a major threat to the country's existence and the justification for massive outlays on national security has been reduced, perhaps, to a major source of political stress. Currently the dispute sets Israelis who are willing to take risks for peace against those who do not want to surrender land won in what they see as a defensive war (1967) and who do not trust the intentions of recent enemies.

The problems centered on Jerusalem combine elements of the Arab-Israeli dispute with the problems of religious conflicts among Jews. A substantial part of what stands for municipal government in Jerusalem is actually international relations. Both local and national authorities treat Jerusalem's Christian and Moslem religious leaders as if they were representatives of foreign powers with influence on the international standing of the Jewish state. High on Israeli policy makers' list of priorities is the need to prevent local and international commotions arising out of disputes among the three faiths that view Jerusalem as a holy city. At the same time, religious disputes among Jews in Jerusalem receive a different treatment. Officials do not see these disputes as threatening Jewish control over the city or the integrity of the Jewish state. For this reason, officials allow public confrontations between religious and antireligious activists in the Jewish community to play themselves out in rituals that are repeated again and again.

CHAPTER 4

The Drama and Routine of Immigration

Immigration features prominently in Israel's national legend. Israel, built as a homeland for a dispersed people and as a refuge from persecution, would be nothing without immigration. From the 1880s, when the early Zionist movement attracted refugees from pogroms in czarist Russia, to the late 1980s and 1990s, when the collapse of the Soviet Union produced what may become the greatest wave of immigrants in Israel's history, 2.5 million Jews arrived. No year in recent history has matched the more than 200,000 immigrants who arrived in 1949, and no year is ever likely to approach the 12 percent growth rate in the country's population during the seven and a half months following Israel's independence on 15 May 1948, or the growth rate of 20 percent in 1949. Almost 950,000 immigrants arrived from 1948 to 1959, more than doubling the total population. The immigration that began in 1989, however, may break some records. It has already brought more than 700,000 immigrants to Israel and has increased the country's population by more than 15 percent. The period since 1989 has seen the longest stretch in Israel's history of consecutive years of 50,000-plus immigration and is likely to surpass the Israeli record for the largest number of immigrants in a multiyear wave.

In addition to the two major episodes of Russian immigration described above were other movements sparked by trauma in Jewish population centers. The rise of the Nazi regime in Germany prompted almost 200,000 Jews to come to Palestine in the 1930s. Refugees from the Holocaust and persecutions in Arab lands arrived in the late 1940s and early 1950s. There was a spurt of immigration from Morocco in the mid-1950s. Romania allowed Jews to leave during the 1960s and later in exchange for payments from international Jewish organizations. A temporary thaw in the cold war produced an outflow of Soviet Jews in the early 1970s. Jews from Ethiopia were brought to Israel in two dramatic rescue operations in the 1980s and early 1990s. Smaller waves of immigration were produced by regime changes in Latin American countries and by the problems of South Africa. Throughout the entire period, single individuals, families, and small organized groups immigrated from North America, Western Europe, New Zealand, and Australia in varying numbers for personal reasons. Economic events in overseas countries and in Israel made the Jewish state more or less attractive as a destination. Table 4.1 records the yearly flow of immigrants to Israel, but the bare numbers hide the drama behind the story of Israel as a refuge for Jews fleeing persecution and as a homeland for Jews from stable countries looking for personal or religious fulfillment.

The repetitious character of immigration to Israel has routinized the mass movement of Jews into the country and the transformation of diaspora dwellers into Israelis. For our purposes, we should treat the issues covered in the present chapter as falling within levels 1–3 of the problem types and responses laid out in table 2.1. Over the years immigrants to Israel have had their entry into the country processed by Israeli representatives in their home countries or by clerks at Israeli ports of entry. They have received entry permits as well as help with transportation, the shipment of belongings, housing, language training, medical insurance, and job placement or retraining. They have received loans or grants to help them through the period of acclimatization and unemployment. When a new wave of immigrants appears on the horizon, or manifests itself suddenly in response to a crisis in a Jewish community overseas, the issue of immigration moves up the scale. Israeli officials and politicians argue about various projections and plans before they put into practice an updated version of existing routines. Once a wave is underway, or even in a year that is not marked by significant immigration, immigrants are likely to present demands that differ from those anticipated under the standard operating procedures. Some of these new demands trigger deliberations by committees within the immigration bureaucracy or even a burst of policy discussion by senior civil servants and elected officials, supplemented by media coverage and commentary from academics and independent researchers.

The major bureaucratic players in the management of immigration are the Immigration and Absorption Ministry and the quasi-governmental Jewish Agency. The Jewish Agency is the Israeli arm of the

TABLE 4.1   Immigrants to Israel

1882–1903	20,000–30,000	1967	14,469
1904–1914	35,000–40,000	1968	20,703
1915–1918	n.a. (World War I)	1969	38,111
1919–1923	35,183	1970	36,750
1924–1931	81,613	1971	41,930
1932–1938	197,235	1972	55,888
1939–1945	81,808	1973	54,886
1946–14 May		1974	31,981
1948[a]	56,467	1975	20,028
15 May 1948–31		1976	19,754
December 1948	101,828	1977	21,429
1949	239,954	1978	26,394
1950	170,563	1979	37,222
1951	175,279	1980	20,428
1952	24,610	1981	12,599
1953	11,575	1982	13,723
1954	18,491	1983	16,906
1955	37,528	1984	19,981
1956	56,330	1985	10,642
1957	72,634	1986	9,505
1958	27,290	1987	12,965
1959	23,988	1988	13,034
1960	24,692	1989	24,050
1961	47,735	1990	199,516
1962	61,533	1991	176,096
1963	64,489	1992	77,032
1964	55,036	1993	77,000[b]
1965	31,115	1994	80,000[b]
1966	15,957		

SOURCES: *Statistical Abstract of Israel, 1992* (Jerusalem: Central Bureau of Statistics, 1992), table 5.1; *Jerusalem Post,* 24 March 1993, 2; *Jerusalem Post,* 30 December 1994, 4.

  a. Israel's independence day was 15 May 1948.
  b. Estimate.

World Zionist Organization, which seeks donations from diaspora communities and sends emissaries to Jewish communities where there is a prospect of emigration. The Jewish Agency provides funds and personnel for Jewish education and welfare services in communities threatened by assimilation or economic distress. During periods of political turmoil and physical threat, as have occurred, for example, in the former Soviet Union, Ethiopia, Iran, Iraq, Yemen, Syria, the former Yugoslavia, and Chechnya, there have been dramatic efforts, some of them clandestine, to provide aid for Jews who wished to stay and transportation for Jews who wished to leave. There is no simple or clear division of labor between the Immigration and Absorption Ministry and the Jewish Agency. The Jewish Agency is prominent in raising money overseas, in the transportation of immigrants to Israel, and in running housing and absorption programs for immigrants. The ministry concentrates its efforts on the phases subsequent to initial absorption and offers loans, grants, and programming for housing and job training. The two organizations, however, are locked in a chronic turf war. Immigrants suffer the problem of not knowing which organization is likely to meet the needs of the moment. Some immigrants fall between the cracks and discover that neither organization can help them with a problem.

Israel's Law of Return grants Jews the right of unhindered immigration to Israel. This right also extends to non-Jews with close family ties to Jewish immigrants. Since its passage the law has been amended to keep out Jews deemed undesirable, such as the American gangster Meyer Lansky,[1] but has not been changed to define Jewishness in the way desired by Orthodox activists or to narrow the range of the non-Jewish relatives who may be admitted. Controversy over these issues surfaces periodically, for example in response to the high rate of mixed marriages among immigrants from the former Soviet Union, or in moves by Orthodox activists to bar immigrants converted to Judaism by non-Orthodox rabbis.

The experience of periodic mass immigration has led Israeli organizations to help immigrants in various ways. Transportation links by air and sea have been established, temporary housing has been built at overseas points of departure and in Israel, programs for permanent housing have been instituted, and existing programs concerned with Hebrew language learning, professional retraining, and social service provision have been expanded. Israeli researchers in university social science departments and independent institutes have produced impressive collections of materials on the experiences of immigrants and on the impact of immigration on the economy, society, and politics of

Israel.[2] The State Comptroller, official commissions, and individual experts and journalists subject the operation of immigration programs to critical review and generate proposals covering the spectrum from adjustment of small details to organizational overhaul.

The routines used for handling Ethiopian immigration differed from those used for Soviet immigration. Centrally organized paternalism was the model employed during the Ethiopian episode. This model was similar to the one adopted for the Yemenite and North African immigrants of the 1940s and 1950s. Israelis organized transportation out of Ethiopia for two waves of Ethiopian Jews, numbering 6,000 in 1984–1985 and 15,000 in 1991. Much of this effort was kept secret because of the sensitive nature of the negotiations, which involved Israeli officials, officials and regional war lords in a deteriorating Ethiopia and in Sudan, and officials of third countries friendly to Israel. The immigration of 1984–1985 necessitated long, clandestine treks from Ethiopian villages to staging areas in Sudan. The journeys were difficult, and many died along the way. The immigration of 1991 began with the Jews leaving their homes for camps in Addis Ababa. This was followed by flights to Israel over the course of an intense weekend when the Ethiopian capital was threatened by an invading rebel army. Israeli television filmed thousands of Ethiopian Jews being herded aboard Israeli airplanes. As many as a thousand immigrants were squeezed into Boeing 747s designed for four hundred passengers, and as many as five hundred into Boeing 707s that normally carry two hundred passengers. Once in Israel, the Ethiopians were housed in hotels or other facilities taken over by the Immigration and Absorption Ministry. They received food, clothing, and training, were given day-long familiarization tours of Israeli sights, and eventually relocated by the Israeli authorities. The media carried stories about primitive villagers still unsure about how to use electricity and flush toilets. For some months the immigrants were not allowed to leave their areas of residence, seemingly because it was feared that they would get lost, be exploited, or otherwise suffer because of their lack of preparation for life in a modern society.

In the aftermath of Ethiopian immigration the paternalism of Israeli bureaucrats clashed with the political activism of the immigrants and their allies in Israel. Ethiopians who arrived during the earlier wave of the mid-1980s organized campaigns for more rapid absorption. They called for more language and job training classes, greater attention to the immigrants' need for permanent housing, and more freedom for individuals and families to choose where they would live and what social programs and job opportunities they could take advantage of.

Different routines governed immigration from the former Soviet Union. By 1989 privatization was a theme of Israeli public policy. Privatization in immigration policy de-emphasized the use of immigration centers, where earlier immigrants had been housed for several months and had received Hebrew language training and instruction in Israeli culture. The Israeli authorities believed the Soviet immigrants had the ability to organize their own absorption, with the authorities' role limited to providing financial assistance and counseling, language and job training classes, and referrals for housing and employment.

Immigration is deeply ingrained in Zionist rhetoric and is part of Israel's myth, but it generates problems and has its opponents. Israeli veterans searching for work find themselves competing with thousands of unemployed immigrants. Many immigrants from the former Soviet Union have arrived with impressive professional credentials and with the necessary qualifications for work at all levels of the Israeli economy. Until public agencies can build enough new apartments, a veteran wanting to buy an apartment may find that immigrant pressure on the market (supported by the monthly housing allotments immigrants receive) has raised prices. On occasion the government has financed overbuilding in the belief that an immigration wave will continue, with the result that veterans complain that the value of their property has declined. Immigration also inevitably creates problems caused by language barriers and the clash of cultures. For instance, some local authorities objected to the settlement of Ethiopians in their communities, or said more delicately that lingering social problems created by the North African immigrations of the 1950s would be made worse by the arrival of uneducated Ethiopians.

In immigration even the jokes are routine. Local wits say they support immigration as a national goal but dislike immigrants. Immigrants who have been in the country long enough to learn its banter respond that immigrants love Israel but do not like Israelis.

Some immigrant stories read like comedies created for an audience of Israelis inured to the chaos of Israeli bureaucracy, although the stories are tragedies for the people involved. The wave of immigration that began in 1989 increased the price of rental housing in Israel. A number of veterans' families responded by declaring themselves homeless and erecting tents on a prominent site opposite the Knesset. The Jerusalem municipal authorities gave the protesters access to drinking water, toilets, showers, and electricity. The municipality, the Housing and Construction Ministry, and housing companies owned by the municipality and the ministry said that they were trying to help. The cause of the homeless was not advanced when the mother of one family said on Israeli radio that she could not accept the apartment offered to her because it had only two rooms and lacked a balcony. The "city" of perhaps ten tents became a tourist attraction for Jerusalemites and others. A separate group of religious tent dwellers set themselves up in a religious neighborhood. They refused offers of temporary housing in hotel rooms, arguing that that would interfere with their ability to keep kosher. The tent cities returned to the headlines on three occasions: at the beginning of September, when the municipality assigned the children to schools; when the onset of autumn cold and rain moved the authorities to renew their offer of quarters for the homeless; and in January 1991, when Iraqi missile attacks led the authorities to apply more pressure on the homeless to accept temporary quarters in hotel rooms that could be sealed against poison gas.[3]

The problem of the homeless families rekindled an ethnic and class issue that had simmered since the 1940s. Most of the homeless Israelis belonged to lower-income families of Asian and North African origin. They contrasted the benefits provided to the recent Russian immigrants with the lack of aid that was their parents' lot on arriving in Israel four and five decades earlier. The homeless claimed to be the victims of a social problem created by poor and crowded housing. They argued that Israel had to solve the homelessness problem before turning its attention to helping European immigrants with professional qualifications.[4]

Similarly, a long-standing complaint associated with the Yemenite immigration of the 1940s also erupted in the 1990s. In 1949–1950 tens of thousands of Yemenites were flown to Israel in an operation that involved organizing travel to Aden from communities in the hinterland, flights to Israel, and settlement in temporary tent cities. The problems created by the rudimentary education and poor health of the immigrants were exacerbated by Israel's poverty in the period following the War of Independence and by the simultaneous arrival of many other immigrants. Some Yemenites had died on the way to Aden, and more died in the Israeli tent cities.

In some cases, Yemenite babies who died after being separated from their families were buried by hospital authorities who did not locate their families. Allegations later emerged that Israeli officials had taken Yemenite babies from their families, sometimes under the pretense that the babies had died in hospital, and then had given or sold them to Jewish families in the diaspora eager to adopt a child. Government authorities made several efforts over the years to investigate these allegations, but they could not explain all of the missing-baby cases and thus were unable to lay to rest the Yemenite community's feelings of loss and exploitation. In the 1980s the story gained renewed attention with media appearances by older Israelis who said they had been told in 1949 that their children had died in hospital, but had never seen the bodies. Forty-year-old diaspora Jews with distinctive Yemenite features and skin coloring appeared on Israeli television to explain that they had been adopted by Western Jewish families and had been unable to trace their biological parents. Government officials and Yemenite activists argued about whether the relevant public agencies had opened all their files for inspection and about how many cases of missing children remained unexplained. The continuing uncertainty lent credence to the stories of kidnapping and adoption.

In 1994 a Yemenite rabbi and his armed followers barricaded themselves and refused to end their protest until the government initiated a comprehensive inquiry into the missing-babies issue. The rabbi's critics reported that the protest also involved a quarrel with neighbors about noise coming from the rabbi's yeshiva. During a standoff lasting several days, one person was killed and several injured in confrontations with police. The rabbi and some of his followers were sentenced to several years in prison, where they continued to find their way into the headlines through their public demands to live, study, and pray together in prison and wear distinctive clothing instead of ordinary prison uniforms.

A commission of inquiry began sitting in 1995 to give what it was hoped would be a final hearing to those Yemenites who believed they had been poorly treated forty-five years earlier. Meanwhile, the thaw in Arab-Israeli relations had resulted in better ties with Yemen and the immigration to Israel of most of Yemen's remaining Jews. As in the 1940s, the media focused on the Yemenites' exotic dress and customs and on the government's decision to allow polygamous immigrant families to maintain that status, despite Israeli laws against polygamy and rabbinical doctrine supporting monogamy.

Another problem connected with immigrant housing emerged in the early months of 1991. An area of Pisgat Ze'ev, a new neighborhood of upwardly mobile families, was chosen as a temporary trailer park for immigrants from the Soviet Union. This decision sparked a demonstration by local residents, who noted their support for Soviet immigration but said they were sure that the municipality could find a more suitable place for the new arrivals. The protest fit the NIMBY (not in my back yard) pattern familiar to policy makers in cases where local residents demand that an undesirable facility be located elsewhere.[5] In response, the municipality reduced the planned number of trailers and began to investigate alternative sites. Having been cautioned by the publicity, the city engineer refused to disclose the locations being considered.[6] When the alternative sites, which were in less affluent neighborhoods, were announced a few weeks later, a new wave of local opposition arose. "Why not put them in Rehavia or Beit Hakerem?" was the question asked by one angry resident, referring to older upper-crust areas with little space for the proposed several hundred trailers.[7]

The Hadassah Hospital then intervened by arranging to provide land to the municipality for temporary immigrant housing, on the condition that it could use some of the trailers to house immigrants it had recruited for work in the hospital. As a result, the hospital and its international funding arm, Hadassah Women, won some plaudits for serving the cause of immigration.[8]

When grounds preparation was under way at another trailer site, archaeologists from the Antiquities Authority announced that part of the area had been inhabited from the time of the First Temple (before 587 B.C.E.) to the Byzantine period (dated from the fourth century C.E.). When ancient artifacts are discovered during construction, Israeli law gives the Antiquities Authority time to determine their value and take steps to preserve them. The archaeologists surmised that they would have to halt all site development for at least three months. They also hoped to preserve part of the area for research. Meanwhile, immigrant and homeless families continued to live in the hotels and tents that had been provided as temporary housing.[9]

The vast number of immigrants who arrived in Israel in 1990 and 1991—more than 300,000—overwhelmed the absorption capacity of Israel's existing housing stock and Israel's ability to quickly construct temporary housing. The government commandeered entire hotels, which owners saw as welcome relief from a slump in tourism. Tensions seemed bound to emerge when whole families were put up for months on end in cramped hotel rooms and had to prepare their food in shared kitchens or on tiny electric units. Another problem was the clash of cultures that resulted when several hundred Russian and Ethiopian families were placed in the same Jerusalem hotel. The hotel's name, the Diplomat, added a touch of irony to the stories carried in newspapers throughout the world when the friction escalated to name-calling and fights between children, and then to fights between adults.[10] A few weeks later a similar problem arose at the Hotel Shalom (the Hebrew word for peace), this time pitting Ethiopians against homeless Israelis.[11]

In March 1992 the Housing and Construction Ministry provoked an outburst from Jerusalem's mayor, Teddy Kollek, when Israeli newspapers reported that it was considering a plan to temporarily house new immigrants in trailers in the Old City.[12] This plan, Kollek claimed, would harm the esthetics of the Old City and spark ethnic tensions between the indigenous Palestinian population and the immigrants. Newspaper readers could only hope that the plan was simply a ruse by the ministry to provoke the mayor. Kollek's renowned good humor seemed to be tested to its limits when he was reported as saying at a local council meeting that "the [national] Cabinet was shit."[13]

A building spurt in the neighborhood of Pisgat Ze'ev added to traffic congestion at key intersections and was the background to a religious-secular conflict that occupied the attention of the country's media during the summer of 1993. The problem also reflected Jerusalem's situation as a mountain city where opportunities for road building are limited by a difficult topography of ridges and valleys. One intersection had to handle multiple streams of heavy traffic, including traffic from Pisgat Ze'ev, as well as form other suburbs. Commuters often waited an hour or more to negotiate the intersection during the morning rush hour. Conditions threatened to worsen significantly as apartments for an additional 40,000 residents in Pisgat Ze'ev, many of them immigrants, neared completion.

When excavation work for a two-level traffic interchange was well under way, the contractors uncovered graves from the period of the Second Temple (535 B.C.E.–70 C.E.), which sparked a controversy of a kind familiar to Jews. Those favoring continued construction cited rabbinical sources that allowed reburial of human remains to facilitate urban development, while their opponents cited rabbinical sources that forbade disturbance of the dead. Secular observers asked why these graves should be a barrier to development of a major roadway, when contractors building housing in ultra-Orthodox neighborhoods had managed to find acceptable solutions for handling graves discovered in those areas. When Israel's archaeologists intervened in the dispute by demanding to exercise their legal right to investigate the site and preserve the stone coffins for museum display and further research, their actions triggered memories of numerous conflicts with religious Jews over graves. Some religious leaders seemed willing to move the remains but not to have them subjected to archaeological investigation. Mayor Kollek's opponents charged that the issues were beyond the old man's ability to find a solution. The prime minister, who seemed to side with those who claimed that the problem exceeded Kollek's abilities, appointed a committee of ministers to produce a solution.

What emerged from this committee was a decision to move the planned intersection eight meters west to avoid the graves. This would have added the equivalent of more than U.S.$3.5 million to the cost of the project and would have delayed its completion by six months. The committee's decision did not satisfy the archaeologists, who sued the government to enforce their legal right to excavate the site. Religious leaders, however, were satisfied with the decision, but only until another gravesite was discovered where the new road was supposed to go. But tempers cooled, as they often do in Jerusalem controversies, when a delay in starting construction intervened. Afterwards, the work was able to continue unopposed.

Social dislocation has accompanied immigration in societies other than Israel. Immigration interrupts people's educations and places strains on families. Immigrant poverty increases family problems and contributes to crime and prostitution. Throughout history, people who have had trouble fitting into their native countries have often sought to improve their chances through emigration. Some never become well established in their new society. Jewish immigration to the Promised Land also has its stories of thieves, prostitutes, document forgers, drug dealers, and alcoholics. Sensational stories about the organized crime activities of a Russian mafia in Israel provoked a response by the Russian immigrant community similar to the responses of Italian Americans to media portrayals of the Mafia in the United States. Natan Sharansky and other leading Russian immigrants spoke about the danger of stereotyping and the insults to their community.

Even among the immigrants who acquire Israeli symbols of success (permanent job, apartment ownership, and a reasonably new car), there are many who accept work of a status lower than what they had in their home country, or who remember that they once lived in more prestigious neighborhoods and that their children had access to more desirable schools. Israelis compare these complaints to those of the Hebrew slaves who left Egypt and then complained to Moses about their hardships in the desert. The Hebrews remembered that in Egypt they had had more to eat and a ready supply of drinking water, as well as a more varied diet that included meat, bread, fish, vegetables, and fruit.[14]

Programs run by Israel's Labor Ministry have sought to help some of the many Russian physicians and university scientists who have come to Israel by preparing them for jobs as nurses and high-school teachers. The Jewish Agency and the Ministries of Immigrant Absorption and Education and Culture have provided for some musically talented immigrants by supporting orchestras in Beersheba and the small town of Maalot. They have underwritten the cost of Russian literary reviews, university fellowships for distinguished academics, and exhibitions of photography, painting, and sculpture. While many immigrants welcome the opportunity to work in their fields, in the eyes of others the opportunities are insufficient or not distinguished enough to match what they once had or what they expected from Israeli society.

The Ethiopians believe they have been treated especially poorly by Israeli officials. Even though the Chief Rabbi accepts them as Jews, individual rabbis continue to question the authenticity of their Judaism. The Ethiopians charge that their children are not accepted by some Orthodox schools and in other Orthodox schools are segregated from non-Ethiopian students.[15]

Despite the problems described above, the easy citizenship provisions of the Law of Return and the attractions of life in Israel are seductive for people in poor countries. Some who apply for immigration are Ethiopian Jews who joined the Coptic Church and have crosses tattooed on their foreheads. Others are Jews who bribed Soviet officials to register them as ethnic Russians. In arguing that Israeli society should recognize them as Jews, the Ethiopians cite rabbinical rulings dating back to the Spanish Inquisition of the fifteenth century, which indicate that Jews who leave Judaism under pressure will be welcomed back into the community. Officials of the Interior and Foreign ministries argue that some Jews wanting to immigrate are genuine converts to Christianity and that untold numbers of Ethiopians without Jewish roots are planning to embrace Judaism for the sake of immigration. The Israeli government has sent officials to Addis Ababa to inquire into such suspected cases. The Ethiopian authorities have objected to the prospect of continued emigration to Israel and have erected their own barriers to the process, which, however, were overcome by several hundred Ethiopians in 1993 and 1994.[16]

Concerns about immigration and the Israeli desire for a large Jewish majority in Jerusalem came together when policy makers drew new boundaries for the city after the 1967 war and expanded those boundaries in 1992–1993. Policy makers argued about moving the boundaries eastward or westward. Expansion eastward would take in sizable Palestinian communities. This approach was favored by Jewish nationalists who sought control over as much territory as possible within the boundaries of the ancient Land of Israel. Policy makers who promoted an accommodation with Palestinian national sentiment favored the expansion of Jerusalem westward into vacant areas that could be made into Jewish neighborhoods.

Immigration produces a no-win situation for policy makers. Despite the open-door policy for Jews who wish to become Israelis, and the transportation assistance, financial aid, and language and job training programs they are given, it is impossible to satisfy immigrant demands. There are never enough resources and opportunities to forestall the frustrations that arise when one has to adjust to a new country with its own culture and job requirements. Even immigrants with prestigious credentials from well-to-do Western countries are likely to find themselves outclassed by natives who know the subtleties of Hebrew and the informal rules of government programs, and have personal contacts that give them access to job opportunities.[17] Immigrants from societies lower in perceived cultural prestige experience more severe problems. Israelis became skeptical about Soviet immigrants who described themselves as engineers or physicians. The authorities demanded that such immigrants undergo retraining and pass professional examinations before receiving Israeli professional licenses, yet did not provide enough training opportunities for all who wanted them. The immigrants came to view themselves as victims of discrimination and asserted that professional examinations were made especially difficult to keep them from taking jobs desired by Israeli natives. In the run-up to the 1992 election, Likud bloc leaders seemed confident that they would have the support of the new immigrants on account of the immigrants' nationalist tendencies and the party's posture with respect to maintaining Israeli control of the Golan Heights and the West Bank.[18] The newcomers, however, gave a larger percentage of their vote to Labor than did long-established Israelis, seemingly because they blamed the Likud for the disappointments of immigration.[19]

Episodes associated with immigration resemble earlier periods in Jewish migration from one country to another. Once the Soviet state collapsed and nearly all restraints on Jewish emigration from the former Soviet Union were abolished, the Israeli media carried reports on medium-sized cities in the former Soviet Union where all the physicians were Jewish and had left for Israel. The mayor of Moscow said on a visit to Israel that the emigration of Russian Jews was "a serious genetic blow to Russia," and described Russian efforts to dissuade Jews from leaving.[20] His remarks recalled tales of medieval princes who wooed Jews to their lands in order to benefit from Jewish skills and resources, just as earlier reports of Soviet anti-Semitism recalled princes who, influenced by anti-Semitic priests, burghers, or peasants, banished their Jews. For Israelis who grew up with stories of the heroic smuggling of Jews out of occupied Europe and through the British blockade of

Palestine during World War II, or out of Arab countries after the war, the 1980s and 1990s provided new stories of threatened Jewish communities and clandestine emigrations to Israel. Operations Moses and Solomon brought thousands of Jews from Ethiopia in short bursts, including the weekend, mentioned above, when thirty-three aircraft shuttling back and forth between Israel and Ethiopia rescued 15,000 people.[21] Changing political conditions created by the 1991 Gulf War and the Middle East peace process provided opportunities for the residual Jewish communities of Yemen, Syria, and Iraqi Kurdistan to emigrate to Israel, at first secretly and via third countries.

Jewish Emigration from Israel

Although Israel's response to Jewish immigration has been routinized and ritualized in the national myth, Jewish emigration from Israel is an issue that awaits clear definition. Some describe it as a public problem of major dimensions, while others say it not so much a problem as a phenomenon typical of mature societies and especially countries that have received many immigrants. There are always immigrants who do not adjust to their new surroundings and return home or go elsewhere. Emigration occurred at every stage of Israel's history. In cases where Jews have come to Israel from countries they have been free to return to, perhaps half have found that the Zionist dream is not for them. Now that Russia is a more open society, its emigrants to Israel do not have to renounce their Russian citizenship, and some eventually return home. Other Jews from the former Soviet Union move on to what they perceive as more attractive opportunities in North America, Western Europe, and elsewhere.

As individuals, Israelis more than other people may be less fearful about leaving their homes for another country because of the historical familiarity of Jewish families with the migration process. There is a saying that it is easier to take the Jew out of the diaspora than it is to take the diaspora out of the Jew. Emigration seems to rise and fall in tandem with changes in the economic situation in Israel and overseas. Some describe emigration as a phenomenon that benefits Israel by removing dissatisfied individuals from a society that makes unusual demands on its citizens. Another supposed benefit is that tired diaspora communities in danger of assimilation receive Jews invigorated by Israeli education. Some commentators insist that emigration is best described as a personal issue that affects only the emigrants and their families. Insofar as emigration is voluntary and often brings wealth and personal contentment to the emigrants, it is not clear that emigration is a problem for Israeli policy makers.

The issue of emigration takes its place in the ancient and not always friendly rivalry between diaspora and Israeli Jews. Some words written by Paul Johnson about the diaspora and Judean communities of two thousand years ago have their parallel in what some diaspora Jews say about Israelis today: "While the Jews of Judea ... tended to be poor, backward, obscurantist, narrow-minded, fundamentalist, uncultured and xenophobic, the Diaspora Jews were expansive, rich, cosmopolitan, well-adjusted to Roman norms and to Hellenic culture, Greek-speaking, literate and open to ideas."[22] Israel-centered Zionists concede that more Jews live in the United States than in Israel, but assert that the quality of Jewish life is better in Israel. They charge that American Jews have sought to entice potential immigrants from the former Soviet Union to live in the United States rather than Israel. Diaspora leaders, in turn, charge that the Israeli Declaration of Independence overlooks two thousand years of rich Jewish tradition in the diaspora in its effort to draw a simple link between biblical communities and modern Zionism. Some intellectuals on both sides of the Zionist-diaspora divide concede the complexities. The Israeli novelist A. B. Yehoshua has wondered whether Judaism is not more suited to a diaspora existence than to life in an independent state, where a Jewish government has to wrestle with the tensions created by a situation in which a religion based on ethnocentric doctrines has to coexist with a substantial non-Jewish minority.[23] The Jewish-American historian Norman F. Cantor has identified the competitive interests of Israeli and diaspora communities along with the commonalties that work to create a single Jewish identity.[24]

The absence of clear definitions for emigration confounds analysis. It is difficult to define individuals as emigrants, much less estimate the number of emigrants in a year or the accumulated number over a longer period. The problematic of Jewish emigration from Israel begins with its challenge to national aspirations. Emigration offends those who view Israel as the Jewish national home, which, they argue, should have the loyalty of all the world's Jews. Emigration is seen as a threat by those who worry that the national home might not survive if its Jews leave for greener pastures.

The Israeli educational system and celebrations of national holidays reinforce the emotions focused on the Land of Israel and the ingathering of Jews. Religious festivals recall the biblical homeland. Holocaust Remembrance Day serves as a reminder of the fate of diaspora Jews.

Independence Day and the day for remembering Israelis who fell in the country's defense commemorate the birth of the state and emphasize the association of Israelis with the army that prevents another Holocaust.

There is no official Israeli definition of who is an emigrant. The power of Zionism's hold on Israelis appears in the ambivalent feelings of many emigrants, who are unable to admit to their friends or even to themselves that they have left Israel for good. Instead, they say they are abroad for a year or two to study, acquire professional credentials, or earn enough money to establish themselves back home in Israel. Some Israelis say they are abroad temporarily even when they have been away for years or decades. The convenience of international travel allows periodic family visits. Many emigrants continue to use Hebrew. The children of emigrants come to Israel for summer camp or a year of high school under programs sponsored by the Jewish Agency. Some emigrants' children volunteer to serve in the Israeli army. Thousands of emigrants return to live in Israel each year, taking advantage of programs that help with the costs of moving, offer assistance in finding a job, and reduce import duties on household goods brought from overseas.

During a wave of concern in the mid-1980s, renegade Jewish Agency officials created the Citizens' Organization to Prevent Emigration. They estimated that 500,000 Israelis were living abroad and that 50,000 to 100,000 others would leave Israel in 1984. The organization's members earned their renegade status by insisting on emphasizing the issue of emigration from Israel that threatened the raison d'être of the Jewish Agency to emphasize immigration to Israel. Some Jewish Agency leaders seemed to believe that any treatment of emigration would remind Israelis of the possibility and add to the movement outward. Others believed that creating expanded programs for returning emigrants would induce Israelis to emigrate with the intention of soon returning and claiming the enhanced benefits.

To dissuade Israelis from leaving, the Citizens' Organization proposed improving the benefits offered to returning Israelis and creating new benefits for resident Israelis. The organization demanded increased government expenditure on housing, education, job training, and industrial development, enhanced programs of nationalist education, and counseling for Israelis contemplating emigration. The organization itself provided counseling and referrals for individuals seeking help with jobs, education, and housing. But the organization's prospects were not helped when its members demanded a general improvement of social and economic conditions to dissuade emigration, during a period when the government budget was greatly overloaded and inflation was rising from 100 percent per annum to about 400 percent per annum.

The government responded in a small way to concerns about emigration. Prime Minister Menachem Begin appointed a deputy minister with responsibility for efforts to prevent emigration, but provided him with meager resources and a staff of one. The Jewish Agency and the World Zionist Organization forced the resignation of two senior officials who continued to emphasize the issue of emigration against the policy of those organizations to emphasize immigration.

Israel's Central Bureau of Statistics provides no official figures on emigration. The best it provides are yearly figures on the numbers of Israelis who have remained abroad for various periods. On occasion the Central Bureau of Statistics or independent researchers have estimated the numbers of Israelis who have died overseas and should be removed from the emigrant count, or the numbers who have accepted citizenship in foreign countries. In contrast with the alarmist prediction of the Citizens' Organization that 50,000 to 100,000 Israelis would leave in 1984, a report issued by the Central Bureau of Statistics showed that in 1984 17,000 Israelis left the country and did not return within a year. Research covering the period from the founding of the state to the mid-1980s showed that the numbers of Israeli Jews living overseas were lower in the 1980s than in the period from 1949 to 1964.[25] A newspaper report in 1994 supplied a wide range of estimates on the numbers of Israelis living in the United States. All of these estimates were far lower than the Citizens' Organization claim that 500,000 Israelis were living abroad. The U.S. census of 1990 counted 144,000 people living in Hebrew-speaking homes. The North American Jewish Data Bank estimated that there were 150,000 Israeli emigrants in the United States and Canada in 1993. An American Jewish Committee report estimated 110,000 to 116,000 Israelis in the two countries. Israeli consular officials in North America estimate 250,000 to 350,000. A report by the consul-general in New York noted that since the government dropped its requirement that Israelis abroad register with their local consulates, no figure has been more than an educated guess.

One report noted an increase in returning Israelis, estimated at 5,000 in 1991 and 10,000 in 1992.[26] At about the same time, there was renewed concern about the outflow of immigrants who had arrived from the former Soviet Union since 1989. Some Israelis were especially offended by decisions made by Canadian authorities to grant refugee status to non-Jewish Israeli residents of Soviet origin who claimed that they suffered in Israel because they were not Jews.[27]

Emigration as well as immigration appears to have become routinized in the 1990s. The concern for the emigrants' souls and their contribution to the Zionist enterprise has declined as more and more people know people who have emigrated and as high levels of immigration add greater numbers to the population than emigration drains away. Israeli universities produce more Ph.D.s and M.D.s than the country can absorb. Some of them find professional employment in North America and Europe. The decline in airline prices means, in terms of accessibility, that overseas Israelis are not significantly farther from home than Americans who grow up in New York and move to California. The peace process has lessened the Israeli army's need for every last available soldier. Indeed, the cost of maintaining a large army has led the military to recruit more selectively among females and to avoid enlisting immigrants who arrive in Israel in their thirties and forties.

Immigration is a part of Israel's drama. Yet it is a performance repeated routinely. Policies and programs are defined in laws and regulations and are administered by cadres of bureaucrats who not only recruit and process immigrants but also take coffee breaks and have pension rights. Occasionally one learns about heroic deeds of organizing transport in hostile settings. Immigration rates rise and fall in response to events that affect Jewish communities far from Israel. When immigration increases it triggers an expansion of the immigration bureaucracies and the implementation of plans already developed and polished through use. Offices recruit previous immigrants from the same sources who know the language and culture of the newcomers. When an immigration wave ends, plans are filed, contracts terminated, and workers released.

In contrast with immigration, emigration from Israel remains a backwater in Israeli policy making. In some people's eyes it still is surrounded by a pall of embarrassment or shame. Many emigrants do not admit that they have left, and there are no official surveys or definitions of emigration. There are financial incentives for emigrants to return, but policy makers have opposed giving the problem major attention. From all appearances emigration is more a phenomenon than a problem. Numbers seem to rise and fall in tandem with economic changes at home and abroad. Unlike the situation in earlier periods, emigration may now be routinized and the discomfort removed.

Even further in the background is the issue of non-Jewish immigration. Israel's Law of Return makes it easy for Jews and their non-Jewish relatives to enter Israel, claim residence, and attain citizenship. Non-Jews may apply for entry, but they are subject to procedures and criteria similar to those of other countries that accept but do not recruit immigrants. Israel's status as a Jewish country helps to minimize concern for non-Jews. Israel also faces the specter of Palestinian refugee status claims and the demands of the Palestinians to return to what have been Jewish neighborhoods since the Palestinians fled or were driven out in the wars of 1948 and 1967. This is a part of the Arab-Israeli dispute that surfaces time and again, and may never be resolved or forgotten.

CHAPTER 5

Bringing Peace to the Middle East

A political scientist looking for work in the Middle East can choose from an array of problems. The region lends itself to several geographical definitions, each with its own disputes. The outer boundaries of the Middle East extend from Morocco and Mauritania in the extreme west of North Africa to Afghanistan in the east, and from the Moslem republics of the former Soviet Union in the north down to the Arabian Peninsula and Sudan. More limited conceptions of the Middle East center on the region that extends from Egypt in the southwest through Turkey, Iraq, and Iran in the northeast, and includes the Persian Gulf and the Arabian Peninsula.

In the present chapter the focus is the Arab-Israeli disputes. For much of the period from the 1920s to the late 1970s the disputes appeared insoluble by either violence or political negotiation. The Jews could not be forced or persuaded to leave the region, to limit their settlement in the Land of Israel, or to subordinate themselves to an Arab ruler. The Arabs, likewise, could not be forced or persuaded to leave the Land of Israel or to live as good neighbors with a Jewish state.

Since the late 1970s the conflicts have appeared to be soluble, at least in part, through political persuasion and agreement. Yet the difficulties of their several components have frustrated politicians and provided work for fighters. This cluster of problems illustrates the continuum between violence and politics as ways of settling conflict. It recalls the epigrams attributed to Karl von Clausewitz: that war is a political instrument, a continuation of political commerce, or a carrying out of the same by other means. Mao Tse-tung said something similar: that politics is war without violence, while war is politics with violence.[1]

Of all the chapters in this book that examine ongoing problems, this chapter is the most risky. While the cases of immigration, Jerusalem, and religious conflict all seem to be in a situation of limited change, the Arab-Israeli conflicts are fluid. Israel, Egypt, Jordan, and the Palestinians have all reached agreements, with that between Israel and the Palestinians being an interim agreement requiring much more work. Israel, Syria, and Lebanon have not moved so far, but they have engaged in peaceful negotiations. An additional complication is the Israeli election of 1996. The new government, headed by Likud prime minister Benyamin Netanyahu, has begun its tenure with an emphasis on security rather than further concessions. Arab leaders have alternately expressed worry and satisfaction as a result of contacts with Netanyahu and his ministers. It is too early to determine whether the differences in style from the Rabin-Peres governments signal differences in the substance of Israel's policy.

The history of war, protracted armistice, and agreements already achieved shows that the Arab-Israeli situation encompasses not one problem, but several. They illustrate that each problem attracting public attention is a product of how observers describe many discrete bits of reality. What has been called the Arab-Israeli dispute is actually an amalgam of separate disputes, some of which have proved easier to resolve than others.

Each antagonist involved in negotiations asserts demands that the others cannot accept. Yet the remaining disputes appear to be resolvable, more or less, by the parties entering into agreements similar to those between Israel and Egypt and Israel and Jordan. Each side can give up some of its demands, claim that it has achieved its essential goals, and assert that it is taking risks for the sake of peace. There is no assurance that the parties will reach these positions soon or that the process will be free of additional violence. Rejectionists of peace among groups of Palestinians, Shiite Moslems of Southern Lebanon, and Israelis are the most troublesome to the process. The region seems ready for peace, but elements of the Arab-Israeli disputes may continue to earn the designation of insoluble.

Arab-Israeli disputes have qualified as much as anything as the central problems in the region. They have produced temporary Arab and Moslem unity, or at least a pretense of unity in support of an anti-Israel posture. In reality, the Arab and Moslem blocs contain a number of problems that have produced armed conflict between their members. Saddam Hussein is the latest Arab leader to have used the anti-Israel banner to cover his aggression against an Arab neighbor. In 1991 he gained some support from the masses by claiming that Israel was at the heart of the bloc aligned against him on the issue of Kuwait and by launching Scud missiles against Israeli cities. According to some reports, the Israeli government readied its nuclear strike force as a precaution against the prospect that the Iraqis would equip their missiles with poison gas. This movement toward a nuclear holocaust might have been among the factors prompting Israeli and Arab leaders to begin peace negotiations some months later.

The starting point of the Arab-Israeli disputes is a matter of contention. Israel's Jews point to roots in the land that extend back 4,000 years, and the Arabs claim no less. It is conventional to begin the modern history of the Arab-Israeli disputes with the onset of secular Jewish migration to Palestine in the 1880s. At that time older communities of religious Jews already constituted a majority of Jerusalem's population, and communities of religious Jews were to be found in Hebron, Safed, and Tiberias. The ethos of homeless Jews with a yearning for their Holy Land prompted some diaspora Jews to migrate. The movement was spurred first by pogroms in Eastern Europe, then by the Holocaust and pressures against Jewish communities in Arab lands after Israel gained its independence in 1948. The end of the Arab-Israeli conflicts, or at least the prospect of an end, has come with the collapse of the Soviet Union. Arabs who reject an accord with Israel no longer have a major power providing weapons and political support for their attacks on a country they see as America's neocolonial stooge. Israel, moreover, can no longer count on American aid by playing the role of Middle East bastion against communism.

The Arab-Israeli Problems

Egyptian president Anwar Sadat signaled that the Arab-Israeli conflicts had ceased to be insoluble when he came to Jerusalem in 1977 and from the Knesset rostrum declared "No more war." After Egypt other Arab states and the PLO ceased being enemies of Israel and became adversaries. While enemies are included to fight, adversaries negotiate. Although dissident Arabs continue to use violence, the major Arab governments and the PLO favor negotiations. As in other political controversies, each side makes concessions and claims that it succeeds in satisfying essential demands. What remains are several problems whose level of difficulty means that they will not be solved in the near future. However, the cluster of problems known as the Arab-Israeli disputes no longer appears so intractable as to qualify for the label insoluble.

This chapter does not provide a full history or description of the Arab-Israeli disputes. Instead, it focuses on the period since the Six Day War of 1967, when Israel conquered parts of Syria, Jordan, and Egypt, began the occupation of land settled by hundreds of thousands of Palestinians, and set the stage for negotiations regarding the future of those territories and the more general issue of peace between Israel and its neighbors. In this chapter we review the number and breadth of dimensions that first made the Arab-Israeli disputes insoluble, as well as episodes and conditions that changed the character of the disputes. As was noted in chapter 2, an insoluble problem is likely to involve several parties in a number of intertwined conflicts, the presence of competing goals and strategies, and ambiguous analyses of the costs and benefits associated with each policy option. The rest of this chapter identifies the underlying elements of the disputes as well as the issues in controversy. It describes in general terms what has been agreed and what remains to be negotiated, or perhaps evaded, by national leaders who are prepared to leave some problems unsolved so that the people of the area may live in peace. We will see what is more or less certain, and more or less problematic.

Components of the Conflicts

The Arab-Israeli conflicts comprise several elements: different religions, contrasting cultures, and clashing nationalisms. Israelis know that many Moslems are opposed to the existence of a Jewish state in the Middle East and to the existence in their midst of Jews who do not submit to Arab governments and ruling classes. Moslems, for their part, call Israel a manifestation of Western neocolonialism in an Arab region. In their eyes, Israel's Jews are the tools of foreign governments and economic elites.

Amidst the verbiage of religion, ethnicity, nationalism, and a resilient marxism, the concrete issues are land, boundaries, and settlements. Jewish settlements in the territories occupied during the Six Day War have played a central role in the conflict since 1967.[2] The 1967 war itself was the result of many factors: tensions associated with Arab resistance to Jewish settlement in Palestine beginning in the 1880s; issues left unsettled after the 1948 War of Independence and the 1956 Sinai Campaign, when Israel joined with France and Britain to fight Egypt; and terrorist incursions from Arab countries that resulted in the killing of Israeli civilians and Israeli retaliation.[3]

The present political environment remains so charged with emotion that it is difficult to avoid using loaded terminology. Should the lands taken in 1967 be labeled "conquered," "seized," "occupied," or "administered"? Should the territory on the west bank of the Jordan River bear the ancient Hebrew names Yehuda (Judea) and Shomron (Samaria), as favored by the Israeli right wing; Palestine, as the Arabs prefer; or the more neutral term, West Bank?[4] Should Israelis be allowed to point to prior Arab aggression to justify their actions? Is it appropriate for Arabs to recall that Israel expelled Arab villagers from territory under its control during the 1948 and 1967 wars and that Israel has refused permission for Palestinian refugees from those wars to return to their homes? Or would such claims only get in the way of agreement on other issues?

In June 1967 Israelis were caught up in euphoria over the extent of their country's military victory and were optimistic about the prospects for a political solution. A war launched in the face of Arab threats to liquidate Israel ended in six days with the Israelis in control of what had been the Egyptian Sinai and Gaza Strip, the Syrian Golan Heights, and the Jordanian West Bank. Less than a week after the fighting ended the Israeli Cabinet indicated its willingness to return to the prewar international borders with Egypt and Syria. Israel, however, declared that it would hold on to the Gaza Strip, an area that had been a chronic source of terror attacks. A quarter century later, it was the Gaza Strip that Israel was most anxious to hand over to some other authority.

With respect to the Jordanian border, the Cabinet chose to remain silent.[5] Security and religious issues made the Jordanian border more problematic than the others, and kept the several parties in Israel's government coalition from reaching agreement among themselves on the issue. The West Bank, which was entirely within the biblical Land of Israel, held sizable Arab populations close to Jewish cities, and the history of Palestinian attacks against Jewish civilians made the area a security threat. Many religious Jews believed that it should not be returned to an enemy after being taken in a defensive war. They also pointed out that the Old City of Jerusalem with its Western Wall—sacred to Judaism—had been closed to Jews during the 1948–1967 period of Jordanian control.

The Khartoum Declaration of September 1967 became the definitive Arab statement on the Arab-Israeli situation. There would be no negotiations, no peace, and no recognition of Israel. Once the Arab governments indicated their steadfast opposition to making peace with Israel, Israel's initial indecisiveness on the future of the West Bank hardened into policy. Those Israelis who were "waiting for the telephone to ring" with an offer from the Arab states were pushed aside by those who wanted to "establish facts" in the occupied territories. Violent attacks against Israeli civilians by Jordanian-based terrorists in the years after 1967 and from Lebanon in the 1970s and 1980s added to Israeli distrust of Arab intentions.

The Sinai was removed from the Arab-Israeli agenda in 1977–1981 with the implementation of a peace treaty with Egypt. As for Jerusalem, Israel enlarged the city boundaries in 1967 to include former Jordanian East Jerusalem and considerable vacant tracts in what had been the Jordanian-controlled West Bank. By the early 1990s more than 100,000 Jews lived in previously Jordanian areas of Jerusalem. But only the government of Israel formally recognized these neighborhoods as part of Israel.

Israel's Cabinet alternatively pursued an active policy of establishing Jewish settlements in the West Bank, avoiding an outright proclamation of annexation outside of Jerusalem, and minimizing further settlement activity for other areas of the occupied territories. One reason for the lack of a clear policy was the impossibility of reaching consensus within Cabinets divided by party and factional loyalties. Some officials hoped that a fluid, undecided situation would permit an appropriate response to an Arab indication of willingness to negotiate. Against outright annexation of the are to Israel was the lack of desire to make the Arabs in the territories Israeli citizens, and the international opposition likely to be provoked by further annexations.

Jewish settlers initially wanted to establish themselves in the heart of Hebron. The history of Arab-Jewish relations in and around Hebron has been marked by violence on both sides. Hebron's Jewish quarter was abandoned by its Jewish population after a bloody Arab riot in 1929. The city has significance for religious Jews as the site of the Cave of Machpelah, the burial place of the patriarchs Abraham, Isaac, and Jacob and their wives. The same cave also has religious significance for Moslems. During the long years of Moslem and British domination, Jews had been denied entry to the cave or relegated to worshiping in a subordinate part of the mosque that covered the site. The Labor-dominated government that held power in Israel until 1977 compromised with the settlers and authorized construction of a new settlement called Kiryat Arba, just outside of Hebron.[6]

The Israeli elections of May 1977 were different from previous Israeli elections. As in the past, no party won a majority of the votes. For the first time, however, it was the Likud bloc, not the Labor bloc, that would form the governing coalition. The Likud bloc was led by Menachem Begin and other nationalists. In 1979 the Cabinet lifted the ban against private land purchases by Jews in the occupied territories. As a result, a land rush guided by the profit motive joined the more rarefied motives of nationalist and religious zeal in propelling Jewish settlement in the occupied territories. The new settlement policy emphasized the building of suburbs connected by fast roads to Tel Aviv or Jerusalem instead of the creation of small villages with a minimum of urban facilities. The typical settler of the 1980s was middle class and nonideological, someone looking for an inexpensive home within an hour's commute of his or her workplace. Whereas Labor had built twenty-seven settlements in the West Bank during the ten years of its rule, the Likud Cabinet created fifty settlements during its first four years. This number was doubled again during the second Likud Cabinet of 1981–1984. The Begin government, moreover, acceded to settler demands to establish a Jewish presence in the old Jewish quarter close to the center of Hebron. By the end of 1985 there were 137 Jewish settlements in the West Bank.

A wave of violent Palestinian demonstrations began in Gaza and the West Bank in December 1987 and came to be known as the intifada. Palestinians blocked roads and threw stones and Molotov cocktails. In support of the protests Palestinian merchants closed their shops and Palestinian laborers stayed away from work. The Israeli army greatly increased patrols by regular and reserve units in the territories' cities and villages. At various times the army employed wooden truncheons, tear gas, rubber bullets, plastic bullets, and deadly conventional bullets against the demonstrators. Israel also took social and economic measures against the uprising, including periodically denying the Palestinians entry into Israel and closing schools and universities in the occupied territories. Israelis curtailed their shopping visits to Arab cities and villages. In December 1993 an Israeli human rights organization reported that 1,095 Palestinians had been killed by Israeli security forces since the onset of the intifada. It also reported that 771 Palestinians had been killed by other Palestinians, 109 Israelis by Palestinians, and 76 Palestinians by Israeli civilians.[7]

Some Israelis asserted that the security forces were reacting too aggressively to Palestinian demonstrators. Others demanded a more speedy and thorough repression of Palestinian violence. They charged that the government's policy was too moderate, that it was sending out ambiguous signals that Palestinians read as Israeli weakness and as encouragement to further rebellion. Some Israelis spoke of ending Israel's Palestinian problem by moving the hostile population into Jordan or Lebanon. Some threatened civil war if the Cabinet decided to with-draw from the territories.

The Palestinian uprising dominated the 1988 election campaign. The Labor Party's candidate for prime minister, Shimon Peres, advocated international negotiations in which Israel would be willing to withdraw from parts of the occupied territories in exchange for peace. The Likud bloc, under the leadership of Yitzhak Shamir, opposed any withdrawals.

The election's outcome reflected Israel's continuing division over the Palestinian question. Likud barely outpolled Labor, by forty Knesset seats to thirty-nine. A group of small parties that leaned toward an alliance with Labor won ten seats.[8] The same number was won by another group of small parties that favored the Likud.[9] Eighteen seats were won by religious parties, five of which went to the NRP. Although some analysts would argue that the seats won by the religious parties represented votes for Likud's position on the occupied territories, it is likely that some NRP voters, and most of those who voted for the other religious parties, were concerned not with the occupied territories or international relations but with domestic religious issues such as the enforcement of dietary laws or government support for religious educa-tion.

Israeli politicians responded to the closeness of the vote by forming a government of national unity that included Likud and Labor members in key positions. As the new government was being formed, the PLO moved to satisfy what the U.S. government defined as the minimum demands for PLO participation in a peace process. A meeting of the Palestine National Council in Algiers produced a declaration of an inde-pendent Palestinian state and a document ambiguously renouncing ter-rorism and recognizing Israel. The initial American response was to reject the PLO statements as insufficient and to deny Yassir Arafat the visa that would have allowed him to address the United Nations Gener-al Assembly in New York. This forced the General Assembly to con-vene in Geneva to give Arafat a hearing. Within a few days, the United States announced its satisfaction with clarifications that Arafat made and initiated its first open and formal discussions with his organization.

Complicating the process was the refusal of some PLO factions to support a peaceful settlement with Israel. Some PLO leaders spoke more aggressively in Arabic than in English or French. Armed bands continued to attempt infiltrations into Israel to seize civilian hostages. When the mayor of Bethlehem suggested ending the intifada as an expression of good faith, Arafat threatened to kill him.

The leaders of both major Israeli parties refused to accept the PLO's

Algiers statements and insisted that the organization was still committed to terrorism. Labor leader Shimon Peres, who became finance minister in the new government, left open the prospect of changing his position. A number of Israelis indicated that the PLO's statements merited a more serious response and demanded that their government begin talks with that organization. After the Labor Party left the government coalition in 1990, the Likud housing and construction minister began a new wave of expansion of Jewish settlements in the occupied territories, which may have added to the pressure on the Palestinians to reach an accommodation with the Israelis. It was in this context that representatives of Israel, Jordan, the Palestinians, Syria, and Lebanon began negotiations under the prodding of U.S. Secretary of State James Baker.

The results of Israel's 1992 election were not a dramatic victory for one perspective or another. Likud and the right-of-center parties won forty-nine seats in the Knesset, Labor and the left-of-center Meretz Party fifty-six, the Jewish religious parties (which lacked a clear position on territorial issues) ten, and the Arab-dominated parties five. However, the government that emerged from parliamentary negotiations was much different from its predecessor. Yitzhak Rabin put together a coalition of Labor and Meretz, with intermittent participation by SHAS (the Sephardi religious party) and amorphous commitments from Torah Judaism (a Jewish religious party) and the Arab parties. One of the new government's central concerns was to advance the peace process. It was able to enter into an accord with the PLO in its first year and a peace treaty with Jordan in its second year.

As was mentioned in an earlier chapter, the 1996 election was the first in which Israeli voters cast two ballots, one for the prime minister and one for a party list of Knesset candidates. The election produced a narrow victory for Likud's prime ministerial candidate Benyamin Netanyahu, whose campaign rhetoric and first statements as prime minister signaled another change in Israel's relations with its neighbors. Netanyahu emphasized the increase in Israeli casualties from terrorism in the wake of the Israel-PLO accord of 1993 and promised to strengthen Israeli security in contrast to the record of a more accommodationist Labor government. He asserted that he would not divide Jerusalem, allow the Palestinians to make Jerusalem their capital, or accede to Syrian demands for a complete withdrawal from the Golan Heights. Initially the Palestinian Authority and Arab governments were severely critical of Netanyahu. They charged that he was abandoning the principle of trading land for peace and endangering the peace process.

By 1995, 145,000 Jews in the West Bank and Gaza (more than

300,000 if East Jerusalem is counted) were estimated to be living on what others persisted in calling Arab land.[10] Israeli security forces have been able to give these Jews a fair measure of physical security. Yet the domestic and international controversies that rage about their homes deprive them of quiet certainty about their future.

Israel's Neighbors

This part of the chapter presents a survey of Israel's relations with the Arab governments and Palestinians who are its neighbors. It is selective rather than comprehensive and identifies the more typical and stable conditions, not the fluid details of the latest crises. In devoting a great deal of attention to Lebanon and the Palestinians, it parallels the allocation of effort in recent Israeli policy making. Jordan, too, warrants attention because of the fascinating ambiguities of peace and hostility that prevailed until the signing of a formal agreement with Israel. The especially difficult issue of Jerusalem will be treated briefly here and more thoroughly in chapter 6.

A review of the Arab entities that remain at odds with Israel reveals the complexity that existed under a label that implied that there was a single Arab-Israeli dispute. This complexity both worsened and lightened the burdens on policy makers on all sides. On the one hand, it frustrated efforts to solve the conflicts through one comprehensive agreement. On the other hand, the differences between the disputants have provided the opportunity for dealing with the issues piecemeal. As the Jordanian case illustrates most clearly, this complexity has also provided opportunities for entering into informal peace arrangements before formal agreements can be signed.

Egypt

At one time Egypt's large population and army made that country Israel's major threat. However, in 1977–1981 Egypt negotiated and implemented a peace treaty with Israel, which led to the two countries establishing full diplomatic relations. Israelis quarrel about how warm or cold the peace with Egypt is. The Egyptian press frequently dips into the most virulent of anti-Semitic caricatures for its portrayals of Israelis, and the Egyptian government can be acerbic in its comments on Israeli policy. Yet Egypt's ambassador to Israel is a prominent figure in the Israeli diplomatic community and is seen as a friendly critic. The peace has held through several crisis periods, including massive Israeli incursions into Lebanon. The Israeli army continues to station troops at bases close to the Egyptian border, but not to the extent that marked the period before 1977. Israelis rank among the world's most frequent visitors to Egypt. At first it seemed that Egypt was boycotting Israel, but recently thousands of Egyptian tourists have come to Israel each year. Both governments reported that 200,000 Israelis visited Egypt and 30,000 Egyptians visited Israel in 1995.[11]

After several years of being an outcast among Arab states because of its peace with Israel, Egypt has emerged as a leading Arab country with good connections with Israel and the United States. It has used its position to broker deals between Israel and Arab countries by pushing Israeli and Arab negotiators to become more accommodating.

Jordan

Jordan's contribution to the lessons of policy making that can be learned from the Arab-Israeli conflicts is one of demonstrating the existence of conditions that seem to be at odds with one another. Israeli-Jordanian relations were marked by overt enmity and covert cooperation, a combination that confused foreign observers and regional policy makers. For years before the formal peace agreement of 1994, Jordanian actions varied from the quietly cooperative to hostile and uncooperative. Covert meetings between high-ranking Jordanian and Israeli officials took place during the 1948 war and later. The two countries cooperated in the administration of the territories occupied by Israel in the 1967 war, and on issues of trade, economic development, and security. Jordanian and Israeli military officers appreciated the benefits that each country provided to the other. At times the two countries' military forces may even have helped each other.[12] Publicly, however, Jordan adhered to the standard Arab posture of no peace and no relations with Israel, and the public statements of its leaders and journalists were often hostile to Israel.

Jordan resembles Israel in that it lacks the natural resources and the large population that would allow it to impose its will on a hostile and unstable region. Both countries have been more dependent than dominant. In Jordan's case the dependence began with the country's creation by the British as something of an afterthought in the period following the end of World War I. What became Jordan was a largely empty tract that the colonial power made into a kingdom for one of the sons of an Arabian chieftain who suffered defeat in the competition for a richer prize, the future Saudi Arabia. After Jordan's establishment Britain provided an annual subsidy and the officer corps for the new country's army. The United States took over as the major provider of aid when

Britain's financial power weakened after World War II. Oil-producing Arab states also provided financial because of Jordan's status as front-line state against Israel. Moreover, for Jordanians and Jordanian-Palestinians the Arab oil states have been and continue to be a source of better-paying jobs than they can find at home. The funds that these workers send back to their families in Jordan are a major source of foreign exchange for the Jordanian economy.

Jordan is an absolute monarchy. The king, who convenes the Jordanian parliament, can also dismiss that body. He also appoints and can dismiss government ministers. However, Jordan is a "soft" authoritarian regime whose ruler copes with forces that enjoy independent bases of power. A major rift exists between the Palestinians, who possibly constitute two-thirds of the population, and several bedouin tribes. Other sources of tension arise between secularists and those who wish to Islamize the country's laws and policies, between people who call for Israel's elimination and people who are prepared to live alongside it, and between people of different levels of wealth. The concepts of "natives" and "outsiders," "majority" and "minority" have limited application in Jordan. Members of the royal family, which arrived in the 1920s, are only marginally more "native" than Palestinians who arrived in the 1940s. Intermarriage adds to the confusion in the ethnic landscape, as does the fact that King Hussein has married and had children with Palestinian, British, and American women. To date, Jordan's monarchs have succeeded in keeping their country together despite its tensions. People who worry about the future of Jordan recall the assassination of King Abdullah by a Palestinian in 1952 and the several attempts to end the life and the government of his grandson Hussein.

Jordan has faced external pressures from Syria, Egypt, Iraq, and Saudi Arabia as well as Israel. Jordan has found itself caught between, on the one hand, contenders for the leadership of Arab countries that want to maintain a united front against Israel, and on the other, threats of Israeli retaliation for attacks coming from Jordan. Scathing anti-Jordanian campaigns in the media of other Arab countries and military confrontations with the forces of Saudi Arabia and Syria have also been Jordan's lot. During the Iran-Iraq War Jordan lined up with Iraq against Syria and Iran. This Iraqi-Jordanian alliance was repeated during the Gulf War, when Jordan again stood by Iraq and Syrian troops were sent to help the Saudi-Egyptian-Western alignment against Iraq. The Gulf War led Saudi Arabia to terminate its financial aid to the Jordanian government and to curtail employment opportunities for Jordanians. But King Hussein's most serious political error occurred earlier, in 1967, when he sided with Egypt against Israel. According to some reports, he was misled by President Nasser into believing that the Egyptian air force had destroyed the Israeli air force. After Hussein's soldiers opened fire on civilian neighborhoods in Israeli West Jerusalem, the Israelis retaliated, and the king lost those parts of Jerusalem and the West Bank that his grandfather had annexed to Jordan in 1948.

Although Israel captured East Jerusalem from the Jordanians in 1967 and then formally annexed it to Israel, both countries cooperated in its administration. The pragmatic reality was bizarre in contrast to Israel's declarations of annexation and Jordan's assertions of steadfast loyalty to the Arab cause.[13] The borders between Israel, the West Bank, and Jordan remained opened for truck and taxi services. Palestinians in East Jerusalem were allowed to operate businesses and practice their professions on the basis of their Jordanian licenses, without having to apply for Israeli documents. Palestinians in East Jerusalem continued to use Jordanian dinars despite Bank of Israel regulations that prohibit residents of Israel from holding foreign currency. The Israeli tax authorities imposed their demands gradually on East Jerusalem after the 1967 reunification, by seeking to accustom Palestinian businessmen to Israeli levels of assessment over a period of several years.[14] Jordan's Alia Airline had an office in East Jerusalem and the Arab Chamber of Commerce functioned as a Jordanian consulate, providing passports and other official documents to Jerusalem residents who preferred to retain Jordanian status. Secondary schools financed by Jerusalem's municipal government and the Israeli Education and Culture Ministry offered Jordanian curricula and prepared students for the Jordanian examinations that were the stepping stone to university attendance in Arab countries. The municipality and the Israeli police hired a number of Palestinians who had been Jordanian government employees when the city was unified. Those employees took some risks by allowing themselves to be identified with the Israeli regime, but they facilitated a peaceful transition from the one administration to the other. They also continued to receive salaries from Amman, as a symbol of Jordanian's continuing claim of sovereignty over East Jerusalem.[15]

The political relations that followed the signing of the Israeli-Jordanian treaty in 1994 were warmer than those that followed the signing of the Israeli-Egyptian treaty or the Israeli-Palestinian accord. High-ranking Jordanians, led by the king, came to Israel for working visits and ceremonial occasions. They continued to express their support for regional peace, and their public comments on Jerusalem fell short of endorsing Palestinian claims to part of the city. King Hussein was so popular among Israelis that he might have outpolled either of the major contenders for leadership of the Israeli government if he had run in the 1996 election.

Lebanon

At one time Lebanon seemed to be the simplest element in the Arab-Israeli disputes. After Israel's War of Independence the Israel-Lebanon border was well defined in the minds of the countries and not subject to any outstanding territorial claims. It was common for Israelis to speculate that Lebanon would be the first Arab state to make a formal peace with Israel, or perhaps the second, once another Arab state had legitimized the possibility. However, Lebanon's internal problems made that country a launching pad for armed attacks against Israel, triggering limited Israeli retaliatory strikes and finally major military incursions intended to gain control of the border from the Lebanese side. At present, the issues surrounding Israel's relations with Lebanon remain unresolved. Israel's occupation of Lebanese territory has fed Arab claims about Israeli expansionism, and attacks against Israel from Lebanon have heightened Israeli suspicions about the ability of Arab countries to keep their territory from being used against Israel. Israel's war in Lebanon has also contributed to mistrust between the right and left wings in Israeli politics.

The events leading up to Israel's war in Lebanon, which began in 1982, provide their own insights into the fractions and fluidity in the Middle East. The immediate background was the result of two events: first, the movement of the PLO's headquarters and principal bases from Jordan to Lebanon as a result of Jordan's military action against the PLO in September 1970 (Black September), and second, the Palestinians' use of Lebanese territory to launch raids into Israel. Earlier the PLO had expanded its base of operations in Jordan and provoked Israeli retaliation. Rather than see his country come under the sway of the PLO, King Hussein sent his largely bedouin military against the PLO.

The more distant background of the Israeli war in Lebanon can be traced to several ingredients that produced sharp divisions in Lebanese society and a central government too weak to assert its control over the country. One ingredient was the existence of a sizable Christian population descended from early Christians who resisted conversion to Islam and were reinforced by the Crusaders who arrived in the eleventh century.

Another was the divisions within the Lebanese Christian community, which were traceable to theological splits in world Christianity and to social and geographical variations in Lebanon itself. Divisions among the Moslems of Lebanon, which produced substantial minorities of both Sunni and Shiite Moslems and a Druze minority, also contributed to the background to the Israeli war in Lebanon, as did the patchwork of communal settlement patterns that prevented a clear demarcation of regions under the control of one group or another.

Another ingredient was the history of communal rivalry and warfare under feudal or family leadership for control of shared or abutting regions, compounded by memories of massacres and countermassacres. A final ingredient was the periodic intervention of foreign elements, most notably the French, who entered Lebanon at various times after 1860 and defined the boundaries of modern Lebanon to include areas also claimed by Syria. In 1958 the Americans intervened to calm a flare-up of domestic violence. The Syrians and Israelis entered Lebanon after 1975, and at the time of writing remain there. Both countries claim that they are defending their vital interests, and both say they cannot leave because of the other's presence.[16]

The conclusion that emerges from a consideration of Lebanese history is that Lebanon is one of three things: a place but not a country, a country without a government capable of keeping order, or a simmering tragedy always about to explode. From the mid-1940s to about the mid-1970s a semblance of stability existed in a political framework based on a finely balanced allotment of power among the country's ethnic and religious groups. Restive elements among each of the communities that desired to improve their economic or political positions were dormant.[17] The movement of the PLO headquarters and several thousand PLO personnel to Lebanon following the PLO's expulsion from Jordan in 1970 overloaded an already tense situation. The entry of an aggressive Palestinian element into Lebanon and several other developments combined to upset the Lebanese ethnic and political balance. Within the large Shiite population, which had been characterized as poor and passive, there was restiveness. Shiites migrated to Beirut from the south, partly in response to the new Palestinian element in the south, but also to the dangers created by Palestinian attacks on Israel and Israeli reprisals. Beirut became the focus of elements that differed sharply on issues of economics, ideology, ethnicity, and religion. The civil war that broke out in 1975 thus seemed bound to occur sooner or later. The lack of an effective central government in Lebanon, combined with the country's multiplicity of religious, ethnic, regional, ideological, and clan divisions, produced, according to foreign observers, 90 to 124 private armies.[18] The existence of these armies, and the competition between them for resources and prestige, provided a further impetus to civil war.

The greater sense of power felt by Moslems in the wake of assertions of Egyptian victory in the Yom Kippur War of 1973 and the rise in prestige of the OPEC petroleum cartel may have added to the assertiveness of various groups in Lebanon. When the 1975 civil war reached the point where the Lebanese Army, itself beset by ethnic and religious divisions, could not provide the minimum conditions necessary for civil peace, the Syrian army intervened under the auspices of a formal invitation from the Lebanese government and financing from other Arab states. At various times the Syrian contingent amounted to 30,000 troops, and alternately cooperated with and fought against Christian, Palestinian, and Lebanese Moslem forces.

With the expulsion of the PLO from Jordan, Lebanon became the principal headquarters of the Palestinian organization. It was also the base from which the PLO fired artillery shells and rockets into Israel's north and sought to infiltrate Israel by sea or land. Israel retaliated with artillery and air attacks, training and matériel for friendly Lebanese Christian militia units, and army patrols into southern Lebanon. In response to a PLO raid in March 1978, the Israeli army moved a substantial force to the Litani River, twenty-five kilometers into Lebanon.[19] However, the Israelis withdrew from all of southern Lebanon under an international agreement that placed United Nations military contingents in the region.

The United Nations Interim Force in Lebanon (UNIFIL) did not contribute significantly to Israel's security. In June-December 1980 sixty-nine military operations were conducted against Israel from the UNIFIL zone. United Nations troops typically did not interfere in the PLO's activities. When PLO personnel fleeing the Israeli army turned themselves over to UNIFIL, the United Nations forces would usually give them refuge and then return them to PLO headquarters in Tyre. A particularly intense period of cross-border rocket and artillery fire in 1981 hit twenty-nine Israeli settlements and left six civilians dead and fifty-nine wounded.

In Israel, the replacement of a Labor government by a Likud government in 1977, followed by Likud's move to the right after the election of 1981, produced a greater inclination within the Israeli government toward active involvement in Lebanon as a way of protecting Israel's northern settlements. The key men behind this new policy were Prime Minister Menachem Begin, Defense Minister Ariel Sharon, and the military Chief of Staff Rafael Eitan.[20] At their disposal was the impressive military power that Israel had built up since the 1973 war. From 1973 to 1982 the number of military personnel in Israel's standing forces had grown from 75,000 to 172,000, and the number who could be mobilized from reserves from 275,000 to 450,000. Where Israel had once had 1,225 tanks, it now had 3,825, and the number of armored personnel carriers had risen from 500 to 4,000.[21]

The immediate prelude to the war that began in June 1982 was an assassination attempt against the Israeli ambassador in London, heavy Israeli bombing of PLO targets in Lebanon, and a renewed wave of PLO rocket and artillery attacks against northern Israel. In Israel today controversy continues to rage over what the Israeli Cabinet's initial war plans really were and how its aims evolved as the war unfolded. The controversy may never be resolved. Advocates of a minimalist approach sought a modest operation that would eliminate PLO bases able to launch artillery and rockets against northern Israel. The minimalists also sought a prohibition against Israeli forces engaging Syria's troops in Lebanon. The maximalist approach associated with Defense Minister Sharon would have expelled the PLO and the Syrian military from all of Lebanon and created a strong Lebanese central government controlled by Maronite Christians beholden to Israel and willing to sign a peace treaty with Israel. The Sharon plan also envisioned that the PLO's humiliation in Lebanon would weaken support for the PLO in Israel's occupied territories, bring about the Palestinian overthrow of King Hussein, and result in the creation of a Palestinian state in place of Hussein's kingdom.[22]

When a policy is ambiguous, determining whether it has succeeded or failed can be difficult, as is deciding who should be praised or criticized. In Israel's Lebanon invasion, disagreements over war aims erupted soon after the war began. On each side were members of the Israeli Cabinet who were present when the aims were said to have been decided, high-ranking military officers, and members of opposition parties.[23] The lack of clarity at the top apparently made it difficult for Israeli commanders to coordinate their efforts, because the commanders seemed to be operating under varying conceptions of the army's mission.[24] Arguments about the war also signaled Israel's enemies that national resolve was lacking. This may have produced greater military efforts on the part of the PLO and the Syrians and more resistance in the bargaining positions taken by the Lebanese who negotiated with Israel.[25] By 1985 the Israelis had withdrawn to a security zone in the extreme south of Lebanon. Along with its allies in the South Lebanon Army, Israel continues to occupy that zone. Israel and its allies occasionally penetrate farther into Lebanon to ensure the safety of Israeli forces and civilian settlements in the extreme north of Israel.

Lebanon's weakness continued to be a factor even after the PLO signed its accord with Israel in September 1993. By then Israel's main enemies in southern Lebanon were not the Palestinian dissidents but the Lebanese Shiites. Analysts quarreled about what lay behind the Shiites' actions against Israel. Was it the Islamic fundamentalists, who combined religious fanaticism with Lebanese nationalism in opposing a continued Israeli presence in Lebanon, or Iran and Syria, both of which had their own motives for keeping the pressure on Israel. Whatever the explanation, Israel and the Shiites continued to fight each other. Seventeen Israeli soldiers were killed in southern Lebanon in the first eleven months of 1994, and a similar casualty rate prevailed through the first half of 1995.[26] In April 1996 an upsurge in cross-border rocket and artillery attacks against Israel prompted the Israelis to launch Operation Grapes of Wrath, a two-week operation that included massive air, artillery, and naval bombardments and the closure of Lebanon's airports and harbors. One shell struck a United Nations observer camp in which Lebanese civilians had taken shelter, killing more than ninety. This, and a prolonged closure of Israel to Palestinian workers from Gaza and the West Bank in response to suicide bombings, seemed to produce dismay among Israeli Palestinians about the intentions of the Peres government. Arabs voted for the prime minister at a lower rate than anticipated and thus contributed to Netanyahu's narrow victory.

The Palestinians

The Palestinians are the Israelis' most intimate neighbors, and together they evolved into the core of the Arab-Israeli disputes. Israelis view Palestinians as prominent sources of terrorist attacks against civilians since the 1920s and the initial cause of Israel's incursions into Lebanon since the 1970s. The Palestinians, in contrast, view Israelis as aggressive foreigners who came to Palestine, took the land, and forced the Palestinians into exile or made them second-class residents in their own land. These stereotypes serve the needs of the nationalists in each group who wish to portray the other side as an implacable and brutal enemy.[27]

The hypocritical claim by Arab governments that they are protecting Palestinian interests has served as a vehicle for producing at least temporary Arab political unity. During the 1948 war King Abdullah of Jordan proclaimed that he was fighting for the Palestinians, yet cooperated with the Israelis in dividing Palestine between his country and Israel.[28]

Egypt's 1979 peace treaty with Israel contained expressions of support for the Palestinian cause, but its substantive clauses provided for the return of territory to Egypt only, not to the Palestinians.

The size of the Palestinian population and the question of who qualifies as a Palestinian are both matters of dispute produced by the uncertain boundaries and population shifts. Should the label of Palestinian be given to a family of migrants who arrived from Syria, Egypt, or Arabia in the late nineteenth or early twentieth centuries and left in 1948 or 1967, or to the children of a marriage between a Palestinian and a non-Palestinian in Lebanon, Jordan, or another place outside the boundaries of the former Palestine?[29] Communities that identify themselves as Palestinian are to be found not only in every Middle Eastern country but throughout the world. Of all the countries that took in Palestinians after 1948, only Jordan has offered them a general grant of citizenship. Elsewhere in the Middle East many Palestinians have not been formally integrated into the countries that claim to fight for their cause. They live in refugee camps that have become urban slums. The periodic demands of Palestinians for a right of return typically produces the official Israeli response that the birth of Israel produced Jewish refugees from Arab lands and that each new host society should take on the task of absorbing its own refugees.

It is important to make a distinction between Palestinians who are Israeli citizens living within the borders of pre-1967 Israel, those living in sections of Jerusalem annexed to Israel in 1967, and those living elsewhere in the West Bank and Gaza.[30] Non-Jews make up 18 percent of the Israeli population. Most are Palestinians, but there is some dispute about whether the term Palestinian includes the bedouin and the Druze. Israel's non-Jews have a lower standard of living and receive fewer policy benefits than Israeli Jews. The average income of Israeli Palestinians is two-thirds and education levels three-quarters those of Jews.[31] Israeli Palestinians have limited their political leverage by voting mostly for the communists and other antiestablishment parties. Few East Jerusalem Palestinians have accepted Israeli citizenship and thus cannot vote in Knesset elections. Most have also declined the opportunity granted to noncitizen local residents to vote in Jerusalem's municipal elections.

In the long run Jerusalem's Palestinians may be able to maintain their distance from the Israeli regime and thus remain ready for the possibility that they will become citizens of a Palestinian state. In the short run, however, they have lost the opportunity to translate their 25–30 percent share of the city's population into a significant voting bloc that could improve conditions with regard to housing, education, and social service provision. The mayors of Palestinian cities and towns in Israel have become active on the political scene. They embarrass the Israeli government and attract international media coverage by organizing demonstrations that emphasize the low level of aid given to their municipal projects. Jewish politicians respond by describing the low taxes that Arab communities levy on their residents.

The PLO has asserted that Palestinians are united under its leadership. The organization's primary focus is the Palestinians of the West Bank, Gaza, and East Jerusalem. Without a state to impose discipline on its factions, the PLO was long unable to present a united front behind a reasonable negotiating position. Caught until the 1990s in an Arab vortex that identified anyone who proposed compromise with Israel as a traitor, the PLO demanded maximum results but achieved little. The 1993 accord boosted the PLO's legitimacy, gave it control of Gaza and substantial areas of the West Bank, allowed it to establish an internal security force, and made Palestine a state in all but name. Subsequent killings of Israelis by Palestinians and of Palestinians by Israelis combined with charges by both Israeli and Palestinian officials that the other side was not fulfilling all of its agreements. Yet the accord held, and its strength was attested to by periodic public statements of support by Arafat, Rabin, Peres, and Netanyahu. At present, negotiations continue with respect to Israel's handing over of additional sections of the West Bank, the boundaries between Israel and the Palestinian territories, the future of the Jewish settlements in those territories, and the status of Jerusalem.

Neither Israeli portrayals of total Palestinian enmity nor the PLO's claim that it represents all Palestinians seem to reflect the evolving reality. Research into Palestinian organizations reveals a number of struggles between groups and individuals that are more or less marxist, more or less Islamic, and more or less willing to compromise with Israel.[32] The numerous factions and the fluidity of their status within the Palestinian community both facilitate and complicate the process of finding a solution to the Arab-Israeli conflicts. The Palestinians include extremists whose statements and actions reinforce the postures of Israelis who see no future in peaceful accommodation. The accommodationists among the Palestinians reinforce parallel groups among the Israelis. The progress in peace negotiations after 1991 is explained by the fact that accommodationists were in the ascendant among both Israelis and Palestinians. However, there remain Palestinians more willing to engage in violence than to compromise. The increased number of terrorism-related civilian casualties among Israelis in 1994–1996, many of them caused by suicide bombers affiliated with Islamic extremist groups, was a key reason why Likud won the election of 1996.

Also contributing to Likud's victory was a lower level of support for Labor among Israel's Palestinians. The explanations for this trend focused on the Palestinians' assessments of the Labor government's responses to violence in Lebanon and Israel. In Lebanon Operation Grapes of Wrath was directed against Shiite Moslems who attacked Israeli soldiers in southern Lebanon and launched rocket attacks against northern Israel. On several occasions following Palestinian suicide bombings, the Rabin and Peres governments closed Israel's borders to the daily inflow of Palestinian workers from Gaza and the West Bank. And even when access was eased, the Israeli authorities put in place tighter entrance criteria and sanctions against Israeli employers who hired illegal Palestinian workers. The result of all of this was a sharp decline in the number of non-Israeli Palestinians working in Israel and economic hardship in Gaza and the West Bank. At various times 10,000 to 50,000 non-Israeli Palestinians were allowed into Israel, compared to 140,000 before the wave of suicide bombings.

To meet its labor needs, Israel began to rely more heavily on foreign workers. Newspaper reports indicated that 100,000 non-Arab workers were legally in Israel. Most were construction and agricultural workers from Romania, Thailand, Turkey, and the Philippines. Perhaps another 100,000 were in the country illegally. Most of the non-Arab guest workers were males who came without families. Occasional articles in the Israeli press commented on the moral problems associated with the poor treatment of foreign workers by Israeli employers and the movement to Israel of prostitutes, mostly from Eastern Europe.[33]

Syria

Syria's behavior in the Arab-Israeli conflicts has been the opposite of Jordanian subtlety. Syria is the heavy among Israel's neighbors, a harsh confrontationalist and a source of uncompromising anti-Israel rhetoric. Intra-Arab politics have made Syria the military adversary of Iraq, Jordan, and factions within the PLO. Syria and Libya are Israel's most intense enemies. Yet Syria can be reasonable. Its shared border with Israel prevents it from indulging in the sort of pure oppositional stance adopted by distant Libya and the more implacable factions of the PLO in the Palestinian diaspora.

Israelis are distressed by their proximity to a harsh regime that killed

20,000 of its own people in the course of putting down disturbances in the city of Hama in 1982. On the other hand, Israel benefits from the fact that the Syrian regime has been more effectively authoritarian than Jordan or Lebanon. The Israeli-Syrian border has not been as open as Israel's other borders to raids or bombardments by Palestinians and their supporters.[34] During the long years of overt hostility, Syria has provided a pedantic observation of cease-fire agreements with Israel. Despite extensive negotiations in 1992–1996 between Israeli and Syrian officials aided by American intermediaries, no significant progress in relations between the two countries was apparent to the public. Press reports indicated that the Rabin-Peres government was amenable to a substantial withdrawal from the Golan Heights, but not to the extent demanded by the Syrians. Syrian President Hafiz al-Assad seemed unwilling to make the kind of statements that would encourage support among the Israeli public. He endorsed the right of Lebanese Shiites to oppose by force the Israeli occupation of their country and allowed them to operate in Syrian-controlled areas of Lebanon. At the beginning of its tenure, the Netanyahu government announced that there would be no total Israeli withdrawal from the Golan Heights. Syrian officials continued to demand such a withdrawal as the minimum requirement for a peace agreement.

Americans and Others

The tensions of the Middle East, and the region's importance to outside powers, have long attracted the attention of would-be peacemakers. But the peacemakers have had their own motives, which sometimes have included obtaining a portion of the Middle East for themselves. The prestige of overseeing the holy places, the development of the Suez Canal as a strategic waterway between Europe and the East, and oil have made the problems of the Middle East those of the world powers. Competition between Europeans and North Americans, and between Middle Eastern countries themselves, has seemed to guarantee a condition where foreign powers involve themselves in regional disputes without being able to dictate the outcome, and where Middle Eastern countries are unable to stabilize the region without seeking the involvement of foreign powers.[35]

An observer of contemporary affairs should not forget the Crusades or the Crimean War. The European Crusaders explained their conquest of Jerusalem in 1099 as a fitting response to Moslem attacks on Christian pilgrims and the violation of Christian holy places. The Crimean

War, involving Russia, France, Great Britain, and Turkey, was justified partly by the necessity to protect Greek Orthodox and Roman Catholic claims to Christian holy places. Russia sought to ensure priority for the claims of the Greek Orthodox Church, while France supported the Roman Catholic Church. Modern historians quarrel about both the Crusades and the Crimean War. The harassment of pilgrims in the Middle East long predated the Crusades and did not cease once the Christians had established their kingdom in the Holy Land.[36] Scholars who doubt the Crusaders' own explanations argue that a situation in Europe of too many gentry and too little land spurred the Crusaders to seek their fortunes elsewhere by taking land from others.[37] With respect to the Crimean War, a number of historians conclude that the holy places were more an excuse than a genuine cause of a war that was fought to halt the expansion of Russian influence.[38] Whether cause or excuse, the holy places of Jerusalem proved their capacity to ignite passions and to justify organized slaughter and huge outlays of matériel.

The United States is the most recent foreign power to see itself as a potential peacemaker in the Middle East. For Israel the United States is a welcome source of economic assistance and military weaponry and an attractive ally because of its promise to work for a secure Israel within defensible borders. It is respected by the Palestinians and other Arabs as the sole country able to pressure Israel into making concessions. Many Israelis and Arabs, however, are suspicious of the intentions that lie behind American statements.

Like others who have tried to make peace in the Middle East, the Americans' record in this regard is mixed. Along with promising declarations and ceremonial signings presided over by Presidents Jimmy Carter, George Bush, and Bill Clinton, other efforts to offer mediation have been turned down by the locals more or less politely. Secretary of State William Rogers initiated a proposal when Israel was involved in a war of attrition with Egypt in 1970. President Ronald Reagan promoted a peace plan during the first summer of Israel's Lebanon war in 1982. Neither Rogers's plan nor Reagan's found support among Israeli leaders.

In 1988, one year into the intifada, Secretary of State George Shultz sought to arrange negotiations between Israeli, Jordanian, and Palestinian representatives. Shultz, however, encountered difficulties in dealing with the PLO and was faced with a division at the heart of Israeli politics during the period of the government of national unity. The Labor Party, under Foreign Minister Shimon Peres, supported wide-ranging international negotiations and announced its willingness to give up some of the territories occupied in 1967. The Likud Prime Minister,

Yitzhak Shamir, offered a limited version of Palestinian autonomy but held to his party's commitment not to withdraw from the occupied territories.

The Shultz proposal was an occasion for the Jews of the diaspora to express their disagreements. The presidents of major American Jewish organizations promoted the secretary of state's mission by saying that the incumbent American administration was likely to produce a better deal for the Israelis than the administration that would emerge from the 1988 elections. One group of diaspora intellectuals, led by Saul Bellow, supported the Labor Party position on international negotiations. Another group, led by Nobel laureate and Holocaust survivor Elie Wiesel, supported Likud. Former U.S. secretary of state Henry Kissinger advised the Israeli government to keep foreign journalists out of the territories and to put down the intifada harshly and with dispatch.

Another foreign influence that affected the Middle East was the arrival of several hundred thousand immigrants in Israel from 1989 on. One effect of the immigration was that it seemed to spur the Palestinians and other Arabs to enter into a peace process out of concern that additional thousands or perhaps millions of Jews would eventually tilt the balance of economic and military power in the Middle East even further in Israel's favor. The cost of absorbing so many newcomers led Israel to ask the U.S. government for $10 billion in loan guarantees. This request for assistance gave the Americans additional leverage over the Israeli government. In September 1991 the Americans postponed their decision on the loan guarantees and seemed to link a favorable decision to a freezing of Jewish settlements in the occupied territories. The Israeli response, however, was an increase in the rate at which Jewish settlements were built in the territories. But after the Israeli election of 1992 the tone in Jerusalem changed and the government's construction of new settlements stopped (though as the Palestinians complained, the private-sector construction of new settlements continued, as did construction work in established settlements and Israeli government support for continued building in East Jerusalem).

The very fact of the peace process that began with the Madrid conference in 1991 gave a boost to Israel's formal status among countries that wanted a share in a great international event. First the Soviet Union, then China and India agreed to establish full diplomatic relations with what had been a pariah state, and thereby won Israel's agreement to their participation in multilateral discussions to settle the Middle East's outstanding regional issues. Many newly independent states in Eastern Europe and Central Asia and several African states that had adhered to the Third World's anti-Israel stance concluded formal agreements with Israel. A number of Israel's new diplomatic contacts were countries with substantial Moslem populations. It was difficult to avoid the view that an exaggerated perception of the power wielded by international Jewry contributed to the rapprochement. Countries that had viewed Israel as a lackey of the West as long as the Soviet Union could orchestrate the Third World now seemed to view good relations with Israel as a way of gaining legitimacy in the West and entry to North American and Western European markets via international Jewish contacts connected with Israel.

Post-Madrid developments also affected two sensitive topics to be considered in the following chapters, namely Jerusalem and the role of religion in Israel. When the Vatican joined the wave of states that were concluding diplomatic relations with Israel, both the Greek Orthodox clergy and the ultra-Orthodox Jews of Jerusalem expressed concern that the Roman Catholics would gain a dominant position in the Old City.[39]

The Arab-Israeli dispute is a label given to a large bundle of quarrels, some of them setting Arab governments and factions against one another in a way that complicates resolving the conflicts between Arabs and Israelis. Israel's conflicts with the Arab states seemed insoluble until the breakthrough created by Anwar Sadat's 1977 visit to Jerusalem. Since then, the Israeli-Palestinian dispute and the Israeli-Syrian dispute have at different times seemed to defy resolution and to provide hope for one. For students of policy making, the disputes demonstrate that what seems to be one problem can actually be a nesting of numerous distinct issues; that violence may push (or exhaust) the parties involved in severe quarrels to the point where they are willing to consider political compromises; that extreme expressions of hostility, for example those that Israel and Jordan hurled at each other, can exist alongside operational cooperation; and that a problem's status can change from insoluble to soluble as a result of changes in the perspectives of the parties and linked global events such as the collapse of the Soviet empire, the weakening of the Arabs' military options, and the mass migration of Jews to Israel.

CHAPTER 6

The Difficult Problems of Jerusalem

Jerusalem is not a conventional city. Israel asserts that Jerusalem is its national capital, but major nations adhere, at least formally, to United Nations decisions of the 1940s requiring international control of Jerusalem.[1] One source of tension derives from ancient Christian and Moslem claims to Jerusalem's holy places. Another source of tension comes from the clash of modern nationalisms that sets the Palestinian minority against the Jewish majority and the Jewish authorities. Palestinian nationalism is also intensified by religious emotions among those Palestinians who are observant Moslems or Christians. And insofar as Palestinians draw support from the wider Arab nationalism of the Middle East, the threat of a military crusade on their behalf is not an impossible one. When activists in other cities use the term crusade they may be thinking of efforts to clean up the streets or combat conventional crime. In Jerusalem the term conveys the threat of yet another military onslaught by government-assisted fanatics who want to march on the holy city, slaughter the infidels, and restore religious purity.

Jerusalem's policy makers also worry about more conventional issues that disturb the officials of other cities. There is never enough money to meet demands for services and maintenance. The municipality seeks to maximize its autonomy vis-à-vis national government ministries that exercise formal controls over local activities. It is necessary to steer a difficult course between those who want to develop sites for luxury housing, commerce, or industry and those who want to preserve the landscape or historic buildings. In the context of weightier issues of national survival and international relations, however, these features of Jerusalem's politics pale in significance and will not concern us here.

The geopolitics of Jerusalem adds to its problems. Assuming that negotiations between Israelis and Palestinians will result in the creation of a Palestinian entity or state throughout much of the territory occupied by Israel in 1967, Jerusalem will be on the eastern edge of a small country, right up against a hostile hinterland. Jerusalem will figure prominently in the negotiations because the Palestinians demand part of the city for their national capital.

The present chapter overlaps with and repeats some of the material in the preceding and following chapters. Jerusalem is part of the Arab-Israeli conflicts and the greatest point of contention in the national argument among Israeli Jews about religion. Yet the city deserves its own chapter. It illustrates the mixture of many issues that come together within its modern municipal boundaries (sixteen kilometers from north to south and eight kilometers from east to west) and even more within the confines of the Old City (which covers about one square kilometer).

Jerusalem might not be so problematic if the three religions that compete for it were not so heavily grounded in theological notions of monopoly and exclusivity. Each faith, however, also incorporates elements of universalism, and all three share a belief in peace and fellowship. On the other hand, notions of exclusivity also reveal themselves at points of religious and political conflict and provide support to those who will not compromise.

The key to managing Jerusalem's problems is to keep the peace among potentially warring factions. Among the Jews the factions are based on religious identity: ultra-Orthodox, Orthodox, secular, or aggressively antireligious. Some Moslems say that their demands will be satisfied once they gain control of their holy places, especially the Haram-Esh-Sharif plateau, which contains the Mosque of Omar (the Dome of the Rock) and the al-Aqsa Mosque. The Jews call the same place the Temple Mount, and some of them want to destroy its Moslem structures to clear the way for a new temple. Solomon built the First Temple in the tenth century B.C.E. The Babylonians destroyed it in 586 B.C.E. Returnees from the Babylonian Exile began the construction of the Second Temple after 537 B.C.E. This building was refurbished by Herod (who reigned in 37–4 B.C.E.) and destroyed by the Romans in 70 C.E. Some Palestinians may want only to plant a Palestinian flag in Jerusalem and have a national capital building, but others want a substantial part of the city or all of it. Some may hope to repeat the practice of some previous occupiers and exclude the Jews.

The issues that excite Jerusalem are not always apparent at first. The history and sensitivities of the city can turn a mundane neighborhood quarrel or an administrative blunder into high drama. It is never clear what starts an international crisis or what is simply being used as an excuse by those who want a crisis. A crisis can begin with the discovery of ancient bones at a construction site, with a Jewish or Palestinian family moving into the wrong neighborhood, with the opening of a Chinese restaurant that serves pork and shrimp, or with the placement of an advertising poster showing a woman in short sleeves. When ancient bones were discovered at one construction site, Christian churchmen threatened to cause a scandal in the United Nations.

The mixture of municipal and world problems, old religious conflicts, and the threat of violence justifies placing Jerusalem's problems in level 4 or higher in table 2.1. The problems have multiple dimensions. Jerusalem's political violence and the history of calls for armed crusades to capture the city (calls most recently heard from the Shiite Moslems of Iran), suggest a placement in level 5 (low-threat insoluble problem) or level 6 (high-threat insoluble problem).

Jews and Jerusalem

The importance of Jerusalem in Jewish memory and aspiration begins with the story of its capture by David about 1,000 B.C.E. and with his unrestrained joy while bringing the Ark of the Lord to Jerusalem.[2] One of the oldest subjects of Jewish mourning is Jerusalem's destruction by the Babylonians in 586 B.C.E. According to rabbinical tradition, the Book of Lamentations was written at that time by the prophet Jeremiah. Years later, after Jerusalem had been destroyed again by the Romans and Jews were forbidden to enter the city, Jewish pilgrims would gather on the hills overlooking the Temple site and weep as they recited the Book of Lamentations: "How solitary lies the city, once so full of people! Once great among nations, now become a widow; once queen among provinces, now put to forced labor!"[3]

For the better part of two millennia, Jewish prayers during Passover have expressed the sentiment "next year in Jerusalem." "Next year" occurred in 1967 with the conquest by the Israeli army of the entire West Bank, including the Old City of Jerusalem and its Western Wall. For many Israelis, memories of the 1967 war revolve around pictures of mass graves being prepared for the planned Arab slaughter of Jews, followed by pictures of Jewish soldiers crying at the Western Wall. The exclusive side of Judaism is expressed in the comment that "Jerusalem has a far more powerful corporate meaning for Judaism than for Christianity and Islam. Christians have Rome and Muslims have Mecca, but Jews have only Jerusalem."[4] Recalling his walk through the Old City soon after the battle that won it from the Jordanians, the novelist Amos Oz expresses the universalistic, humanistic side of Judaism: "With all my soul, I desired to feel in Jerusalem as a man who has dispossessed his enemies and returned to the patrimony of his ancestors . . . Were it not for the people. I saw enmity and rebelliousness, sycophancy, amazement, fear, insult and trickery. I passed through the streets of East Jerusalem like a man breaking into some forbidden place. Depression filled my soul."[5] The Western Wall is not only a symbol of Jewish history and Jewish claims to Jerusalem, but a site where Reform and ultra-Orthodox Jews, each claiming to be properly religious, have quarreled about the rituals to be permitted there. Sometimes their arguments have involved pushes, punches, and appeals to the Supreme Court backed up by pronouncements from their supporters overseas.

Christians and Jerusalem

For Christians Jerusalem is the site of Christ's agony and his resurrection. Early Christians viewed Jerusalem as cursed, not holy. They interpreted its destruction by the Romans as the Lord's punishment of the Jews for rejecting Christ. Jerusalem became a sacred Christian site after the Emperor Constantine converted to Christianity in 324 C.E. His mother claimed to have located the places of Christ's crucifixion and burial and began construction of the Church of the Holy Sepulchre. Seven hundred and seventy-five years later, the emotions of the Crusaders were apparent in a passage attributed to a knight who participated in their purge of the city: "Some of our men—and this was the more merciful course—cut off the heads of their enemies; others shot them with arrows so that they fell from the towers; others tortured them longer by casting them into the flames . . . men rode in blood up to their knees and bridle reins. Indeed, it was a just and splendid judgment of God that this place should be filled with the blood of unbelievers, since it had suffered so long from their blasphemies."[6]

Ideas about brotherhood and neighborly love have not kept the peace among the city's Christian communities. The Roman Catholic and Greek Orthodox inhabitants have often been at odds with one another over the control of the holy sites. A late-seventeenth-century traveler left the following report of violence during a religious ritual: "Greeks and Latins . . . in disputing which party should go in to celebrate their Mass . . . have sometimes proceeded to blows and wounds even at the very door of the sepulcher, mingling their own blood with their sacrifices."[7] Arguments about which Christian authorities have the right to make necessary repairs to the holy sites have continued into the Israeli period. The severe winter of 1991–1992 damaged a structure on the roof of the Holy Sepulchre. This structure was shared by the Ethiopian and Egyptian Coptic Churches. Senior officials of the Jerusalem city government and of the Israeli Religions Ministry, as well as the local leaders of both churches, were involved in negotiations to decide how the churches would divide the repair work.[8] The lack of Christian unity in Jerusalem is apparent in the number of congregations that maintain churches, schools, hospices, and other institutions. These include Armenian Orthodox, Armenian Catholic, Greek Orthodox, Greek Catholic, Roman Catholic, Ethiopian, Coptic Orthodox, Coptic Catholic, Syrian Orthodox, Syrian Catholic, Maronite, Anglican, Lutheran, Baptist, and Mormon.[9]

Moslems and Jerusalem

For Moslems Jerusalem is the site of Mohammed's ascent to heaven and the center of a region that should be controlled by the faithful. Ninety-five percent of the city's Palestinians are Moslems. Like the Christians and Jews, the city's Moslem community is divided, and these divisions have international implications. The early months of 1992 witnessed a row between the kings of Jordan and Saudi Arabia over who would have the honor of financing repairs on the Haram-Esh-Sharif. King Hussein, a member of the Hashemite family, claimed priority on account of his family's traditional responsibility for the Moslem holy places of Jerusalem. The Saudi royal family, which ousted the Hashemites from the Arabian holy cities early in this century, seemed intent on scoring more points in intra-Moslem rivalries. Yassir Arafat gambled on improving his own status when he publicly thanked Saudi king Fahd, but not Hussein, for offering to finance the repairs. In late 1994 the Palestinian Authority and the Jordanian government each appointed a mufti for Jerusalem. The Palestinians' appointee occupied the main officey while Jordan's mufti settled into an anteroom. In this matter Arafat accused the Israelis of favoring Jordan.

Some Moslems adopt extreme rhetoric in challenging Jewish control over Jerusalem. According to the Islamic Council of Europe, "The Zionist usurpation and continued occupation of Jerusalem and Palestine . . . has perpetuated untold human misery and unleashed a seemingly unending reign of terror in a land held sacred by Moslems, Christians and Jews alike. As a result, more than a million men, women and children have been hounded out of their homes and forced to become refugees, while merciless Zionist persecution goes on throughout the length and breadth of their homeland."[10] Another statement holds, "Despite Israeli propaganda, there are in fact no important Jewish monuments of religious significance in Jerusalem. It is true that there is a Jewish ritual of mourning at the Wailing Wall, but this in fact is a portion of the wall of the Haram Esh-Sharif, and is actually Muslim property."[11]

Jerusalem as an Israeli Municipality

Jerusalem is Israel's most populous municipality. The population was 544,200 at the end of 1991, which was substantially larger than Tel Aviv's 353,200 and Haifa's 251,000. When population calculations are made with reference to metropolitan areas rather than municipalities, the Jerusalem area's population of 600,900 is less than half the Tel Aviv area's 1,131,700. The Jerusalem metropolitan area is also less populous than the Haifa-Akko metropolitan area.

Changes in the size of the city's population over time provide the best measure of its changing importance through the ages, despite the shortcomings of the data for earlier periods (table 6.1). The pre-1920s figures in table 6.1 are estimates, with those for the distant past being the least reliable. Before the twentieth century the population was highest in three periods: the years preceding the destruction of the Second Temple, when Jerusalem was the capital of a crusader kingdom, and after the onset of major Jewish immigration in the latter part of the nineteenth century. During most of the long period of Moslem rule from the seventh century to the middle of the nineteenth century, Jerusalem was important as a site of Islamic holy places and religious institutions but was politically and economically subordinate to Cairo, Damascus, or Constantinople, and never acquired a large population.

The city's importance has reflected the changing status of that imprecise geographical area called the Land of Israel. The city has experienced its greatest development when it has been the religious and political capital of a Jewish nation. On those occasions Jerusalem has been close to the geographical center of the country, at the junction of

TABLE 6.1   Jerusalem's Population

1000 B.C.E.	2,500	1900	70,000
700	6,000–8,000	1913	75,200
600	24,000ᵃ	1928	62,700
537	10,000	1931	93,100
0–70 CE	30,000	1946	164,400
1099–1187	30,000	1961	243,900ᵇ
1200–1300	5,200	1967	267,800
1500–1600	4,700–15,800	1972	313,900
1800	8,000–10,000	1988	493,500
1834	22,000	1990	504,100
1840	15,000	1991	544,200
1860	20,000	1992	556,500
1876	25,000		

SOURCES: Howard F. Vos, *Ezra, Nehemiah, and Esther* (Grand Rapids, Michigan: Zondervan, 1987); Joachim Jeremias, *Jerusalem in the Time of Jesus: An Investigation into Economic and Social Conditions during the New Testament Period* (London: SCM Press, 1969); Yehoshua Ben-Arieh, *Jerusalem in the 19th Century: The Old City* (New York: St. Martin's Press, 1984); Amnon Cohen, *Jewish Life under Islam: Jerusalem in the Sixteenth Century* (Cambridge: Harvard University Press, 1984); Karl R. Schaefer, "Jerusalem in the Ayyubid and Mamluk Eras," Ph.D. diss., New York University, 1985; U. O. Schmelz, *Modern Jerusalem's Demographic Evolution* (Jerusalem: Hebrew University Institute for Contemporary Jewry, 1987); F. E. Peters, *Jerusalem: The Holy City in the Eyes of Chroniclers, Visitors, Pilgrims, and Prophets from the Days of Abraham to the Beginnings of Modern Times* (Princeton: Princeton University Press, 1985); *Statistical Abstract of Israel, 1990,* (Jerusalem: Central bureau of Statistics, 1990); *Statistical Yearbook of Jerusalem, 1988* (Jerusalem: Municipality of Jerusalem and Jerusalem Institute of Israel Studies, 1990); *Statistical Yearbook of Jerusalem, 1991* (Jerusalem: Municipality of Jerusalem and Jerusalem Institute of Israel Studies, 1993); *Statistical Yearbook of Jerusalem, 1992* (Jerusalem: Municipality of Jerusalem and Jerusalem Institute of Israel Studies, 1994).

   a. After the arrival of refugees from the north following the Assyrian conquest.
   b. Israeli and Jordanian sectors.

north-south and east-west routes. At other times Jerusalem has been merely a regional market center, with modest agriculture to the west but a desert to the east, and forty kilometers from major coastal plain routes connecting Cairo, Lebanon, and Damascus.

After 1967 Jerusalem was again at the strategic heart of a country thickly settled by Jews, for the first time since its destruction by the Romans. A book on the geopolitical importance of the city notes that it protrudes prominently into the center of Palestinian settlement on the West Bank. In what may be too final a conclusion, the author writes that no Palestinian state can be viable without the Jerusalem that Israel will never concede.[12]

Religion and ethnicity are the most obvious of Jerusalem's social categories. Table 6.2 provides estimates of varying reliability for the size of the city's major religious groups from 1525 to 1992. The Jews were the largest of the city's communities by the middle of the nineteenth century and have been a substantial majority throughout the twentieth century. Now they make up 72 percent of the population. Of the country's major cities, Israel's capital has the highest percentage of non-Jews. Non-Jews are 9 percent of the population in Haifa and 4 percent in Tel Aviv. We shall see in the next chapter that Jerusalem's population is also distinctive in having a larger proportion of ultra-Orthodox Jews than the country as a whole. Although a precise figure for the ultra-Orthodox population is not available, in the election of 1992 ultra-Orthodox parties won 22 percent of the vote in Jerusalem, against 8 percent of the vote nationally.

The city's most prominent minority is variously described as Moslem, Arab, or Palestinian.[13] The terms overlap to some extent, although the Arab and Palestinian designations include a sizable minority of non-Moslems (mostly Greek Orthodox Christians and Greek Catholics). From 1967 to 1992 the city's non-Jewish population grew faster than the Jewish population. The total Moslem and Christian population increased by 119 percent as opposed to a 104 percent increase for the Jews. The Jewish share of the population dipped from 73.5 percent to 72.1 percent during that period.

The demographic data for the Jerusalem municipality does not include Palestinian settlements in the occupied territories. Israel crafted the municipal boundaries in 1967 to exclude a number of Palestinian settlements and to maximize the Jewish percentage of the Jerusalem population. Due partly to Palestinian opposition, there has not been a census of the occupied territories since 1967. The number of Palestinians from the territories who have acquired residence illegally in Jerusalem remains unknown. Israeli regulations have permitted Palestinians from the occupied territories to make day trips to Jerusalem and other Israeli cities to work, shop, or visit, but have barred them from establishing residence within Israel. Enforcement is haphazard. Estimates by municipal and Interior Ministry officials of the number of residents of the occupied territories living illegally in Jerusalem range from 10,000 to 100,000.[14] Being without proper documentation, the illegals do not qualify for the social services available to East Jerusalem Palestinians, but they have no problem finding work, renting a dwelling

TABLE 6.2 Jerusalem Population by Religion

	Moslems	Christians	Jews	% Jews
1525	3,670	714	1,194	21
1553	11,912	1,956	1,958	12
1806	4,000	2,800	2,000	23
1844	5,000	3,390	7,120	46
1870	11,000		11,000	50
1876	7,560	5,470	12,000	48
1910	25,000		45,000	64
1913	10,050	16,750	48,400	64
1922	13,400	14,700	34,100	55
1931	19,900	19,300	53,800	58
1946	33,700	31,300	99,300	60
1948	40,000	25,000	100,000	61
1967	58,100	12,900	196,800	73
1985	115,700	14,200	327,700	72
1990	131,900	14,400	378,200	72
1992	155,500		401,100	72

SOURCES: Yehoshua Ben-Arieh, *Jerusalem in the Nineteenth Century: The Old City* (New York: St. Martin's Press, 1984); F. E. Peters, *Jerusalem: The Holy City in the Eyes of Chroniclers, Visitors, Pilgrims, and Prophets from the Days of Abraham to the Beginnings of Modern Times* (Princeton: Princeton University Press, 1985); U. O. Schmelz, "Modern Jerusalem's Demographic Evolution" (Jerusalem: Hebrew University Institute of Contemporary Jewry, 1987); Schmelz, "Jerusalem's Arab Population since the Mandatory Period (1918–1990)," in Aharon Layish, ed., *The Arabs in Jerusalem: From the Late Ottoman Period to the Beginning of the 1990s—Religious, Social and Cultural Distinctiveness* (Jerusalem: Magnes Press, 1992), 6–42, Hebrew; Sarah Markovitz, "The Development of Modern Jerusalem: An Evaluation of Planning Decisions and the Effectiveness of the Planning Process" (Princeton University School of Architecture and Woodrow Wilson School for Public and International Affairs, 1982); *Statistical Yearbook of Jerusalem, 1988* (Jerusalem: Municipality of Jerusalem and Jerusalem Institute of Israel Studies, 1990); *Statistical Yearbook of Jerusalem, 1992* (Jerusalem: Municipality of Jerusalem and Jerusalem Institute of Israel Studies, 1994).

in a Palestinian neighborhood, or sending their children to a Jerusalem private school. Israel's Central Bureau of Statistics estimated that 20,000 Palestinians a day entered Jerusalem from the territories to work in 1989.[15]

The concept of metropolitan Jerusalem is a vague and sensitive one. Jerusalem's hinterland to the north, east, and south is heavily Palestinian. As we shall see below, metropolitan Jerusalem is likely to figure prominently in negotiations between Israel and the Palestinian Authority. It may provide a location for a Palestinian national capital in what the Palestinians will call "Jerusalem." Estimates of the non-Jewish population of the metropolitan area range from 42 to above 50 percent.[16]

Jerusalem's economy is weakened by a lack of natural resources and by the fact that it is not close to a large market that could absorb industrial output. Yet the economy is strong enough to serve as a magnet for the Palestinian population of the West Bank. Although East Jerusalem experienced an economic decline when under Jordanian control in 1948–1967, a Palestinian intelligentsia remained and continues to be a source of nationalist activity. Jerusalem's Palestinian newspapers and opinion leaders are more prominent than their counterparts in the occupied territories. The al-Aqsa Mosque is both a national symbol and a place of worship that attracts thousands of Moslems from the surrounding area each Friday and on Islamic holy days.

Outwardly, East Jerusalem has remained more peaceful than the West Bank. According to one observer, much of Jerusalem's Jewish-Palestinian violence has been imported from elsewhere in the occupied territories.[17] The Palestinians of East Jerusalem have several reasons to accept the status quo or at least to avoid violence. They benefit from Israeli social services that are not available to residents of the West Bank. They are closer than West Bank residents to the economic opportunities offered by the city and not kept from work by occasional Israeli closures of the country's borders to Palestinians from the West Bank and Gaza. Jerusalem's Palestinians have not been roused to violence by the extensive building of Jewish suburbs. This may be because Palestinians have benefited economically by doing almost all of the manual labor involved in the construction and because the Israelis have built mostly on vacant land.

The Jordanian government has been a conservative influence on the Jerusalem Palestinian community through its connections with the religious establishment (the Waqf) and the Arab Chamber of Commerce. So far, East Jerusalem's Palestinians have not moved in large numbers to Islamic fundamentalism.

This description of East Jerusalem's relative calm should not lead to the optimistic conclusion that East Jerusalem is entirely different from other Palestinian communities in Israel or the occupied territories. Palestinian neighborhoods in Jerusalem have witnessed stone throwings, tire burnings, political killings within the Palestinian community, and casualties in encounters with Israeli security forces. There have been stabbings of Jews by Palestinians and suicide bombings directed against Jews on Jerusalem buses. Public opinion surveys find widespread hostility to the Israeli establishment among Jerusalem Palestinians.

Social contacts between Jews and Palestinians in Jerusalem are rare. With few exceptions members of the two communities live in their own neighborhoods, read their own newspapers, send their children to their own schools, and use their own bus lines and taxi companies. Generally speaking, Palestinians in East Jerusalem academic high schools prepare for higher education in Arab countries, not Israel, and few have the command of Hebrew that is typical of Palestinian students elsewhere in Israel. As a result, most of the Palestinians who study at the Hebrew University are from outside Jerusalem. Intermarriages are discouraged in both the Jewish and the Palestinian communities and are rare.[18]

Jerusalem's Jewish municipal government has dealt with the Palestinians partly through the institutions of the traditional mukhtar (village headman) and the modern neighborhood association. Jerusalem's Palestinians have not formed their own municipal political party or stood for election to the municipal council. Most of the Palestinians who were included within the city when Israel annexed a large area of Jerusalem after the 1967 war have refused the national government's offer of Israeli citizenship.

The extent of the Jerusalem Palestinian community's willingness to identify with Israel can be judged by comparing national election voter turnout in the non-Jewish areas absorbed in 1967 with voter turnout in Jerusalem as a whole. Such a broad-based analysis, however, does not provide a conventional measure of voter turnout because it does not take into account age differentials within the various sectors of the population. Nevertheless, the contrast between the non-Jewish voting pattern in the absorbed areas and the pattern for the city as a whole is so stark that it cannot be ignored.

In the 1988 Knesset election the residents of the Old City's Armenian Quarter demonstrated their greater rapport with Israel by participating in the vote at a higher rate than other non-Jewish residents of post-1967 neighborhoods, although even their rate was less than half the rate in predominantly Jewish areas of Jerusalem. The voting data for the Old City's Christian Quarter (whose population in 1990 was 85 percent Christian and 15 percent Moslem) revealed the small degree to which Christian Palestinians exceeded Moslem Palestinians in their support for Israeli institutions. The rate of participation in the Christian Quarter was only 3 percent of participation in predominantly Jewish areas.[19] The 1988 election participation of post-1967 neighborhoods that were predominantly Moslem varied from 0.4 to 1.7 percent of the norm in predominantly Jewish areas.

In Jerusalem, noncitizen Palestinians can vote in municipal elections and stand as candidates for election to the municipal council by virtue of being city residents. However, since 1967 there have been no Palestinian candidates for municipal office, and most Palestinians refuse to vote in local elections. An estimated 7,500–8,000 of the 35,000 Palestinians (21–22 percent) who were eligible voted in the 1969 municipal election, which seemed to indicate that the election boycott called for by some Palestinians had failed. In the 1973 election, held soon after the Yom Kippur War, only 3,150 of 43,000 eligible Palestinian voters participated (7 percent). In the 1978 election the numbers were 7,000–8,000 of 55,000 (14–15 percent). The 1985 election saw voting by 10,000–11,600 of the perhaps 66,000 Palestinians who were eligible (18 percent). The next election, in 1989, occurred almost two years after the onset of the intifada, and the boycott held as never before, the total Palestinian vote dropping to 3,000.[20] The 1993 election came two months after the signing of the accord between Israel and the PLO. An aged Teddy Kollek, mayor since 1966, had announced his retirement before the election was held, but gave in to pressure from his Labor Party colleagues to run again in order to keep Likud out of the municipal administration. The city's Palestinians seemed torn between wanting to oppose the Likud candidate in the context of the Israel-PLO accord but not being able to endorse the Israeli regime in Jerusalem with their votes. Seven percent of the eligible Palestinians voted, more than in the intifada election of 1989 but less than in the elections of 1969, 1978, and 1985.

Israeli and Palestinian Dilemmas

We saw in chapter 2 that the concept of a dilemma is problematic. It requires us to judge the intensity of participants' feelings about different options and to decide that two or more alternatives are equally undesirable. In the Jerusalem case, however, the accumulated pressures of competing nationalisms, aggravated by religious fanaticism, justify the use of the term dilemma to convey the impossibility of satisfying all demands.

It is also difficult to decide whether the Israeli or the Palestinian dilemma is more severe. From the perspective of Israeli officials, the stressful situation of Jerusalem is marked by ethnic-religious tensions within the local population and a lack of certainty about whether the Jewish regime can retain control of the city. A Jewish population share of 72 percent within the municipal boundaries favors the regime, but the non-Jewish population is increasing at a greater rate. In the larger metropolitan region the ratio of Jews to non-Jews is unknown but may be tilted against the Jews. And of course, the ratio of Jews to non-Jews in the entire Middle East is sharply against Israeli control of Jerusalem.

The Palestinian dilemma appears in the squeeze between Palestinian nationalist demands to place the Palestinian capital in Jerusalem and the refusal of the Israelis to even bargain on the issue. Israel has offered the PLO peace, Gaza, and substantial areas of the West Bank outside Jerusalem, but the PLO feels pressure from non-Palestinian Moslems and Palestinian nationalists to insist on recovering part of Jerusalem. The rejectionists' implicit threat to engage in violence cannot help but remind PLO leaders of the long road already traveled and of the failure of violence to earn them more than a mixture of international support and condemnation and Israeli rejection.

Israelis and Palestinians Coping

Jerusalem is a city that invites policy makers to cope. As was discussed in chapter 2, coping is a word often used in the literature on public sector problems and policy making, but typically without a great deal of specificity. "Engagement coping" and "avoidance coping" are useful categories. Engagement coping refers to efforts by individuals or organizations to salvage something from a difficult situation. It displays flexibility in its pursuit of achieving the most important goals at the expense of lesser ones. It also may employ ambiguity in order to reach working accords, without spelling out terms so clearly that they generate opposition. "Avoidance coping" responds to stress with confusion, rigidity, or a hasty choice of options without considering costs and benefits. Instances of engagement and avoidance coping in Jerusalem can be found in the actions of Jewish and Palestinian leaders. Their behavior also demonstrates that both forms of coping may be present at the same time and that it may be difficult to determine which is more prominent.

Israel has controlled the entire city since 1967, but a sizable minority of the local population opposes its rule. Added to the stresses on Israeli policy makers are the numerous foreign governments that do not formally recognize the status quo. Moreover, the dominant Jewish population is itself riven by chronic and highly emotional disputes. History weighs heavily on contemporary rulers. A former deputy mayor writes that the city has changed hands thirty-seven times as a result of armed conflict.[21]

Here we consider the actions of Israeli policy makers and Palestinian nationalists. The goals of other bodies with interests in Jerusalem add to their stresses. They include several Moslem and Christian religious organizations, which have competing interests with respect to the holy sites; the governments of Jordan and Saudi Arabia, which express different preferences with respect to the Moslem holy sites; European governments, which assert conflicting claims to a protective role vis-à-vis the Christian holy sites; the United States and other governments that see wider implications in the conflicts surrounding Jerusalem; the United Nations; the European Community; and international Jewish and Arab organizations. Some have coped more successfully than others with the problems involved in getting their voices heard amid the emotion and noise, and in placing on the agenda proposals that seem capable of realization.

From 1967, when Israel took control of the entire city, until the beginning of serious Israel-PLO negotiations in 1993, engagement coping predominated in the actions of Israeli policy makers, while avoidance coping was more prominent among Palestinian nationalists. Control of the city also reflected differentials in military, economic, and political dimensions of power. Thus, Israeli and Palestinian choices with respect to coping strategies may also have reflected current positions as the stronger and weaker of competitors for the city.

The signing of an accord between Israel and the PLO in September 1993 represented a marked shift to engagement coping on the part of the Palestinians. A mixture of engagement and avoidance coping by Palestinians continued in Jerusalem through the municipal election of November 1993. More than in the period before the accord was signed, it became difficult to judge which side was marked more by engagement, and which by avoidance coping.

Israeli Policy Makers

Controlling Jerusalem has been the highest goal of Israeli policy makers. However, they have coped with realities by lessening their conception of control. Ambiguity has proved useful in dealing with disputes among Jews, Arab-Israeli conflicts, and the sensitivities of Moslem and Christian religious leaders. The Jerusalem municipal government and several Israeli government ministries have their own priorities with respect to Jerusalem. Important Israeli officials do not always see eye-to-eye on what is best for Jerusalem and sometimes act in ways that seem contradictory.[22] The authorities avoid defining some policies precisely. Nonetheless, what follows is an effort to describe the five most prominent Israeli policies with respect to Jerusalem.

One major Israeli policy is to maintain Jerusalem as a predominantly Jewish city and as the capital of Israel. The two elements of this policy are connected to each other. Should the Jewish percentage of the Jerusalem population fall below a certain level of dominance it may not be feasible to maintain the city as the national capital.

The concern to establish a large Jewish majority in Jerusalem appeared in the boundaries drawn for the city after the 1967 war, which left a number of Palestinian settlements outside the city and included large vacant areas that were later made into Jewish neighborhoods. The vacant areas were intended to attract more Jews to the city and to act as a buffer zone between the city core and its major transportation arteries on the one hand and the outlying Palestinian settlements on the other. The Israeli government expanded the municipal boundaries again in 1992 in an effort to increase the Jewish share of the city's population above 72 percent. The 1992 expansion extended the city's boundaries westward, away from areas where Palestinians were concentrated.

Critics of the Israeli regime have accused it of avoidance coping on the grounds that national officials avoid confronting the implications of the large Palestinian population in Jerusalem's metropolitan hinterland. However, engagement coping appears more dominant by virtue of Israelis' focusing on their principal goal of strengthening their control over the city of Jerusalem and that part of its metropolitan area that is or can be settled with Jews.

A second policy goal is to satisfy the essential demands of the major communities in Jerusalem and keep the peace between them, even at the expense of limiting achievements by the Jewish majority. This policy is connected to the policy of maintaining Jerusalem as a predominantly Jewish city and as the capital of Israel.

Engagement coping appears in the efforts of Israeli officials to satisfy at least the minimum demands of the city's major communities, even if that requires sacrificing lesser goals for the sake of achieving more important ones. Allowing non-Jews to administer Christian and Moslem holy sites, without conceding formal sovereignty, is a strategy that seeks to minimize friction between the city's religious communities. The policy began when some of the first Israeli soldiers to enter the Old City in the war of 1967 raised the national flag on the Haram-Esh-Sharif plateau (the Temple Mount). Defense Minister Moshe Dayan ordered the flag taken down and the government left the administration of the site in the hands of the Moslem religious authorities. In keeping with this policy, Israeli authorities have used the police against nationalist and religious Jews who would pray on the Temple Mount or try to build a new temple.

Israeli ministries and the Jerusalem municipal government have distorted or ignored their own rules in order to accommodate hostile Palestinians.[23] As was mentioned above, Palestinians living in East Jerusalem neighborhoods that were annexed in 1967 have been allowed to use Jordanian licenses for operating businesses and practicing their professions, without having to conform to the requirements of Israeli professional associations and licensing bodies. The Jerusalem municipal government and the Israeli Education and Culture Ministry gave up efforts to impose Israeli Arab curricula on the local schools. Jordanian banknotes circulate freely in the Arab sections of the city, in violation of Israeli regulations respecting foreign currency.

The municipality has encouraged housing segregation in order to minimize friction between the major communities. The issue is complex and sensitive and demonstrates the imperfections in coping. In the background are international concerns for segregation as defined in the United States and South Africa. Palestinians and ultra-Orthodox and secular Jews are not forbidden by law from moving into one another's neighborhoods. When a group of Jews moved into an apartment near the Church of the Holy Sepulchre just before Easter in 1990 they provoked a suit by the Greek Orthodox Church to have them removed. The mayor chastised the Jews for their timing and spoke about the usefulness of separate neighborhoods in the mosaic of Jerusalem. In proceedings that have languished for more than six years, a Jerusalem court ordered the removal of several Jewish families from the building over which the Greek Orthodox Church claims ownership, while allowing some Jews to remain there to guard their claim to legal residence.

The third major policy with respect to Jerusalem is to keep the city beautiful. This goal touches religious and aesthetic concerns. It has appeal in its own right and serves to quiet a number of the local and international sources that can make trouble for the present regime. In some people's eyes, the beauty of the city also includes the richness of its cultural offerings. Beauty and culture both appealed to the sensitivities of former mayor Teddy Kollek and added to the success of his Jerusalem Foundation in raising money overseas for social and cultural projects in Jerusalem. In the Jerusalem context no less than elsewhere, however, beauty and culture are topics that invite condemnation as well as applause. The sacred and the profane do not mix well in the city, especially on the Sabbath, near a holy site, or in a religious neighborhood.

The fourth goal is to develop the city's economy. It is not enough to build houses for Jews. It is also important to provide a livelihood for Jews willing to live in Jerusalem and to give the non-Jewish minority an economic reason for keeping the peace. Policy makers must take account of the economic disadvantages of Jerusalem, a city located some distance from the country's major markets, sources of industrial supply, and international ports. Moreover, economic development cannot proceed at the cost of Jerusalem's sanctity or beauty.

The final policy goal is to postpone the settlement of the Jerusalem issue. National policy makers have said that the Jerusalem issue should be last on the agenda of Arab-Israeli issues scheduled for resolution and be dealt with after the conclusion of formal accords with Syria, Lebanon, and the Palestinians.

On its face, this policy seems to be a case of avoidance coping. However, it is a key element in a strategy that fits the conception of engagement coping. It has elements of postponing a formal resolution of Jerusalem's status while maintaining de facto control and building support for a resolution favorable to Israel. Israeli leaders assert that Jerusalem's problems will be the most difficult to solve. Because they are concerned that further concessions on Jerusalem might be demanded during negotiations on Israel's borders, they do not want to make such concessions until they have settled the border issue. They hope that goodwill and trust between Israelis, Palestinians, and other Arabs can grow as a result of other agreements that will come first. They also hope that the world's tolerance of Israel's control over Jerusalem will grow along with the continued development of the city and Israeli management of its affairs. International de facto acceptance of Israeli control over Jerusalem may be the most the regime can achieve, if it cannot formally solve the problems of national borders and other outstanding issues.

Events in Jerusalem since the signing of the Israeli-Palestinian accord in 1993 provide additional illustrations of ambiguity as a coping mechanism. Israeli insistence on control over Jerusalem did not keep the government from agreeing that Palestinian residents of the city could vote in elections for the Palestinian Authority. Israeli insistence that the Palestinians' Orient House not be used for political activities gradually gave way to an acceptance of ceremonial visits there by high-ranking officials from foreign governments. Municipal and national education authorities funded schools in the Palestinian sector and appointed the teachers and administrators, but consulted with PLO representatives on issues of importance to the Palestinians. Israeli insistence that the Palestinian police not operate in Jerusalem was at odds with reports that Palestinian opponents of the PLO were picked up in the city by Palestinian security operatives and transported elsewhere for detention and investigation. An article in a Jerusalem newspaper expressed the ambiguity of policing with headlines that described "Joint Patrols (Almost) of the Border Police and the PLO in the Eastern Part of the City" and "Full Coexistence Even if Not a Formal Coordination."[24] Critics chastised the Israeli establishment for its failure to plan and formulate policy rationally and to solve its problems. Another view was that an acceptance of ambiguity reflected an acquired cultural capacity of Israeli Jews to cope with vexing problems.[25]

The concept of coping involves responses to stressful situations that are likely to be intense and fluid. Coping may involve emoting as well as material adjustments. It seems likely to appear in different shades of gray rather than as discrete categories such as engagement or avoidance. Although the major policy actions of the Israeli authorities with respect to Jerusalem fit the description of engagement coping, some have resembled avoidance coping.

One example of avoidance coping by Israelis appeared when policy makers turned down a proposal to erect a fence between an Arab neighborhood and a Jewish one after terrorist attacks against Jews. The reason offered was that Israel cannot divide any part of Jerusalem, for that might lead to the situation which prevailed in 1948–1967, when there was no contact between the Jewish and Arab sectors. But if a reasoned consideration of the facts had prevailed over emotion, the policy makers would have noticed other places in the city where fences or major roads already separated Jewish and Arab neighborhoods. Such barriers do not seal off one section of the city from the others, but simply make neighborhoods less convenient targets for terrorism.

Mayor Teddy Kollek acquired a reputation for an openness to non-Jewish concerns that fits the description of engagement coping. However, he exhibited avoidance coping when a member of his coalition on the city council collaborated with a prominent Palestinian in proposing to divide Jerusalem into separate Jewish and Palestinian municipalities. For the mayor this was too much of a concession to Palestinian aspirations. Yet it differed only in degree from his own proposal to create Palestinian and Jewish boroughs in Jerusalem. The mayor announced that he would break off all contact with this council member and sought to deprive him of his oversight of the municipal transportation department.

The Jewish city council member who provoked the mayor's anger was a prominent critic of Israel's Jerusalem policy and earlier had produced a study that is relevant to the present discussion of coping. By documenting behavior by city residents that pointed to a minimum of economic and social contact between the Jewish and Arab sectors of Jerusalem, his study highlighted the limited success that Israeli policy makers could claim for their actions in the city. He found that Jerusalem remains under Israeli control, but the assertions by Israeli officials that it is unified or united are not true with respect to conventional meanings of economic or social interactions.[26] Coping is a way of managing problems whose solutions appear elusive and may remain ambiguous. The priorities of Israeli policy on Jerusalem have dictated that maintaining control over the city is more important than ensuring a high level of economic and social integration.

Palestinian Nationalists

Opinion polls reveal the stresses in Jerusalem's Palestinian community. Eighty-six percent of a sample of Palestinians living in Jerusalem answered "no" or "not at all" when asked whether they were satisfied with the services provided by the Israeli municipal government. Almost 90 percent chose "Palestinian state" when asked, "If confronted with a choice, which would you choose: Palestinian state, economic well-being, family and community, or religion?" Fifty-five percent said that the city should be divided into eastern (Palestinian) and western sections.[27] At the time the survey was taken, all major political parties in Israel opposed the creation of a Palestinian state and insisted that Jerusalem remain the undivided capital of Israel.

A prominent sign of Palestinian avoidance coping appears in the calls by their community leaders to refuse the political opportunities offered by Israel. Almost all the Palestinians who were included within the city when Israel annexed a large part of it after the 1967 war refused Israeli citizenship. No local Palestinian political party has emerged in Jerusalem and most Palestinians living in areas annexed by Israel in 1967 have refused to vote in local elections.

Events that took place in September–November 1993 provided mixed clues about Palestinian coping with respect to Jerusalem. In September Israel and the PLO departed from their long-standing enmity and signed an accord that committed them to reaching a peaceful settlement of their disputes. A crucial feature of the agreement, which helped convince the Israelis to cede control over sections of the occupied territories (Gaza and Jericho), was the PLO's willingness to postpone resolving the Jerusalem issue. As the November date for Israel's municipal elections approached, some Palestinian leaders called on their community to participate in the Jerusalem election to oppose the most nationalist Jewish candidate. But more authoritative voices in the Palestinian community endorsed a continuing political boycott as a way of demonstrating the Palestinians' claim on the city, and only 7 percent of the eligible Palestinians voted.

The long run may demonstrate that coping by Jerusalem's Palestinians has involved engagement with respect to their most important goals of maintaining their distance from the Israeli regime. Until now, however, their coping seems to have taken the form of avoiding opportunities.

Even after the beginning of negotiations between the PLO and the Israeli government and the implementation of the Israeli-Palestinian agreements, some Palestinian organizations expressed their hostility toward the Israeli regime through violence directed against Jewish civilians and security personnel in Jerusalem. Before the onset of negotiations, terror was conducted by mainstream as well as fringe elements within the PLO.

Violence in Jerusalem, as elsewhere, is difficult to evaluate in conjunction with the categories of engagement coping and avoidance coping. From one perspective, terror appears to be a quintessential manifestation of avoidance coping, reflecting the frustration and rage of those who employ it. Terror stiffened the resolve of Israeli victims and added to their support among Western democracies.[28] Yet terror is one of the power elements that may bring adversaries to the bargaining table. Whether the intifada was terror or successful will be an issue for historians to debate. On the one hand, it did not bring Israel to its knees. Palestinian casualties during the intifada were ten times greater than Israeli casualties, and 40 percent of the Palestinian casualties were attributed to violence within the Palestinian community.[29] On the other hand, the intifada persuaded many Israelis that they could not resolve their conflict with the Palestinians by force alone. Perhaps the violence and the frustrations led Palestinians as well as Israelis to support engagement coping through negotiation.

Assessing Israel's Accomplishments

The complexities of Jerusalem give us an opportunity to assess Israeli policy accomplishments in the context of difficult problems and sharp antagonisms. Issues related to Jerusalem touch the most important goals of Israeli foreign policy and Palestinian nationalism. Jerusalem is associated with hopes and anxieties for Israelis who want to preserve their country as a Jewish state but also aspire to reach an accommodation with Palestinians and other Arabs.

This section makes an effort to judge Jerusalem's record in the period since 1967. It does so in recognition of the emotions that cloud judgment. Palestinian and Jewish residents split on their support for the Jewish regime. People the world over look to the city with spiritual aspirations and the feeling that the worldly city should be more ideal than others. Expectations are inflated by religious images of Jerusalem as the city of David and Christ, the city that figured in the dreams of Mohammed, and the city where religious Jews and Christians await the messiah. There is no obvious list of criteria that the antagonists could agree on in judging those who control the city. This book's evaluation of Jerusalem policy making judges the government authorities on the basis of their own goals. The focus continues on Jerusalem below, and not the "Jerusalem above" (a metaphor for paradise) where all groups' aspirations are optimized.

The Palestinians are the Jerusalemites least served by the municipal government and Israel's national ministries. They also are the segment of the Jerusalem population who have most clearly removed themselves from the political process that determines who gets what in the city. Israeli policy makers take account of Palestinian sentiments out of a sense of what foreign observers in Western democracies would expect to be offered a hostile minority, or what it would take to minimize Palestinian disaffection.

The lack of East Jerusalemite participation in the local politics of Jerusalem and the national politics of Israel adds to the technical problems in evaluating Israeli policies on Jerusalem. There is no authoritative list of Palestinian demands that might serve as a basis for judging how well the municipality addresses the desires of Palestinian individuals or neighborhoods for public services.

Other technical issues also make it difficult to judge how far current policies serve local residents. Most Israeli opinion polls fail to include respondents from the sizable ultra-Orthodox and Palestinian communities of Jerusalem, which are closed to outsiders and suspicious of conventional polling techniques. Even if questioned by Palestinians or religious Jews, with an additional concern that only male or female pollsters contact male or female informants, it is doubtful that the responses would be as candid as those gathered in surveys of Western secular communities, where the political issues are less emotional.

While remaining aware of the limitations, one can evaluate certain features of public policy and other aspects of living conditions in Jerusalem. Some traits can be examined by adopting approaches widely used in political science. One can compare Jerusalem to other places or to itself in the past. One can also compare the benefits received by different groups in the city's population, or look at policy makers' intentions in the light of their achievements.

But what places can be compared with Jerusalem? Other cities that have been idealized, such as Paris, London, New York, and Berlin, are the capitals or showpieces of countries much wealthier than Israel and have not been subject to bitter claims relating to national ownership. Troubled cities, such as Belfast, Beirut, and Nicosia, lack the spiritual aura that leads overseas Jews, Christians, and Moslems to contribute toward Jerusalem's improvement despite ethnic and religious tensions.

The most appropriate comparisons appear to be with other large cities in Israel or with Israel as a whole. Israel provides most of the public resources used in Jerusalem. A comparison restricted to Israel will show how Jerusalem fares in relation to communities that rely on the same national economic base. And insofar as the city has changed hands violently on a number of occasions and is subject to rival claims for control, it is appropriate to assess the stability of the current regime.

The following discussion is more suggestive than definitive. It identifies issues and measurements that are relevant to evaluating Jerusalem, without claiming to resolve issues that are beset with contrasting readings of historical and contemporary reality. The most sensitive Jerusalem issues do not lend themselves to evaluation on the basis of standard statistics available for relevant cities or population groups. The data in table 6.3 provide some quantitative indicators bearing on the question of "who gets what in Jerusalem?"

How do the benefits provided to the city's residents compare with those enjoyed by other Israelis? This kind of question is commonly asked by political scientists and is appropriate for Jerusalem. To be sure, it is a limited question in the sense that it does not address the concerns of those nonresidents who view the place as the world's city or the possession of all the world's Moslems, Christians, or Jews.

Jerusalem's air is better than that of other Israeli cities, thanks in

TABLE 6.3 Jerusalem and Israel: Selected Indicators

| | Jerusalem | | | | | |
	Jews	Non-Jews	Entire City	Tel Aviv	Haifa	All Israel
Air quality						
Sulpher dioxide index			10	21	56	
Nitrogen oxide index			20	37		
Health: infant mortality per 1,000 live births	7.4	11.4	8.7			9.8
Divorces per 1,000 population	1.5	0.7	1.3			1.4
Standard of living						
Average net income per household			3,710	3,620	3,990	
Households with two or more persons per room (%)	13.1	14.2		7.3	6.0	
Unemployment (%)	9.2		10.9	11.0	13.9	10.6
Education						
Years of education of head of household			13.8	12.6	13.0	
Average no. of primary school pupils per classroom	24–32	30				26
Traffic accidents involving injuries			1,385	3,728	806	
Crime rates						
Crimes against the person, per 1,000 population			.71			1.31
Crimes against property per 1,000 population			.15			2.29

SOURCES: *Statistical Abstract of Israel, 1990* (Jerusalem: Central Bureau of Statistics, 1990), 31, 583, 618; *Statistical Yearbook of Israel, 1990* (Municipality of Jerusalem and Jerusalem Institute for Israel Studies, 1990), 205, 242; *Statistical Yearbook of Israel, 1991* (Municipality of Jerusalem and Jerusalem Institute for Israel Studies, 1991), 67, 70, 107, 116, 124–25, 222.

part to policies that have kept heavy industry out of the city. The air quality also owes something to mountain winds and to economic conditions that discourage industrialists from investing in a city located some distance from the country's economic centers and ports.

Jerusalem's crime rates are generally lower than those for Israel as a whole. The explanation may lie in the culture of a city that is heavily populated by religiously inclined Jews, Moslems, and Christians, and in the heavy police presence in a city troubled by terrorism. It is tempting to compare Jerusalem's crime rates with those of the United States, which also suffers from multicultural tensions. The 1992 murder rate in Jerusalem was 0.02 per 100,000 residents, while the rate for all of Israel was 1.97. In the United States the rate was 9.8, but 80.1 in Washington, D.C., 68.9 in New Orleans, 65.0 in St Louis, and 59.3 in Detroit.[30]

There are substantially fewer traffic accidents involving injuries in Jerusalem than in Tel Aviv, although more than in Haifa. This may reflect the lower number of motor vehicles in the city, which in turn reflects lower family incomes.

There seems to be more parks and cultural facilities in Jerusalem than in other Israeli cities, although residents of Tel Aviv might quarrel about the relative merits of the theaters, orchestras, and museums in each city. Heads of families in Jerusalem are somewhat better educated than those of Tel Aviv or Haifa. However, class sizes in Jerusalem's state primary schools for Jews are in the upper part of the 24–32 range shown in table 6.3 (ultra-Orthodox schools for Jews have smaller classes) and are larger than the Israeli average.

Do various groups in the city's population benefit or suffer from existing policies? The answer to this question is that all groups—Jews, Christians, and Moslems—both benefit and suffer. All suffer from being denied sole control over their holy city and its sacred sites. Rivalries between Christian sects, between Moslem religious authorities, and between secular and religious Jews are only marginally less intense than the more prominent rivalries that characterize relations between the Christian, Moslem, and Jewish communities. Jerusalem's Palestinian nationalists are frustrated by having to live in Israel's capital. Jews are nervous about the world's respect for Palestinian claims. Jews must always be on the alert for an abandoned package that could be a bomb or for a Palestinian who might suddenly shout "God is great" and attack them with a knife. After a successful act of Palestinian terror, Palestinians worry about Jews seeking revenge.

Housing congestion is more of a problem in the Palestinian sector than in the Jewish sector. This state of affairs is a result of meager public resources being devoted to the construction of houses in Palestinian neighborhoods and problems in providing construction permits for the private building of Palestinian housing. These policies in turn are caused by official Israeli reluctance to allow an expansion of the city's Palestinian population and Palestinian reluctance to deal with the Israeli authorities.

Divorce rates may be seen as a general indicator of social stability. In Jerusalem they are substantially lower among the Palestinians than among the Jews. On the other hand, infant mortality is substantially lower in the Jewish community. Some Israelis assert that the average Jerusalem Palestinian is better off materially and politically than most residents of Arab countries. Few Palestinians would agree that such a fact, if true, is sufficient cause for them to lessen their desire for nationhood.

Jerusalem's Palestinians appear to benefit from more and better educational and cultural opportunities than are available in other Palestinian communities in Israel or in the occupied territories. Nevertheless, the city's Palestinians prefer to compare what they receive from government with the more substantial services that the Jews receive.

Information on how the Jewish and Palestinian communities use publicly funded schools is one indicator of the extent to which Palestinians opt out of the Israeli service network. In per capita terms, non-Jewish Jerusalemites aged five to nineteen attend publicly funded schools in much smaller numbers than Jewish Jerusalemites of the same age group.[31] The municipal government has tried on several occasions to attract Palestinians to its schools and away from church-supported and other private institutions. Many Palestinian parents have rejected the offer of a free education for their children, presumably because the municipal schools are tainted by their Israeli curriculum and links to the Israeli state.

How does Jerusalem's current condition compare with its condition in the past? This is an elementary question for policy analysts who are concerned that officials do not, at the very least, make things worse. It is also a question that would bring a more positive response from Jews than Palestinians. The conventional indicator of population size suggests a level of economic development that surpasses Jerusalem's record in any previous era. Since 1967 Jerusalem has thrived under Israeli rule. The population more than doubled by 1992. Resources have come to the city from Israeli taxpayers, overseas donors, and investors both at home and abroad. There has been a surge in the construction of houses and public facilities more impressive than anything since the days of Solomon or Herod. Jerusalem ranks as a modern city that meets European or North American standards with respect to housing, access to clean water, electricity, communications, transportation, and other public services.

Jerusalem's current situation is immeasurably better than what prevailed a century or more ago under Ottoman rule. A visiting physician in 1834 found neither doctor nor dispensary in the city. The Christian and Jewish quarters were in decay, and the Moslem authorities refused to permit new construction of churches and synagogues or even their repair. Dead animals and piles of rubbish were left to rot in the streets. The water was generally foul and usually in short supply. Mark Twain's observations are widely quoted: "Rags, wretchedness, poverty, and dirt, those signs and symbols that indicate the presence of Moslem rule more surely than the crescent flag itself, abound. Lepers, cripples, the blind, and the idiots, assail you on every hand, and they know but one word of but one language apparently—the eternal 'bucksheesh.'"[32] A British officer reported that the city was "one of the most unhealthy places in the world . . . [because of] the inferior quality of the water and the presence of an enormous mass of rubbish which had been accumulating for centuries."[33] As late as 1910 it was reported that 25 percent to 60 percent of the population suffered from malaria.[34]

As for the Jerusalem's holy sites, the current situation is better than in any earlier era. There has been no purge of Christian or Moslem sites under Israeli rule. Each religious group controls its own holy sites, although some sites have been subject to competing Christian, Moslem, and Jewish claims. Antagonists claim that the Israelis ruined the city's skyline, expropriated Palestinian homes to make way for a plaza fronting the Western Wall, and took Palestinian land for the development of Jewish neighborhoods. Jews respond to these charges by describing Jerusalem under Jordanian rule in 1948–1967, when Jewish graves and synagogues were desecrated and Jews were denied access to the Western Wall. Most of the new Jewish neighborhoods have been built on vacant land not suitable for agriculture. Israelis do not respond gently to United Nations bodies that have condemned Israel without taking into account distorted Arab propaganda and Arab terror against Israelis.

Have the Israeli authorities achieved their policy goals for Jerusalem? This is anoter question without a clear answer. Most of the policy goals listed earlier in this chapter are not amenable to precise measurement. We cannot tell whether the authorities have simultaneously managed to preserve the city's beauty and natural environment, meet the essential demands of the major religious communities and weaker socioeconomic segments, and develop the economy to its maximum potential. Confining our analysis to the period since 1967, it is possible to argue that both positive and negative indicators can be found to apply to each policy goal. Things could have been much worse, but they can be made better.

The national government has been successful in postponing the settlement of the Jerusalem issue. It is not yet clear whether postponement will facilitate the more basic goal of ensuring continued Israeli rule over the whole of Jerusalem.

Efforts to maintain Jerusalem's status as a predominantly Jewish city and as the capital of Israel can be examined in several ways. At first glance these goals seem to have been achieved. In 1992 the municipality had a sizable Jewish majority of 72 percent. This represented a decline of 1 percent since 1967 but an increase of 11 percent over 1948. Ongoing building of Jewish neighborhoods and immigration from the former Soviet Union may continue to increase the Jewish majority in the years to come. However, attempts to measure Jerusalem's Jewish majority are clouded by the artificial nature of the city's boundaries. For the true metropolitan area, which is defined by commuting patterns and extends beyond the municipality's formal boundaries, the proportions are not known with any certainty, because Israel has never been able to conduct a full census in the occupied territories. Estimates of the Jewish population in the metropolitan area range from 58 percent to only 50 percent or less. As for the second goal, Israel has not, in formal terms, gained wide international recognition for its insistence that Jerusalem is its capital, although there is a greater degree of informal recognition. Almost all countries maintain their embassies in Tel Aviv, but ambassadors and visiting heads of state come to Jerusalem to meet with Israeli officials. Thus, Israel appears to have been successful in making Jerusalem its de facto national capital.

Critics of the Israeli regime emphasize the artificiality not only of Jerusalem's borders but also of the city's unity. The formal municipal borders act as a demographic wall around a city that is predominantly Jewish only because substantial Palestinian settlement has been kept out. The borders are effective only because the Israeli regime remains strong and can enforce the lines it has drawn. A recent book based on conversations with Israeli Arabs makes the point that although Jews are a large majority within Israel, Arabs are a much larger majority in the Middle East and can bide their time until a change in regime.[35]

The fact that there is minimal contact between the Jewish and Palestinian sectors in Jerusalem mocks the Israeli claim of a united city. Frequent police inspections of Palestinian identity documents discourage Palestinians from entering Jewish areas other than to work. They rarely shop in Jewish areas. Jerusalem's Jews ceased shopping in Palestinian areas with the onset of the intifada and altered their travel patterns to avoid having their vehicles stoned. Vehicles registered to Israeli citizens

(Jewish and non-Jewish) carry yellow license plates, while those registered to non-Jewish residents of the occupied territories carry blue plates. Stone throwers attempt to distinguish Jewish from Palestinian Israeli vehicles by looking at the type of vehicle and the appearance of the occupants. Sometimes they err.

Jerusalem Scenarios

The dangers of Jerusalem begin with religion and ethnicity. The city is holy to three faiths, each of which incorporates elements of monotheism and doctrinal exclusivity. The city also lies on a cultural divide. For other democracies the boundary between east and west may be an ocean or a mountain range. In Jerusalem it can be a street or even the wall that separates one unit from another in the same apartment building. The city's history dissuades reasonable politicians from using the rhetoric of crusade or holy war, yet some individuals continue to speak in those terms. Such rhetoric may not have any real impact when employed in distant Iran, Iraq, or Libya by leaders who use Jerusalem as a symbol to divert the attention of restive populations from local issues, but their words resonate among Israeli politicians and make those politicians less politically flexible.

In what may seem to be an irony, the intensity of faith that complicates Jerusalem also works in favor of using ambiguity as a policy tool. Religious doctrines include concepts of Jerusalem above and Jerusalem below. Jerusalem above refers to the holy city. It is a synonym for Paradise and has connotations of the otherworldly and the afterlife. Jerusalem below refers to the earthly city, with its traffic sounds, the scurry of cats around garbage, and the tensions of political competition. The optimistic feature of this situation is that politicians might reach agreement on the management of Jerusalem below, while leaving the faithful of each community to remain steadfast on how Jerusalem will be governed once the messiah or prophet arrives.

Although some religious leaders are zealots who wish to impose their version of the truth on the earthly Jerusalem, others seem willing to wait until they reach the heavenly Jerusalem. Jordan's prime minister, Dr. Abd-al-Salam al-Majali, demonstrated a facility with language and political concepts that offer the ingredients of compromise: "Human brains that create problems can create solutions, too. . . . The word Jerusalem is derived from sanctity or places of worship. . . . Political Jerusalem is different from the religious Jerusalem that is sacred to the three religions. Thus, a political solution is possible."[36] Yassir

Arafat spoke in a similar manner on the eve of negotiations for a permanent solution to the Israeli-Palestinian conflict. Against Israeli insistence that Jerusalem not be discussed, he said that Palestinians could not be prevented from dreaming of Jerusalem as the capital of their state. Israeli prime minister Shimon Peres responded that he did not object to Palestinian dreams.

The city's recent history works in favor of the agility and suppleness that are associated with ambiguity and coping. The concessions made by Israeli officials after 1967 reflect their sensitivity to the feelings of the city's Palestinians. The relative quiescence of the city's Palestinians during the intifada suggests that they recognized limits to what could be achieved in Jerusalem. Jerusalem's Palestinians have made no secret of their opposition to the Israeli regime, but they may appreciate their relatively placid existence in Jerusalem and the social services and economic opportunities they enjoy.

The elemental requirements of coping are to avoid impossible aspirations and to continue with the theme of accommodations where they already show signs of evolving. It appears to be beyond the realm of possibility to define fixed boundaries between the Israeli and Palestinian sectors within the present municipal boundaries of Jerusalem or to neatly assign people and government functions to separate municipal authorities. The lines dividing Jerusalem's ethnic and religious neighborhoods (Palestinian and Israeli, Christian and Moslem, ultra-Orthodox Jewish and secular Jewish) are irregular and discontinuous and often change their character from one block to the next, from one apartment building to the next, or even from one apartment unit to the next.

It is unrealistic to expect the Israeli regime to abandon the neighborhoods constructed since 1967 and to return Jerusalem to a status quo ante of whatever date. By 1990, 132,000 Jews lived in new Jerusalem neighborhoods constructed on land that had been under Jordanian control before the 1967 war.[37] In the eyes of some people this reflects the Israelis' lack of concern for justice. In the eyes of others it is the result of legitimate Israeli concerns in the face of Arab threats against Jerusalem and Palestinian rejection of the political opportunities offered by Israel.

Assertions about past injustices frustrate accommodation. Palestinian pragmatists will seek whatever potential for satisfying Palestinian concerns within the outline of what exists. One set of opportunities lies just outside Jerusalem's present municipal boundaries. Neighborhoods and villages to the north, east, and south (from Ramallah to Bethlehem and Beit Jallah) are encompassed by the area assigned to the Palestinians. They contain a sizable Palestinian majority. By building up this area, Palestinians can say they are developing "Jerusalem" without infringing on the Israeli city. This creates the potential for the creation of a binational metropolitan area bearing the magic name "Jerusalem." In this area, utility and sewage systems could be administered by authorities with representatives of both national entities. The Israelis and Palestinians could also develop a mandate for jointly sharing tax revenues and creating a unified and mutually beneficial scheme with respect to water use, budgeting for urban development, and the appointment of civil servants. The following accommodations would depart little or not at all from what already exists within the municipal boundaries of Jerusalem:

• Control of Christian and Moslem holy places by the religious authorities of each community. The present de facto arrangement could be formalized in law, perhaps, as former mayor Teddy Kollek suggests, under a United Nations resolution adopted as Israeli law by the Knesset.

• Recognition of Orient House as the government seat of the Palestinian state. Orient House could have all the trappings of government authority—flags, armed guards, and, for visiting dignitaries, red carpets.

• Devolution of control over sensitive local services, such as education, to individuals vetted by the Palestinian authorities.

• Giving Jerusalem residents the opportunity to choose which national entity they want to associate with for civic purposes (or the opportunity to associate with both). This scheme would cover voting, taxes, and social welfare provision and might be sweetened by providing for protection against double taxation and by allowing Palestinians to vote in both Israeli and Palestinian elections at the local and even at the national levels. The status of Jerusalem's Palestinian residents could resemble that of Israelis who also are citizens of the United States or other countries that permit dual citizenship.

By their very nature, coping and the use of ambiguity as a coping technique give rise to arrangements that are neither flawless nor free of tension. Choosing which Moslem religious authorities will be awarded control of the Haram-Esh-Sharif, or which Christian authorities will be awarded control sections of the Church of the Holy Sepulchre, will demand the same spirit of diplomacy and accommodation as is needed to resolve conflicts between ultra-Orthodox and other Jews.

None of these proposals is likely to be accepted without severe criticism from communal leaders who proclaim that they are not receiving enough from their adversaries or are conceding too much to them. Within both the Israeli and Palestinian communities there are many leaders and followers whose tolerance for ambiguity is limited. Prominent among those who oppose political concessions are people who have been injured or have lost family as a result of intercommunal violence. Yassir Arafat regularly asserts that Jerusalem must be the capital of his Palestinian state. His use of the term jihad creates its own problems of ambiguity. Whereas he asserts that jihad can mean a nonviolent campaign on behalf of a spiritual goal, it can also mean holy war, which implies mass hysteria and violence.

Statements made during the run-up to the 1996 Israeli national election testify to the emotions associated with Jerusalem. The opposition Likud Party began its campaign by accusing Prime Minister Peres of seeking to divide the city and give part of it to the Palestinians for their national capital. The Labor Party's response was to deny any such intention and to assert that it was committed to maintaining a united city under Israeli rule. The internal security minister announced that he would tighten control over Orient House and forbid the kinds of visits by foreign dignitaries that had previously been permitted. What was missing from the Labor Party response was an effort to educate the Israeli public on the complexity of the issues surrounding Jerusalem and on the possibility of addressing those issues by recognizing the multiple meanings of "Jerusalem."

Why the shrill and stubborn response from the Labor Party? Perhaps its leadership wanted to maintain a strong position on Jerusalem in preparation for negotiations with the Palestinians, whose own leadership had staked out a demand for a national capital in the city. If this was the Labor leadership's thinking, it seemed weakened by comments made by members of the party's left wing and of the Meretz Party (Labor's coalition partner), who said that considerations of equity and pragmatism required compromise with the Palestinians. More persuasive is a political explanation for the Labor Party's formal position on Jerusalem, namely its fear of the Jewish electorate's concern for the city.

Did this mean that the party was lying to the voters? Perhaps not, as long as it did not specify what it meant by Jerusalem, and what it meant by not dividing it. Eventually it may be possible to explain a Palestinian government site in Jerusalem, and measures of autonomy for the Palestinian population that differ little if at all from practices already in place. Even easier to explain will be Palestinian developments in greater Jerusalem, much of which has already be assigned to the Palestinian Authority.

It is neither natural nor inevitable to expect that Palestine's capital will be all in one place. The Palestinian Authority could accept a small symbolic site in the Israeli municipality and continue developing its administrative offices in the suburbs. The Federal Republic of Germany had its legislative chamber and key executive offices in Bonn but placed its supreme court in Karlsruhe and its central bank and state audit office in Frankfurt. South Africa has its legislative chamber in Cape Town and executive offices in Pretoria. Even Israel compromises on its insistence that Jerusalem is its capital; it has kept the Defense Ministry in Tel Aviv while moving other ministries to Jerusalem.

There is nothing inevitable about a city containing only one capital or the territory of only one national entity. Brussels is the seat of the European Union and of the Belgian monarchy. New York City houses the headquarters of the United Nations. The territory and accredited personnel of the United Nations enjoy a form of sovereignty in New York City that does not challenge national sovereignty over the remaining land. The same is true of countless embassies in national capitals. Thus the Palestinians could develop a ceremonial site at Orient House in East Jerusalem, emphasize their spiritual connection with the Moslem-controlled holy site of Haram-Esh-Sharif, and develop other government sites elsewhere in greater Jerusalem, Gaza, and the West Bank. Allowing a Palestinian seat of government at Orient House or some other site within Israeli Jerusalem would not compromise Israel's claims of sovereignty over its national capital.

There may be no avoiding Palestinian charges that such arrangements would be too similar to the allegedly unfair status quo now maintained by Israel. Nor will Israeli nationalists avoid making the charge that their government has departed from the Zionist ideal of a united Jerusalem under Israeli control. Pope John Paul II has a point when he says that Jerusalem is the world's city. The intensity of international identification with Jerusalem is greater than that which applies to other world cities such as New York, Paris, or London. On the other hand, Jerusalem has had a Jewish majority since the latter half of the nineteenth century and has been predominantly Israeli since 1967. The Israeli regime has already demonstrated that it can make concessions on spiritual and symbolic issues. Palestinian leaders as well as Moslem and Christian clerics have shown themselves to be concerned with spiritual and symbolic accomplishments, if not entirely satisfied with them.

Jerusalem's history has been marked by intense competition for control of the city and a disinclination on the part of the contending parties to be moderate in their demands. Whether the city's rulers have been Romans, Crusaders, Moslems, or Israelis, there has been a lack of willingness to compromise on points relating to formal authority. No Jerusalem regime has ever been so accommodating as to create an environment of egalitarian pluralism in which all groups are genuinely equal in their access to political power. Yet pragmatic arrangements have allowed subordinate groups a certain measure of autonomy, geographical and otherwise. Such has been the case with respect to Israeli concessions to the Palestinians in the areas of education, professional regulation, and currency use. The Israelis have also adopted a pragmatic approach to the control of Christian and Moslem holy places. Perhaps such a mixture of rigidity on the unity of formal rule in the city, along with practical concessions is the most that can be expected for Jerusalem.

Most Jerusalem Moslems and Christians live peacefully under the Israeli regime, but may be biding their time until there is another upheaval in the city's history. It may take a year, a decade, or a millennium, but they or their descendants will be in Jerusalem to enjoy it. Policy strategy in the city may not become more fully accommodating, to the point of being egalitarian, until the city's contending parties can agree on the spiritual goals they are pursuing. In the meantime, policy analysts perhaps will claim that many of Jerusalem's problems have been solved, in the sense that reasonable expectations have been met. Others problems remain unsolved and perhaps insoluble.

CHAPTER 7

Insoluble Religious Disputes Among the Jews

Religion remains a vital force in economically developed Western democracies two centuries after the Enlightenment that was supposed to mark its decline. Secular intellectuals proclaim God's death and wonder at the continued capacity of preachers to attract the faithful and place the faithful's concerns at the center of political discourse. However, observers who believe that religion remains dominant are no more accurate in their assessments than those who view religion as a withering relic. It seems more accurate to say that religion and secularism have reached a standoff, not that one dominates the other.[1]

Several of Israel's traits make it likely that religious issues will be prominent. Israel proclaims itself a Jewish state and gives control over sensitive personal matters to the religious authorities of its Jewish and other communities. Much of its population is only a generation or two removed from pre-Enlightenment conditions, or still immersed in them. And Jerusalem, even more than Israel as a whole, provides a setting for the intense expression of religious interests, on account of its history, holy sites, and a population that includes greater proportions of religious Jews, Moslems, and Christians than other Israeli cities.

As elsewhere in Israel, however, religious and secular interests exist in the holy city in a condition of chronic tension. Neither dominates the other. Religious and secular (including antireligious) activists are capable of putting religious issues on the political agenda, but none of them can dictate how controversies will end.

Among Israel's Jews, policy disputes that involve religion are conflicts with no apparent solution. The case of religion serves as a vehicle for assessing whether an apparent conundrum truly can be insoluble. It also shows the usefulness of the scheme laid out in table 2.1 as a support for comparative analysis. Parallels with Israeli religious disputes can be found elsewhere, but differ in ways that suggest the influence of particular religious doctrines and national cultures.

The continued tension surrounding religion in the Israeli Jewish population has produced chronic political disturbances of moderately high intensity. The killing of Prime Minister Yitzhak Rabin by a religious Jew in November 1995 testified to the strength of the passions involved. Some observers see the potential of civil war, but the conflicts have to date been marked more by verbal than by physical violence between religious and secular Jews, and neither camp has been able to score clear victories. This condition seems to reflect a great variety of doctrines within Judaism, including an element of ethnicity that allows even those individuals who proclaim their lack of belief in any Jewish religious doctrines to remain part of the Jewish community. Also important is Israel's use of proportional representation in electoral politics, which gives a voice to the religious and antireligious camps but denies either one a position of dominance.

The issue's claim for insolubility rests on its longevity. Religious and secular Israeli Jews have argued about public policy since the state gained its independence in 1948. Disputes that still appear on the political agenda date back to the prestate period of the British Mandate in Palestine, when the Jewish community was allowed only limited self-rule. Some have older roots in the Jewish communities of Europe, particularly those of the period beginning at the end of the eighteenth century, when many Jews left the isolation of urban ghettos or small towns to pursue a secular education. Other conflicts have even older roots in the clashes between Jewish cosmopolitans and religious zealots under Greek and Roman rule in Judea from the second century B.C.E. to the first century C.E.[2]

The long history of Judaism and its spread throughout much of the world have also contributed to cultural diversity and the proliferation of religious disputes. In *Death and Birth of Judaism*, Jacob Neusner claims to identify eight varieties of Judaism, although in fact he seems to have found ten: early Judaism; the Judaism of the dual Torah, which begins in the fourth century C.E. and is based on the written Torah (the first five books of the Bible) and the oral Torah (the accumulation of rabbinical commentaries on the written Torah and the religious law derived from those commentaries); Reform Judaism; Conservative Judaism; Orthodox Judaism; Zionism; Jewish socialism; American

150 Insoluble Religious Disputes Among the Jews

Judaism; Israeli Judaism; and a Judaism of "reversion," which advocates a fresh encounter with the Judaism of the dual Torah.[3] In an article on the Jewish experience in the United States, Neusner compromises his own concept of American Judaism by asking whether it is Jewishness without Judaism. He calls some efforts of American Jews "grotesque" but concludes that they represent a group's efforts to survive that so far have been successful.[4] The Israeli Judaism that Neusner describes should itself be divided into various degrees of religiosity, as will be shown below.

The plurality of Judaisms makes for a great deal of political disputatiousness about religion in Israel. The agenda includes several clusters, each of which comprises numerous disputes:

• Which aspects of religious law should be enforced by state authorities, and which bodies should have the final say in determining the nature of religious law or its application to individual cases? This cluster of disputes revolves around the prohibition of work, public entertainment, and transportation on the Sabbath and on religious holidays; the availability of nonkosher food; laws governing abortions, autopsies, burials, marriages, and divorces; the question of who should be considered a Jew; and the question of who should be allowed the title and authority of rabbi to perform marriages and arrange divorces and conversions to Judaism.

• What should be the rights and privileges of non-Jews? This question includes issues related to opportunities for government employment and access to the resources provided by public programs.

• What should be the rights and privileges of the various categories of Jews? Israelis Jews of many kinds—religious, secular, Asian, North African, Ethiopian—believe they have been mistreated by some other group of Jews.

• How much of the imprecise landscape of the biblical Land of Israel should remain inviolable in negotiations with the Palestinians and other Arabs or bargained away for the sake of peace? Not the least of the issues in this cluster is Jerusalem with its Jewish, Christian, and Moslem holy places. The history of that city has made both religious and secular Jews suspicious of gentile intentions. It is this cluster of issues that holds the greatest potential for bloodshed among Jews, that is, between those who insist on holding on to all of the Land of Israel currently under Israeli rule and building Jewish settlements in Palestinian areas, and those who would give substantial tracts to the Palestinians.[5]

What Is Religious? What Is a Policy Victory?

It is no simple task to determine what is a religious dispute rather than an issue colored by religious rhetoric. This is especially true in Israel, where more than 80 percent of the population is Jewish and where there is an important element of ethnicity in Jewish doctrine. Virtually every policy issue considered by Israel's Cabinet includes a Jewish component, although not every issue involves conflict over religious doctrine. The contending parties in political arguments about welfare policy, fiscal policy, or defense often emphasize the need to safeguard the state's Jewishness or wrap their demands in what they call Jewish norms or traditions. No government budget can pass without the religious parties making a pitch for religious education or housing for religious families, and a secular politician responding that the religious parties are using an unfair electoral advantage to blackmail the secular majority.

Just what is meant by a *policy victory* is a matter of some dispute, especially in the context of religion. *Public policy* refers to what government does or proposes to do, and places an emphasis on what are widely viewed as the "important" actions of government. An issue may be important on account of the resources involved, the number of people affected, or its political sensitivity.[6] Symbols are statements or other things that represent abstract ideas and often have strong emotional content, although not necessarily great financial value: the design of a flag, the words of a song or speech, the content of a ceremony.[7] Policy *substance* refers to the moneys or to the tangible goods and services that are distributed as a result of public policy decisions, and to the use of law to impose controversial forms of behavior or restrict the behavior of the entire population. There is no doubt that religion affects issues whose symbolic content is extensive. What is less certain is the capacity of religious interests to determine the outcome of controversies that have significant implications for policy substance.

A distinction between policy issues that are symbolic or substantial is useful in considering the interface of religion and politics, but only to an extent. A policy that involves moneys, services, or regulations is not necessarily more important than a policy concerning the design of a nation's flag, the words of a prayer in an official ceremony, or the statement of a national leader about what is good, true, or just. In the eyes of a religious or antireligious citizen, a state's official stance (or failure to adopt a stance) on a point of religious doctrine, or an individual's behavior (or failure to behave) in accordance with a religious convention, may be matters of the utmost importance. In 1977 the NRP withdrew from the Israeli governing coalition and caused a political crisis ostensibly because a military ceremony had concluded too close to the onset of the Sabbath. In the election that followed, Likud ousted Labor and initiated many substantial changes in Israeli government policy.

Some political issues combine symbolic and substantive elements, as in the case of Jerusalem. Safeguarding the unity of Jerusalem under Israeli rule is not only one of the platforms of several political parties, but involves tangible issues relating to municipal and national boundaries and the question of who should benefit from the municipality's public services. For a Palestinian, legal residence within the boundaries of the city means access to Israel's social welfare programs, including a monthly payment of about U.S.$40 for every child under age eighteen, medical insurance, and old age pensions. Jerusalem residency also provides access to work in Israel when the border with the West Bank is closed in response to a terrorist attack. The location of the U.S. embassy in Jerusalem concerns not only a symbolic site for an office building but carries weight in international politics. Palestinian success in attracting foreign government officials to Orient House helps bolster the Palestinian claim that Jerusalem is their capital. In the nineteenth century, conflict between the Russian Orthodox and Roman Catholic churches over the Church of the Holy Sepulchre led Russia and France to take sides and ultimately was one reason for the Crimean War.[8]

It is also the case that some matters handled by religious authorities involve both symbolic and material benefits. Where the management of religion is the state's business, as in Israel, political patronage, in the form of money and jobs, comes into the hands of the state religious authorities. In Israel the Religions Ministry and the Chief Rabbinate decide who will be appointed community rabbis, inspectors of kosher food production, and judges in the religious courts. They also decide how much government money will be allocated to the construction or refurbishing of particular synagogues, churches, and mosques.

Jews and Gentiles

The holy sites of three faiths, as well as Christian, Moslem, and Jewish residents provide several points of friction within Israel and affect its foreign relations. A group of American Catholic clerics complained to the White House about the continued construction of Jewish neighborhoods around Jerusalem. In response, leaders of American Jewish organizations complained about the tone of the clerics' letter. This led the clerics to issue a clarification indicating that it was not their intention to threaten Israel's status in Jerusalem or to increase Vatican influence in the city. All they wanted, they said, was to protect the future of their coreligionists in Israel and to facilitate the Arab-Israeli peace process.[9]

The Latin patriarch of Jerusalem, an ethnic Palestinian, presented a broader agenda to the Israelis. He called on them to give Jerusalem's non-Jewish religious leaders a say in city government and to free 10,500 Palestinian prisoners as a sign that Israel was sincere about making peace. On his list of prisoners to be freed was a leader of an Islamic fundamentalist group identified with acts of violence against Israelis.[10]

The complications in Jewish-Christian relations began to be apparent in the response of a Greek Orthodox cleric to the Latin patriarch's statement. He showed that Christians themselves worry about one another's advantages: "If the Christians shared in the [municipal] administration, the Vatican would set the tone."[11]

When some Jews moved into an empty building near the Church of the Holy Sepulchre just before Easter in 1990, they provoked a statement of condemnation from Greek Orthodox clerics that recalled the Christian persecutions of the Jews under Crusader rule, when no Jews were permitted to live in Jerusalem, and under Moslem rule, when Christians stoned Jews who wandered near the Church of the Holy Sepulchre. This in turn led Israel's president Chaim Herzog to send a public letter to the Greek Orthodox Church, one that revealed the strength of feeling that existed between two religious groups with a long history of antagonism:

I do not propose to go into the rights or wrongs of the action taken by those claiming a right to residence in the building. . . . I am, however, very disturbed by the behavior of the Greek Orthodox Church on this issue and by the very unpleasant innuendoes which have been publicized abroad by the officials of the Church. . . . I must say that the sight of a priest in clerical garments, standing on a ladder, ripping down a Star of David from a Jewish residence, cheered on by an enraged mob, is a horrible reminder of what our people lived through in history on many sad and tragic occasions. . . . I have been horrified to receive organized mail from the United States, in which it is alleged that the Greek Orthodox Patriarch has been subject to physical assault by Israelis. This is a blatant lie which is being published abroad without any basis whatsoever. The issue centers on a dispute in a real-estate deal which is being contested in the courts of law in Israel and in respect of which over $5 million changed hands. For a Church to turn such a real-estate transaction, to which it is privy and a party, into a defamatory anti-Jewish campaign, is nothing short of disgraceful and despicable.[12]

Negotiations between Israel and the Vatican concerning official recognition of the Jewish state and an exchange of ambassadors also raised suspicions among the Jews. In April 1995 the Council of Torah Sages, the supreme body of the Agudat Israel, an ultra-Orthodox political party, published a condemnation of what it believed was an initiative on the part of Foreign Minister Shimon Peres to grant the Vatican spiritual authority over the Old City of Jerusalem, and called on all Jews to resist this action. The foreign minister formally replied to the council that he had undertaken no such initiative.[13]

The Rituals of Jewish Religious Disputes

Although Israel is witness to religious disputes that pit different communities of Christians and Moslems against one another, or that cause problems among Jews, Christians, and Moslems, it is religious disputes within the Jewish that are most prominent. These disputes will occupy our attention for the remainder of this chapter.

It is partly because of the concern for intercommunal violence that intracommunal issues among the Jews are the most prominent and most amenable to analysis. The Israeli security forces are responsible for anticipating Arab demonstrations. Religious disputes involving only Christians or Moslems are handled mostly by state authorities and communal leaders. The communal leaders seem willing to get what they can from the authorities and to minimize mass action. To avoid provoking the Moslem population, the police prevent religious Jews from praying on the Temple Mount, where the Dome of the Rock and the al-Aqsa Mosque now stand.

It is religious disputes among Jews that are most likely to cause visible disturbances, which are allowed to play themselves out because they produce only noise and inconvenience and do not lead to mass violence or threaten the security of the state. A scenario that is so routinized as to be ritualized is likely to begin with a charge by religious or antireligious activists that there has been a violation of the status quo. This accepted policy of no change on matters involving religion is designed to limit disputes, but the status quo is ambiguous. The policy of the status quo supports a continuation of the conditions that existed in 1948 when the state was created. But critics ask, what about activities in cities or neighborhoods created since 1948? Or technologies introduced after 1948? When a dispute takes hold, there is likely to be a difference of opinion as to what the status quo really is. There will then come an escalation in rhetoric, with religious and secular spokespersons proclaiming that the other side is anti-Semitic and has provoked a confrontation by threatening the status quo. This routinely escalates further into street demonstrations in which dumpsters are overturned, the two sides fight each other with sticks, stones, and fists, and mounted police intervene to minimize the property damage and jail the most extreme demonstrators for a few hours.

There is no simple way to determine how many Israeli Jews are secular or religious, or, among the religious, how many are Orthodox, ultra-Orthodox, or traditional (in Israel "traditional" means identifying with some but not all of the practices of Orthodox Judaism). The Central Bureau of Statistics provides a breakdown of the population between Jews and non-Jews, but does not record more than that about their religious identity. A survey of 1,287 Israeli Jews conducted by a Tel Aviv University sociologist supplied the following breakdown: ultra-Orthodox, 10 percent; Orthodox, 10 percent; traditional, 29 percent; secular, 51 percent. Another survey, which employed a different categorization scheme, found that 14 percent of the respondents defined themselves as "strictly observant," 24 percent as "observant to a great extent," 41 percent as "somewhat observant," and 21 percent as "totally nonobservant." Yet another survey reported 20 percent "religious," 41 percent "traditional," and 37 percent "secular." The same survey reported that 18 percent of the respondents claimed to "observe most of the commandments," 40 percent to "observe some of the commandments," and 32 percent to "not observe any of the commandments."[14]

Antireligious Israelis worry about the growth of the ultra-Orthodox community, especially in Jerusalem. Ultra-Orthodox parties polled 22 percent of the city vote in the 1992 national election, compared with only 8 percent nationwide. Fifteen years earlier, in the election of 1977, ultra-Orthodox parties had won only 8 percent of the Jerusalem vote. Even more striking are the changing patterns of Jewish primary school enrollment in the city. The number of students in ultra-Orthodox primary schools increased from 17 percent to 42 percent of the total Jewish school population from 1972 to 1992, while the proportion of the total Jewish school population attending Jewish secular schools dropped from 53 percent to 32 percent.[15]

One of the reasons why religious issues are chronically on the Israeli government's agenda is that activists and policy makers concentrate their efforts on particular disputes without resolving the fundamental controversies that underlie those disputes. They will, for instance, manage to settle a dispute about the use of a particular road on the Sabbath, or about ancient bones discovered at a construction site, but sooner or later there will be another road or another gravesite to fight over. In some instances, if one group of rabbis signals its satisfaction with an agreement, a dissenting group will seize on that fact to demonstrate that its members are more observant of religious law.

The secular interests of Israel are generally able to keep religious interests from determining outcomes of issues that generate great intensity. Secular Israelis can rely on help from competing factions within the religious community. Several things get in the way of the religious community developing a united front: disputes on matters of religious principle; competition between religious political parties, religious academies (yeshivot), and synagogue congregations; and personal animosities between rabbis.

The role of religion in marriage and divorce illustrates the muddled status of religion in matters of public policy. Jewish, Christian, Moslem, and Druze religious functionaries oversee the regulation of marriage and divorce within their respective communities in accordance with their religious laws. Israelis who want to marry or divorce in some other fashion, however, can do so outside the country—not a great inconvenience or financial burden in an age of cut-rate air travel. The Interior Ministry will officially record a marriage or divorce evidenced by a certificate obtained outside the country. A couple can thus have their marriage recognized in Israel even if such a marriage could not have taken place in Israel (such as, for instance, in the case of interfaith marriages). Some Israelis have married by mailing the necessary information to a lawyer in Paraguay and receiving a marriage certificate in return. Divorces, too, can be obtained through the mail from foreign lawyers. Alternatively, a couple can live together without any marriage and have their union recognized by an Israeli court in the event of a dispute over property, child support, or inheritance.

Highly Emotional Issues

There is no doubting the prominence of religious issues with high emotional content on Israel's political agenda. On one day in March 1995 the following items appeared on two inside pages of the daily newspaper *Ha'aretz*. The quarrels underlying the details had been matters of public interest for some time.

• Three hundred male and female Reform rabbis were making preparations to pray together near the Western Wall. This was an action likely to provoke Orthodox and ultra-Orthodox Jews, who object to men and women praying together and fail to recognize Reform rabbis as true rabbis. Women who claim the status of rabbi provoke special ridicule among the Orthodox.

• A religious official in the Justice Ministry, whose responsibility was to give advice on the interpretation of Jewish law, made a politically incorrect comparison between homosexuals and men who have sex with animals, citing Leviticus 20:13–15 in support of his comments. The homosexual lobby protested and the Israeli civil service commissioner began disciplinary proceedings against the official for expressing an unauthorized opinion. A week later the commissioner backed down under criticism from the justice minister and others who said that the official was, after all, paid to supply advice on Jewish law.

• The court of an ultra-Orthodox congregation laid a curse on anyone aiding a construction project that allegedly was desecrating Jewish graves. The curse promised cancer, mental illness, and bankruptcy.[16]

Knesset debates offer evidence of the sensitivities of religious politicians and the willingness of some to engage in ritualized disputes. Religious parliamentarians have criticized government officials for not wearing a head covering at the appropriate times, for eating in non-kosher restaurants, and for working on the Sabbath. Some rabbinical members of the religious parties were outraged (although others laughed) when, in opposition to their proposal to strengthen the laws against pornography, a secular parliamentarian read from the biblical Song of Songs: "Thy neck shall be as a tower of ivory . . . thy breasts shall be as clusters of the vine."[17] Another Knesset member provoked an outburst from religious parliamentarians when she referred to the love between David and Jonathan in support of homosexual rights.[18] Foreign Minister Shimon Peres set off a shouting match when he said he could not defend all that King David had done, especially with respect to Bathsheba. Religious members of the Knesset asserted that this was an unacceptable insult to the author of the psalms, and one entered the Knesset clinic with what he claimed was a heart attack.[19] Calmer observers noted that God's own prophet Nathan considered David a sinner and that over the centuries rabbis have pondered the difficult questions raised by David's activities.[20]

Knesset member Shulamit Aloni was a lightning rod for the antagonism between religious and secular Israelis when she served as the head of Meretz Party under the Rabin-Peres governments of 1992–1996. Initially she was made education and culture minister in the Rabin government, but her statements and actions infuriated religious activists. Prominent in their dossier against her were the following items:

• A photograph taken of her sitting at a table laden with bread and beer in a restaurant in the Arab city of Nazareth during Passover in 1993.

• Her proposal that references to God should be removed from the memorial prayer used at military ceremonies.

• Her opposition to teaching that the world was created in six days.

• Her remark that Israel's two chief rabbis were the country's popes and her contention that most Orthodox Jews do not accept their rulings.

• Her comment that it is no longer necessary to keep kosher in Israel, for Jews now live in their own sovereign state and the laws of kashruth were meant to distance Jews from non-Jews.

• A remark that the site revered by some religious Jews as Joseph's Tomb was actually the tomb of one Sheikh Yusuf and perhaps no more than two hundred years old. She based her assertion on archaeological evidence.[21]

• Her complaint that the government was excessive in bribing the ultra-Orthodox, or paying them to move step by step toward a "Khomeinistic" state.[22]

• In a reference to the religious Zionists who had settled in parts of the West Bank and Gaza, her plea to the government to stop the "vile, contemptible methods of rioting and Jewish intafada" which endangered not only the peace process but Israeli society.[23]

• When the army declared a curfew against Arab residents of Nablus so that religious settlers and two Likud members of the Knesset could pray at Joseph's Tomb, her comment, "This is human rights? That they put 120,000 people under house arrest [that is, the curfew] for 24 hours, so that [Likud members] Tzahi Hanegbi and Dov Shilansky could dance with a Torah scroll on Sheikh Yusuf's tomb near Nablus and say 'It's all mine,' without anyone interfering? This is human rights?"[24]

• Her comment on another occasion about the Jewish settlers in Hebron: "Some of the people living there are racists who want to expel the Arabs. . . . We remember how in the night they threw out the people who were living there. They urinated on them, destroyed their houses and shot at them."

Eventually, Prime Minister Rabin gave in to the demands of Aloni's religious opponents by taking the education portfolio from her and demoting her to culture and communications minister. An NRP member of the Knesset, not satisfied with Rabin's move, responded with a call for Aloni's dismissal as culture and communications minister and referred to her as "mentally unstable."[25]

Eliezer Schach is an aged Ashkenazi rabbi and head of an ultra-Orthodox congregation who rails against various groups of religious and secular Israelis. When Aloni was just beginning her tenure as minister of education and culture, Schach prophesied that she would do to Israeli youth what Hitler had done to one million Jewish children fifty years earlier.[26] In a similar vein, the spiritual leader of SHAS, Rabbi Ovadia Yosef, said that he would "declare a celebration and throw a banquet the day that wicked woman Shulamit Aloni dies."[27] Aloni responded that she hoped the rabbi would live "a very long life, so that he would one day indeed get to throw the banquet he wished for."[28]

The harsh comments directed by religious leaders against Aloni led to infighting among religious politicians in the Knesset. A religious member of the Labor Party asked whether Yosef was empowered to pass a sentence of death on anyone.[29] An NRP member remarked that "What Rabbi Yosef said was narrow-minded, immoral incitement and is distinctly un-Jewish. He should not be seen as a Torah great, no matter how many pages of the Talmud he knows by heart. His words drip with personal hatred and have nothing to do with an ideological disagreement." Yosef responded by condemning the NRP: "the NRP's religion can be dumped in the garbage can—it and the NRP both. . . . This party calls itself a bridge? . . . It's a bridge all right—a bridge straight to hell for teaming up with Labor. They are both bound for hell."[30]

Events such as these point to the importance of Jewish symbols in the political discourse of Israel. Yet they are not proof that religious interests are dominant. Instead, they show religious politicians struggling against secular politicians. It is difficult to distinguish between outbursts of true anger or humor and those that are role-playing in an ongoing political ritual. Shouts of protest and expressions of ridicule reflect continuing tension in a standoff rather than dominance by one side or the other.

The Scorecard of Religious-Secular Conflict

An assessment of several issues that have been prominent in recent years reveals chronic conflict over religion, marked by sporadic public demonstrations and victories by both religious and secular activists, but with neither side dominant.

When new roads and a new stadium were opposed by religious

activists, the outcomes were delay or alteration in the implementation of policy rather than total reversal. Some roads were closed to traffic, but others remained open, despite the demands of religious leaders. In the case of one new road, it was decided that an exit which led into a religious neighborhood would be closed on the Sabbath and during religious holidays. A wall was constructed to protect the neighborhood from the sight and sound of traffic.

In another case, involving the burning of bus shelters carrying "indecent" advertising, an agreement between the advertising company and representatives of the religious community took the issue off the public agenda.

Laws prohibiting the sale of nonkosher food are enacted but generally not enforced.

Demands by non-Orthodox rabbis for recognition and funds for their congregations are viewed by the Orthodox as challenges to their religious establishment. Orthodox rabbis continue to exercise a monopoly over Jewish marriages, divorces, and conversions in Israel. However, there has been an increase in the number of Reform and Conservative synagogues and schools, which have received financial support from government and quasi-governmental organizations.

One clear victory for the secularists has come with the opening of restaurants, discothèques, and cinemas on the Sabbath. The municipal bylaws that had kept them closed were overturned in a 1987 court decision. Religious politicians have not succeeded in enacting new measures.

Ultra-Orthodox neighborhoods continue to expand and there has been an increase in the public resources devoted to ultra-Orthodox schools and other institutions. There is no lack of rhetoric surrounding these material benefits. Secular politicians charge that religious political parties inflate their demands and receive excessive material rewards by virtue of their importance in governing coalitions. Religious politicians insist that they continue to receive less than their fair share of resources, and that what they do receive is the result of legitimate politicking. Absolute truth in these matters eludes systematic research. Financing for housing and infrastructure projects in religious neighborhoods and for religious schools and other institutions comes from many programs and is provided for in a number of ministerial and quasi-governmental budgets. Complex bookkeeping discourages a comprehensive and persuasive examination of who gets what.[31]

The present ambiguous standoff between religious and secular Jews is similar to the situation that prevailed in the late 1970s and early

1980s. At that time the religious parties controlled the balance of power between the government and the opposition, and Prime Minister Menachem Begin was inclined to add religiosity to the Jewish nationalist programs of his Likud bloc. Religious politicians demanded an end to abortions, autopsies, archaeological digs (which they said were despoiling ancient Jewish graves), and Sabbath flights by El Al. They also wanted more money for religious institutions, an expansion of the army's practice of exempting religious women from service, and the use of religious law as the basis for determining who is a Jew and qualifies for citizenship under the Law of Return, which fails to define Jewishness and permits the non-Jewish relatives of Jewish immigrants to immigrate.

On several of these issues the religious parties won symbolic victories. El Al ended its Sabbath flights, but other Israeli airlines expanded theirs. The army eased its procedures for exempting religious women from military service. The onus was now placed on the military examining board to demonstrate that a candidate who claimed an exemption was not entitled to one, whereas before the onus had been on the claimant. The criteria for allowing abortions in public hospitals were changed to exclude "social distress," but the Health Ministry rejected a demand that a representative of the rabbinate be included on the boards that applied the criteria in individual cases. Applicants for abortions learned to rely on the still-valid explanation of "emotional distress." The religious parties did not succeed in changing the Law of Return. Then as now, the clearest victory by the religious parties seemed to be a politically pragmatic one—more money for religious schools and housing in religious neighborhoods.[32]

Several problems stand in the way of a systematic, quantitative reckoning of who wins specific confrontations over religion, and of determining whether religious or antireligious interests have been more successful in recent Israeli history. Activists who work for some issues claim that their positions are based on "Jewish norms" or would benefit the Jewish state, but they do not claim that they are religious per se. After a dispute begins there may be public quarrels between Orthodox or ultra-Orthodox rabbis over what constitutes an issue of religious importance and what is the correct view of the religious interest. There is also a lack of unity among religious authorities in Christian and Moslem communities. According to one scholar, the issue is an endemic one in political disputes with a spiritual content: "One special problem has been the other-worldly orientation of these deeply religious people; another problem has been religious particularism, where theological disputes have inhibited political cooperation."[33]

Additional problems arise from judging the outcomes of individual confrontations. Is it a success if one side gets a law enacted but the measure is seldom enforced or is implemented in ways that are criticized by those who supported its enactment? And how does one assess a situation where the same problem (for instance, controversy over public modesty, Sabbath observance, or the availability of nonkosher food) arises again and again, but each time with slight variations in the nature of the demands and subtle differences in the way the issue is resolved. Or what if a particular controversy simply disappears from the public agenda without a resolution? In such circumstances, the most persuasive conclusion is that neither side has won. Religious activists have scored some victories, but so have secular Israelis. It is difficult to weigh the closure of a road against the opening of restaurants, discothèques, and cinemas on the Sabbath. The score is a tie, more or less.

An examination of individual religious-secular conflicts demonstrates the problems that occur in determining who has won and by how much. One road project in Jerusalem generated opposition from several sources: the Antiquities Authority, which was concerned about the despoliation of ancient sites; religious Jews opposed to Sabbath traffic next to an ultra-Orthodox neighborhood; Arabs who objected to construction near their properties; and Likud Party leaders who believed that the road, which was going to follow the pre-1967 border separating the two halves of Jerusalem, would emphasize the division of Jerusalem between Jewish and Arab sectors.

A protest by Anglican, Arab Lutheran, Armenian, Greek Catholic, and Greek Orthodox church authorities that the project would harm Christian holy sites, coupled with a threat to raise the issue in the United Nations, brought an outburst from Mayor Teddy Kollek, who announced that he was angry at and insulted by their criticism of Israel's treatment of the holy sites. Kollek told the leaders, "Your behavior was antagonistic and totally out of proportion. . . . The antiquities found are being treated responsibly and professionally. . . . We let you know about the work. We could have simply covered it up and avoided all the problems, but this is not our way. . . . After all the years of dialog and cooperation, I am angry and insulted that you went to the press with complaints about the Israeli authorities without speaking to me." The gravesite and its bones (believed to be St. Stephen's) were turned over to the Armenian Church. Other artifacts were removed from the site for preservation. Antiquities Authority officials concluded that the site was not important enough from an archaeological point of view to warrant building the road elsewhere.[34]

Jewish religious opposition reached its peak as the road was being completed. It was not enough that the road's planners had included a wall to screen it and its noise from the religious neighborhood and had agreed that an exit leading into the neighborhood would be closed on the Sabbath and during religious holidays. Antireligious Jewish politicians accused the ultra-Orthodox of trying to upset the status quo by demanding the Sabbath closing of major roads near their neighborhoods. Religious activists responded that the status quo has already been upset by the city's secular community, which kept numerous pubs, discothèques, and restaurants open seven days a week. The next stage of the controversy witnessed the playing out of a familiar ritual over the course of several Sabbaths: large gatherings of ultra-Orthodox Jews, shouts about the sanctity of the Sabbath, overturned dumpsters, stones thrown at traffic, the use of mounted police, some injuries among the protesters, counterprotests by secularists, brief arrests of protesters, statements by Teddy Kollek and police officials about the rule of law, and proclamations by Orthodox rabbis about the sanctity of the Sabbath. Finally, the police toughened their posture and reached an agreement with the rabbis to limit the protests to a certain period. Sabbath traffic continued—but not via the exit that led into the religious neighborhood—and the protests died.

Some years later, in a 1995 interview granted by Jerusalem mayor Ehud Olmert to an ultra-Orthodox newspaper, the mayor displayed am abundance of religious symbols against a background of meager delivery of tangible actions. The interview was conducted following Sabbath demonstrations about the closing of Bar-Ilan Street, a major road that bisected an ultra-Orthodox neighborhood. One charge made by the religious and antireligious camps was that the mayor had promised compliance with religious demands concerning road closings in exchange for support from the leaders of religious parties in his 1993 election campaign. As the demonstrations were going on, a committee appointed by the mayor produced a cumbersome proposal that Bar-Ilan Street be closed to traffic only during hours of prayer on the Sabbath and other holy days. This would not have been easy to implement, given that the Sabbath starts at different times from week to week and that out-of-towners and foreign tourists might be taken by surprise to find a major road suddenly closed. In any case, the national government's Ministry of Transportation indicated to the mayor that it had the authority to rule on the closing of major roads, and that the road in question would be kept open. (The same proposal surfaced again after the national election of 1996, when it was endorsed by a member of the NRP who had become transportation minister.)

Part of the mayor's interview was concerned with explaining the failure to close the road and with asserting that he had never promised it would be closed. Another part was concerned with issues of symbolic importance to the ultra-Orthodox community: the mayor's frequent use of religiously correct terminology in his public utterances (such as "with the help of God") and his assertion that the upcoming celebration of Jerusalem's 3,000-year anniversary would feature programs containing religious content and would not see the erection of statues that would violate the religious injunction against graven images. In response to a question on whether he regularly read the psalms, the mayor responded by quoting the first verse from the Book of Psalms: "Blessed is the man that walketh not in the counsel of the ungodly, nor standeth in the way of sinners, nor sitteth in the seat of the scornful." He said that as mayor he was obligated to utter that phrase each day on account of all the temptations that beset someone with his responsibilities.[35]

The conflict among Israel's Jews over religion and religious policy resembles that in other Western democracies.[36] Part of the American puzzle is the fact that a country with one of the most advanced economies in the world and an impressive percentage of adults who have studied in secular institutions of higher education is also among the most religious.[37] American religious leaders can keep proposals with the strongest emotional content on the political agenda without being able to achieve their enactment. Their political agenda features positions on abortion, school prayer, sex education, public support for religious education, the teaching of evolution, pornography, and the rights of homosexuals. A lack of clarity or finality in court decisions about, for instance, placing a crèche or a Chanukah menorah in a public place, adds to the unresolved tensions between religious communities and between the religious and the antireligious. Activists' rhetoric may portray a struggle of polar extremes, but the reality is a process of negotiations that leads to partial victories and losses and to standoffs, not to stunning achievements by either side.[38]

Both the right-to-life controversy in the United States and the sectarian conflict in Northern Ireland have been marked by violence. The Israeli parallel was the killing of Prime Minister Rabin by a religious and nationalist Jew who said he was protesting arrangements made with the Palestinian Authority. Much of the national discussion follow-ing the killing dealt with the significance of the biblical Land of Israel, with how much of it could be bargained away to perceived terrorists in return for the promise of peace, and with how Jews should conduct their disputes over these issues. The assassination and the soul-search-ing that followed were evidence of the passion that Jews can have for biblically rooted political issues. Among the questions at the forefront of the discussion were, can Israel's rabbis and secular leaders dissuade their followers from violence and lead them to rely on persuasion in conducting disputes? Can Israel's security forces deal adequately with people who cannot be persuaded to desist from violence? Will the killing prove to be an anomaly, a departure from the usual pattern of religious-secular disputes, or the beginning of the calamity predicted by some observers, namely a conflict over the Land of Israel that produces a civil war between zealous religious and nationalistic Jews on the one side and Jews willing to compromise with the Arabs on the other?[39]

Before the killing of Prime Minister Rabin, tensions between the reli-gious and antireligious elements in the Israeli Jewish community appeared chronic but did not lead to serious violence. Jews argued about religion without really hurting one another. Israeli society allowed reli-gious Jews to practice their faith (albeit not on the Temple Mount), while allowing nonreligious Jews to avoid the burdens imposed by reli-giously inspired legislation, as in the cases of marriage and divorce. The rhetoric of the participants made it all sound worse than it was in prac-tice. This may have lulled the country's security forces into devoting limited resources to the surveillance of Jewish extremists.

Coping with Religion

The conflict between religious and secular interests in Israel quali-fies as an insoluble problem. The roots of current disputes go back at least as far as the Enlightenment and the clashes between Jewish cos-mopolitans and religious zealots under Greek and Roman rule. The longevity of the problem helps to explain the ritualized nature of cur-rent disputes. No one seriously expects total victory or total defeat. For the past two thousand years, the legacy of an earlier bloody history has helped Jews avoid communal violence. The threat of civil war has not led Jews to solve their problems, but it has kept their inability to reach a solution from boiling over into warfare.

The continued presence of one anti-Jewish movement or another has added to the incentives to keep internal disputes from harming the protections that communal unity provides against outside hostility. The chronic tensions and occasional outbursts within the Israeli Jewish community appear to be the price that Jews must pay for living in a Jewish state. Both religious and secular activists express dissatisfaction with unresolved issues and the annoying monotony with which one incident follows another in disputes about ancient graves or Sabbath observance. The damage resulting from most confrontations takes the form of bruises and insults. The problem is chronic because it is tolerable. It has been ritualized at a low level of suffering.

The plurality that is built into Jewish history is reinforced by the character of Israeli democracy. Jews dominate the political system but individual Jewish factions have been unable to dominate the polity. No party has ever won a majority in a national election. Religious and secular parties argue and bargain in a situation where coalition government is inevitable. The struggle between religious and antireligious activists is often loud, but neither camp has been able to overcome the other. Even in the case of the holy city of Jerusalem, neither the religious nor the secular forces have achieved victory; instead, the situation has been one of chronic tension.

Policy makers cope with the demands of religious and antireligious activists by employing several tactics that have been less than thorough or that treat the details and avoid basic conflicts. The policy makers urge moderation, engage in prolonged discussions, offer concessions, and delay rather than cancel projects. On some occasions delay provides time for splits within the religious or secular camps to show themselves, or wears down the activists. Deliberation focuses on particular instances of conflict. Policy makers do not try to solve in general terms the principles of Shabbat, kosher food, or other general issues that lie behind specific disputes.

The costs of a dispute in treasure and suffering provide an incentive to remove it from the agenda. The accommodations reached between Israel, Egypt, Jordan, and the Palestinians—imperfect as they appear to certain participants or observers—reflect the capacity of policy makers to alter their conceptions and solve important aspects of what had seemed to be an insoluble dispute. The human and material costs of war and terror have led participants on all sides to work toward resolving disputes politically. Religious conflicts among the Jews of Israel indicate that some issues are chronic to the point of being permanent. The costs of compromise are high to the intensely religious and antireligious, while the costs of continued conflict are low. Basic conflicts may remain insoluble even while individual episodes find partial resolution or disappear from the agenda because of the fatigue of the participants. The concept of ritual is appropriate not only because it concerns religion, but because it is repeated time after time, with many of the same assertions and tactics followed by the participants.

The Most Recent Word, but Surely Not the Last Word

Religion per se was not a prominent issue in the 1996 national election campaign, but it may have figured in how some voters viewed the prominent issues of peace and security. Early analyses of Netanyahu's narrow victory indicated that he outpolled Peres by about 11 percent among Jews generally (his overall margin was only 0.9 percent). Netanyahu's support was especially heavy among religious and traditional Jews. The election results increased the number of Knesset seats held by the religious parties from sixteen to twenty-three. Their leaders' statements indicated both a concern to realize key goals on the religious agenda and a desire to calm the fears of secular Jews who perceived a threat to the secular way of life from the religious element. Netanyahu included all of the Jewish religious parties in his government. The NRP received the Education and Culture Ministry and the Transportation Ministry; SHAS was given the Labor and Welfare Ministry and the Interior Ministry. NRP and SHAS agreed to hold the Religions Ministry in rotation. The leading member of United Torah Judaism became deputy minister of housing and construction. Secular members of Likud, as well as members of other parties in the government coalition, readied themselves to resist any far-reaching moves by religious politicians.

The new political party calling itself the Third Way had campaigned on a commitment to accommodate both religious and secular Israelis. Its leader received the post of minister of internal security, which gave him oversight of the police. In his first month on the job he faced renewed demonstrations calling for closure of a major road on the Sabbath. The demonstrations pitted thousands of ultra-Orthodox and secular Israelis against one another and seemed likely to become the major event on the domestic agenda.

The new party of Russian immigrants led by Natan Sharansky received two ministries in the new government, Immigration and Trade and Commerce. The party's agenda addressed an issue tied to religion, namely the problems of marriage and burial faced by the many non-Jews who came to Israel as relatives of Jewish immigrants.

It did not take long for religion to become a prominent issue in the new government. SHAS and NRP squabbled over which party would be given the Ministry of Religions for the first two years of the expected four-year term of the Netanyahu administration. Each accused the other of wanting to be first so that it could scoop up all the benefits that control of the ministry offered—government appointments, budget commitments, and the like—before its rival took charge.

Then the issue of Bar-Ilan Street returned to the headlines. Although the Likud mayor of Jerusalem had promised during his election campaign in 1993 to close the road, the transportation minister in the Rabin-Peres government had refused to approve the mayor's proposal. During the first month of the Netanyahu administration, both ultra-Orthodox and secular Israelis turned the road into a site of weekly demonstrations and low-level violence. Religious Jews said that it would take only two or three extra minutes to travel an alternate route. Secular Jews calculated the extra travel time at twenty minutes or more and quoted religious activists who said that it would only be a matter of time before the forces of religion would force the closure of the alternate route as well as the main road from Tel Aviv to Jerusalem, which also passes by a religious neighborhood.[40] The NRP transportation minister approved the proposal for closing Bar-Ilan Street only during hours of prayer (the proposal his predecessor had rejected), the Supreme Court issued a temporary order against the closure, and the tempo of the demonstrations increased.

The actual outcome of this controversy seems less important than the continuation of conflict that it represents. Indeed, there is not likely to be an outcome of any permanence. Rather, each demand and each demonstration will serve as a stage in a continuing dispute that will erupt sooner or later over one or another site or issue. Each controversy is likely to feature demands by religious or secular Israelis to restore the status quo, but each side will be thinking of a different status quo.

CHAPTER 8

Another Look at Problems, Routines, and Coping Mechanisms

The information presented in the previous chapters shows the utility of dividing policy problems according to their degree of difficulty and of linking the character of a policy problem to the nature of policy making. The more difficult a problem, the less likely that policy makers will employ routines and the more likely that they will cope. Yet anomalies remain. Observers disagree in describing each of the problems considered. Officials succeed in removing many issues from the public agenda, while other aspects of the same issues appear to be insoluble.

The Bits of Public Problems and Policies

The idea of "bits" helps us deal with the lack of clarity. Notions of a problem and a policy are nothing more than abstractions put together by someone who considers many bits of information. The elementary bit of a public problem may be the situation of one individual, as in the case of a person who migrates from one country to another. An observer makes a simple abstraction by summarizing two or more experiences, as in describing migrants' experiences with unemployment. A more complex abstraction links the experiences of numerous individuals with events that impinge on social, economic, or political conditions: describing the influence of migration on the labor or housing markets, inflation, or the popularity of a political party.

The importance of problem bits lies in their helping us to understand how policy makers arrive at contrasting views on the nature of problems and on how to deal with them. It may be obvious that person X has migrated from one country to another and did not work for a period of time after arriving. It is less obvious that there is an association between migration and prolonged unemployment, and even less clear that migration has produced a spurt of inflation or the other phenomena that observers associate with migration. The larger picture does not exist in reality, but is only a construct of numerous bits that observers have assembled. Other observers, who assemble a different group of bits a different way, produce different pictures.

The concept of bits also helps in the comprehension of public policy. Here the elementary bits are the actions of individual officials. Staying with the example of a single migrant, an official's provision of a service is a policy bit. A simple abstraction would report the average grant provided by many officials to many migrants. More sophisticated abstractions would show how grants provided by one clerk vary from one migrant to another, or how the grants provided by many clerks vary from one migrant category to another. There are opportunities for arranging the bits of information differently according to one or another classification of migrants or one or another statistical technique. The results of different combinations would show more or less equality between migrants, greater or lesser correspondence to one or another standard of need. Observers who assemble bits of information pertaining to the actions of officials may produce pictures of public policy that differ from what is perceived in a reading of laws or agency regulations. The explanation lies in the discretion provided to individual clerks, or in the ways that clerks depart from the rules in responding to individual clients.

When different observers put together the bits they observe, they arrive at different pictures of reality, different explanations of what is happening, and different assessments of what should be done. The bits are not like drops of water that become a river running between fixed banks. They are more like droplets of moisture in the air that different observers describe as mist, fog, or light rain. The same point appears in many theoretical commentaries on natural as well as social science.[1] Reality is the discrete events (bits) that observers arrange into abstractions. The abstractions assemble and simplify reality. They have no objective existence outside what observers describe in writing or orally. The abstractions are helpful to the extent that they allow observers and activists to understand physical or social processes and intervene successfully in producing desired changes. They are less than helpful to the extent that they distort more than they reveal and lead activists to intervene in ways that do not produce the desired results.

The idea of bits helps us sort out some anomalies in our discussion of Israel's problems and the character of its policy making. It appears that the Arab-Israeli conflicts were once insoluble but are no longer so, and that the problems relating to Jerusalem and religious disputes between Jews remain insoluble. In fact, these assessments are controversial, and depend on who arranges the bits, and how. For a Jewish family in the occupied territories feeling threatened by negotiations that seem likely to expand the territory under the control of the Palestinian Authority, the problem of the Arab-Israeli disputes may seem to be getting worse rather than nearing a solution. For a Palestinian who dreamed of conquering Israel and returning to an ancestral home in what is now a Jewish neighborhood of Haifa or Jerusalem, the PLO's accommodation with Israel is no solution at all.

One assessment of Jerusalem begins with the contrary demands of Israeli and Palestinian nationalists. Viewing their antagonism in light of the city's long history of cultural conflict and regime changes, what we depict as "the problem of Jerusalem" appears to be insoluble. Yet other assessments that look at smaller bits see in the growth of both Jewish and Palestinian populations some indication of popular satisfaction with the standards of living to be found in the city. Such a picture may depict a problem that is soluble in numerous ways, or is not a problem at all. Other observers may argue that such a picture is distorted insofar as it ignores the reality of conflicts between Jews, Christians, and Moslems. Yet Jerusalem functions despite those conflicts, just as New York functions despite severe tensions between people of different racial and economic groups. No abstraction is a complete picture of reality. Observers differ on what is important.

Religious conflicts among Israeli Jews provide numerous illustrations of how different people combine bits of problems or policies. There is a widely accepted policy of maintaining the status quo in matters of religion. But how much of a variation is a change? And is one kind of change, such as the opening of pubs on the Sabbath, enough of a change to say that the policy of maintaining the status quo is no longer tenable? Religious and antireligious Jews assemble these and other bits in contrasting ways. They also use different standards for evaluating the bits. While a pious Jew may judge issues according to standards that are clear and acceptable to the religious community, antireligious Jews view the same standards as inherently flawed. What to one Jew is the sanctity of the Sabbath is to another a day of enforced boredom.

The notion of bits also explains the observation that routines and coping mechanisms appear at both high and low levels of policy making. In the earlier chapters we put the bits together in a way that supported the conclusion that routines appear more frequently at lower levels of policy making and where simple problems arise, while coping mechanisms appear more frequently at higher levels of policy making and where complex problems arise.

Although that picture appears to be substantially correct, some routines are used at higher levels of policy making. When faced with conflicting demands and political demonstrations by religious or antireligious Jews, high-ranking officials typically employ routines established in dealing with previous demonstrations. Coping also occurs at lower levels of policy implementation with respect to problems that usually are simple. In Israel individual immigrants and organized groups of immigrants present challenges that require lower-ranking personnel to put aside their routines and cope with the stresses. Political scientists owe a debt to Michael Lipsky for his description of street-level bureaucrats. Lipsky emphasizes how teachers, welfare counselors, and police officers use discretion in their encounters with people whose traits are not simple or predictable.[2] Most of their work may involve the routine application of standard operating procedures. However, they also cope with ambiguities in the rules and in the traits of individual citizens, and with coworkers and supervisors who have competing views about the situation at hand and about the actions that are appropriate.

The prominence of routines and coping in one or another of the Israeli situations are those of degree rather than the clear presence of one and the absence of the other. The descriptions of routines and coping in table 8.1 are abstractions that simplify and summarize the Israeli cases and offer hypotheses likely to be relevant in many other situations. Routines are most prominent in the simple decisions of lower-level personnel who deal with individual clients and simple problems. Coping mechanisms appear most prominently in the work of higher-level personnel dealing with complex situations. Coping is likely to be found in political settings created by the demands of organized groups. Although the results of routine policy actions are highly predictable, the outcomes of situations that require coping are less predictable. Those outcomes involve the maneuvers of many people and more creativity than is employed in the application of established routines.

The Arab-Israeli conflicts displayed routines during long periods of antagonism. Groups of Arabs learned and applied the routines of terror. Israeli policy makers and military officers applied their own routines of

TABLE 8.1 Traits Associated with Policy-Making Routines and Coping

Routines	Coping
Lower-level personnel most prominent	Higher-level personnel most prominent
Most prominent in simple decisions	Most prominent in complex decisions
More predictable outcomes	Less predictable outcomes
Most apparent in cases involving individual clients	Most apparent in cases involving groups that are politically organized
Likely to be associated with cases that are less interesting politically	Likely to be associated with cases that are more interesting politically

retaliation. Both sides used the same slogans again and again, slogans that justified their own actions and accused their enemies of vile behavior. These campaigns maintained support from the same groups of locals and outsiders that routinely had endorsed one or the other posture. Coping dominated the conflict at points of change, for instance when a period of escalating conflict required a decision to escalate further, perhaps to the point of a major war, or when genuine negotiations seemed feasible. When negotiations occurred and dissidents engaged in violence, Israeli and Arab policy makers coped with the ambiguities involved in using routines of negotiation and violence at the same time.

Policy makers involved in issues concerned with Jerusalem linked to the Arab-Israeli conflicts show similar combinations of routine and coping behaviors. Jews, Moslems, and Christians routinely assert rights over the same holy city, Jerusalem.

Most local administration is routine: schools open according to a published calendar and teach the expected courses; workers collect the trash and clean the streets; technocrats plan urban development projects and review building contractors' proposals. These routines do not address issues that touch the sensitive nerves of religious or ethnic communities. When a controversy involves the city's Christians, Moslems, religious and antireligious Jews, and their overseas allies, the mayor and even the prime minister swing into action to quiet the protest. Here, too, routines mix with coping. There are standard, routine ways of preaching moderation and halting offensive projects until a committee can review them. Delays may cool tempers or allow modifications that will lessen the intensity of antagonism. Coping involves the choice of the most suitable routine and finding the rhetorical formulations and tangible concessions that will soothe intense activists.

Where religious conflicts among Israeli Jews are concerned, the routines are so well established as to be ritualized. First there are charges that the other side is breaking the status quo, followed by demonstrations and counterdemonstrations, appeals to supporters throughout Israel and the diaspora, the overturning of dumpsters, the throwing of sticks, stones, and garbage, fist fights, use of nonlethal weapons by the police, the arrest and short-term detention of violent demonstrators, calls for moderation by community leaders, delays in project implementation to allow a cooling of passions, and eventually the continuation of the offensive project, with some modifications. In these situations coping is used to find novel formulations and persuade adversaries to accept them. However, the options are likely to be well known and frequently used: insisting on the rule of law, respecting the principle of maintaining the status quo, and recognizing the sensitivities of religious and secular communities. If the decision goes against demands by religious leaders, they may be appeased by a promise of additional funding for schools or housing in their neighborhoods.

Conflicts over traffic on particular roads during the Sabbath, the treatment of ancient graves uncovered by construction projects, or posters viewed as indecent can be solved, but similar issues will come up sooner or later. The larger issue of how Judaism is to be observed in the Jewish state resembles the Arab-Israeli conflicts when they were stuck in one of their long periods of routine posturing, attack, and retaliation. Routines prevail over coping, ritual over creativity. Conflicts between religious and secular Israelis bear some resemblance to those that appeared between Jewish cosmopolitans and zealots during the Greek and Roman periods. The deep-seated nature of these conflicts suggests that they will not quickly disappear. For the time being, religious conflict among Israeli Jews qualifies as an insoluble problem.

Israel in Comparison with Other Polities

Although this book's focus is policy making in Israel, its observations on the general nature of problems and on the general character of policy making are useful for understanding other places as well. We can overlook Israel's particular traits—its identity as a Jewish state, its small size, middling wealth, and intense problems—and concentrate on the international applications of what we have learned. The treatment of each problem examined in this book has parallels elsewhere.

Migration to the United States, Germany, and other countries mixes routine procedures in individual cases and coping at the point where

TABLE 8.2 Measures of Religiosity: International Comparisons from 1981–1983

	Percentage Attending Church Weekly	*Percentage Who Feel Religious*	*Percentage Expressing Belief in God*
Australia	17	58	80
Belgium	30	69	76
Britain	14	53	73
Canada	31	74	91
Denmark	3	56	53
Finland	3	51	—
France	11	48	59
Germany	19	54	68
Hungary	11	42	44
Iceland	2	67	77
Ireland	82	63	95
Italy	32	80	82
Japan	3	24	39
Mexico	54	74	97
Netherlands	25	63	64
Northern Ireland	52	58	91
Norway	5	43	68
South Africa	43	69	95
Spain	40	62	86
Sweden	6	32	52
United States	43	81	96

SOURCE: Adapted from Robert A. Campbell and James E. Curtis, "Religious Involvement Across Societies: Analysis for Alternative Measures in National Surveys," *Journal for the Scientific Study of Religion* 33 (1994): 215–29.

the routines become unsuitable. External events trigger waves of migration, a reconsideration of admission criteria, and arguments among groups with different perspectives on economic emigrants and political refugees. Like the Arab-Israeli conflicts in the Middle East, international disputes in other regions combine the use of routines during periods of stability with coping at points where change seems likely. At all times, in each of these policy fields, officials at all levels of government bureaucracies have to cope with peculiar situations that seem to fall outside routinized categories.

While it is true that there is no city exactly like Jerusalem, other cities present situations appropriate to combinations of routines and coping. The coping is likely to be appear at points of tension between social classes or ethnic groups, or in land use decisions that have implications for environmental protection, historical preservation, and economic development. The echoes of local activity may not spread as far afield or invoke the spiritual echoes of Jerusalem's issues, but the policy-making routines and coping techniques are similar.

Israel's religious problems and activities also have parallels elsewhere. These parallels appear even in societies that are explicitly secular or claim not to treat one faith better than another. Table 8.2 shows the results of surveys on religion in more than twenty countries or regions. There are nine countries or regions where more than 30 percent of the respondents claim to attend church weekly, seven where at least 65 percent feel religious, and six where at least 90 percent say that they believe in God. These patterns are not much different from Israel's, where one survey of Jewish respondents found that 14 percent identified themselves as "strictly observant," 24 percent as "observant to a great extent," 41 percent as "somewhat observant," and 21 percent as "totally nonobservant." American disputes about prayer in schools, abortion, and homosexual rights are not significantly less intense than disputes about kosher food or Sabbath observance in Israel. And as in Israel, the American quarrels seldom move policy in either a religious or an antireligious direction.

Vexatious Problems

The level of a problem's difficulty may change. Problems as difficult as the South African conflict between whites and blacks and the Middle East conflicts between Israelis and Arabs can become soluble, at least in important respects. To be sure, the solubility of such major problems may require a prior change of external conditions of the magnitude of the Soviet Union's collapse. Such events do happen, but rarely.

Vexatious is a label for problems that are very difficult and may be insoluble. The concept of *vexatious problems* is meant to cover issues that appear in the higher levels of table 2.1. The concept includes problems that currently seem insoluble, and others that are, at the very least, predicaments (all options are undesirable), and perhaps dilemmas (all options are equally undesirable). It is possible to use more conventional terms such as *very difficult* to describe problems, but *vexatious* carries a meaning that is especially acute. Vexatious problems are full of trouble or uneasiness.[3] They are the stuff of major political stress and coping.

Several of the Israeli case studies provide lessons that may help to produce more general propositions relevant to vexatious problems. Yet one lesson is that there is a limit to general lessons. Someone who copes with vexatious problems must know their detailed history, including the positions taken, the victories, losses, and insults suffered by the parties, and the implications for each of the parties of the various formulations of the problems and the problems' possible solutions. The material needed for coping with vexatious problems is not likely to be found in standard university courses, but acquired by long apprenticeship close to the arenas of policy making. Along with those reservations, each of the cases offers its own insights into policy making.

Immigration

A prominent lesson from Israel's experience with immigration is the importance of policy stimuli from outside the polity. Another lesson is that immigration may not be a homogeneous problem, but a composite of different migrations, perhaps occurring at the same time.

The collapse of the Soviet Union and the disintegration of Ethiopia had something to do with one another, insofar as the weakening of the Ethiopian regime reflected a lessening of Soviet material support. Some 700,000 immigrants came to Israel from the former Soviet Union from 1989 to 1996, and they continue to arrive at the rate of more than 50,000 a year. Many immigrants from the former Soviet Union arrive with impressive job titles and some have world-class reputations in the arts and sciences. It is up to Israeli institutions to sort out the truly skilled from the less than competent, to identify those who might benefit from further training, and to spot those who submit forged documents. The immigration has created both opportunities and stresses for the immigrants and the Israeli economy. Immigrants have affected the housing market and budget outlays for construction and social programs, added to the competition for jobs, and influenced the results of a national election. They have brought about a decision to establish a symphony orchestra in a small town to provide work for immigrant musicians and have drained the physicians from some cities in the former Soviet Union.

The immigration from Ethiopia was much different. It was smaller and more concentrated, coming in two waves of 6,000 and 15,000 in

1984–1985 and 1991, respectively. Ethiopian immigrants came mostly from poor African villages and had little if any education. Immigration officials employed paternalistic routines for the Ethiopians, while employing free-market routines for Soviet immigrants who were thought capable of using financial grants and their own resources to find housing, jobs, and training programs appropriate to their needs.

The Arab-Israeli Conflicts

Among the myriad details associated with the Arab-Israeli conflicts, several traits have contributed to their long-lasting status as a vexatious problem that on occasion seemed insoluble. A list of these traits may suggest parallels with other regional conflicts involving numerous antagonists animated by long-established rivalries, as in the former Yugoslavia or parts of the former Soviet Union.

- *There is not one dispute but many, which are in part independent of and in part dependent on one another.* Numerous actors have complex agendas. The governments of the region pursue other interests alongside the prominent Arab-Israeli conflicts. Often these other interests take precedence, as when rivals within PLO factions, the Israeli political elites, or Arab governments work toward their own goals or embarrass one another rather than work together to achieve regional accommodation. Egypt could make peace with Israel in exchange for receiving all of its land that had been occupied in the 1967 war. When the Egyptian president claimed to have taken into consideration the needs of other Arab parties, the other Arab states responded with statements of cynical disbelief and by breaking diplomatic relations with Egypt. Some of his own countrymen killed him.
- *History and ideology influence competing perceptions of reality.* The concept of "Arab land" stands against the Zionists' claim of an inheritance from the Hebrew Bible. Both images lead Arab and Jewish extremists to interpret the past in ways that strengthen their dream of a future that is ethnically pure, in contrast to the reality of Middle Eastern history.
- *Ambiguities abound.* For years after PLO speakers claimed to have renounced violence, fighters captured by Israel said that they were sent on their missions by the PLO. The Israeli government did not produce a clear set of war aims for the 1982 invasion of Lebanon. When Israelis, Americans, and Arabs speak about secure borders for Israel, it is unlikely that they are thinking of the same borders.

Jerusalem

Jerusalem is the archetype of vexatious urban problems where social tensions between communities defined by religion, religiosity and ethnicity are especially prominent. The economics of Jerusalem are by no means enviable, even though national authorities and overseas friends have financed impressive growth without creating a fiscal crisis for the municipality. As in few other urban areas, basic issues of sovereignty and regime legitimacy hang over the city, and are mixed with spiritual motivations that seem to get in the way of decision making by more conventional economic or political criteria.

Jerusalem offers coping lessons in how to succeed partially. The Israeli authorities have made their mark by choosing not to pursue a clear and final resolution of basic conflicts. They recognize the problems that arise in keeping control of Jerusalem and have made that goal a high priority. They have decided that a delay in facing the issue is more favorable than head-on confrontation and have compromised conventional elements of sovereignty in order to bolster their control. They have also sought support for their regime among overseas political and religious authorities who might be inclined to demand an international municipality. Israeli officials have sought to convince such figures that Israeli rule is good enough to justify its continuation.

Religion

The case of religious conflict among the Jews of Israel suggests that an issue may remain insoluble because conditions are not so intolerable that policy makers must seriously devote themselves to finding a solution. It is easier to temporize than to solve this problem. Routines exist for removing troublesome issues from the national agenda. More thorough solutions for the entire set of religious issues might push either the ultrareligious or the ultra-antireligious over the edge of established behaviors and into the realm of serious violence. The killing of Prime Minister Yitzhak Rabin indicated the dangers inherent in the issue of Jewish control over the Land of Israel, and its capacity to arouse extreme passions among religious nationalists. Moderate but chronic conflict prevails in regard to other issues of religious-secular conflict, such as Sabbath observance, the availability of nonkosher food, and the rights of non-Orthodox Jews and their rabbis.

The case of religion in Israel also shows both the utility and the limits of international comparisons. Some dimensions of the Israeli situation resemble what occurs in other democratic societies. Religious faith coexists with post-Enlightenment education and technology. Religious activists have no trouble putting issues on the agenda, especially those with great symbolic content and emotional appeal. Yet the outcome is more Shakespearean than biblical: sound and fury signifying nothing.[4]

There are also distinctive elements that derive from the history and culture of Judaism and Israel. Judaism's character as a national religion permits a wide range of positions. People can remain members of the Jewish community even if they do not believe in a deity. Rabbinical teaching tolerates dispute even while it has sought to impose order on Judaism. Jewish culture became even more complex as European Jews left the isolation of closed religious communities in the nineteenth century. In addition to their great cultural variety and tendency toward intracommunal dispute, Jews developed rules of the game that limit conflict. Rabbinical admonitions against sectarian conflict have their roots in reactions to the Jewish civil wars of the late biblical period. To cool tempers during periods of religious-secular tension, religious and secular leaders cite the threats to Jewish existence that arise from the Jews being a minority in the diaspora and a beleaguered population in Israel. The capacity of religious leaders to moderate conflict over the most intense of issues will be tested in the aftermath of Rabin's killing.

The Suitability of Routines and Coping

The emphasis in this book has been on the description of prominent problems and the ways that policy makers have dealt with them. Until now, we have not considered whether routines or coping mechanisms are appropriate for a range of normative concerns. We have recognized that interests receive more or less attention from policy makers and that results benefit some groups more than others. Is the sum total of routine and coping good enough?

The answer depends on aspirations, perspectives, and moral standards. Among the options are:

- an *egoistic, communal,* or *nationalistic* standard (what's good for me or my people?);
- an *egalitarian* standard that values the equal treatment of all individuals and communities;
- an *altruistic* standard that values a concern for the weaker individuals or communities;
- a *utilitarian* standard (for example, the greatest good for the greatest number, or the greatest benefits for the least cost);
- a *pragmatic* standard that values proposals which promise to find

agreement among contending parties or achieve some success amid difficult surroundings;

• a *procedural* standard (such as a concern to follow rules that require democratic selection of key officials, the agreements of certain officials for a policy to go forward, or the public's ratification of major decisions);

• a *legal* standard that requires or forbids particular actions as defined in law that itself has been legislated or proclaimed according to official procedures;

• a *religious* standard (A perceives that God demands X);

• norms of *justice* or *righteousness*, which are complex in expressing a people's sense of what is right, proper, or fair, and may encompass several of the standards listed above.

Israelis and foreigners who judge Israeli policy makers consider them to be perverse, pragmatic, or judicious, depending on how the evaluators assemble the bits of reality and the moral standards chosen as the basis for judgment. Routines and coping per se appear to be value-neutral. Dictators and democrats all have their routines, and all cope with changing reality. Some regimes implement policies that maximize their control and their repression of dissidents, while others seek to maximize political opportunities. For both dictators and democrats, routines seem likely to be used for simple problems and coping mechanisms for more difficult problems. For some problems, neither routines nor coping are satisfactory, and the problems remain insoluble.

As this book goes to press, Israelis are celebrating the three thousandth anniversary of Jerusalem's capture from the Jebusites by King David and are planning for their country's fiftieth anniversary in May 1998. In the span of Jewish history there have been many vexatious problems. That there is a Jewish population to plan these anniversaries says something about the coping tactics that have been learned and then transmitted from one generation to another. The problems remain awesome. To paraphrase the Book of Ecclesiastes, the present appears to be a time of negotiations and peace, but again there may come a time for war. Even during negotiations, officials have used force against those who would kill rather than argue. Both Israeli and Arabs extremists cause stress for policy makers who seek survival by employing the coping mechanisms of ranking goals from the most important to the least important, and avoiding strain on adversaries by demanding too much.

Notes

Chapter 1. Introduction

1. For a discussion of the possibilities and limits of comparative analysis, see Gary King, Robert O. Keohane, and Sidney Verba, *Designing Social Inquiry: Scientific Inference in Qualitative Research* (Princeton: Princeton University Press, 1994), and the symposium on the book in the *American Political Science Review* 89 (June 1995): 454–81.

2. Arend Lijphart, *Democracies: Patterns of Majoritarian and Consensus Government in Twenty-one Countries* (New Haven: Yale University Press, 1984); G. Bingham Powell, Jr., *Contemporary Democracies: Participation, Stability, and Violence* (Cambridge: Harvard University Press, 1982); Peter Y. Medding, *The Founding of Israeli Democracy 1948–1967* (New York: Oxford University Press, 1990).

3. For critical assessments of Israeli democracy by Israelis see Avner Yaniv, ed., *National Security and Democracy in Israel* (Boulder, Colo.: Lynne Rienner Publishers, 1993); Michael Shalev, *Labour and the Political Economy in Israel* (New York: Oxford University Press, 1992); and Baruch Kimmerling, ed., *The Israeli State and Society: Boundaries and Frontiers* (Albany: State University of New York Press, 1989).

4. *Jerusalem Post*, 30 September 1994, p. 5.

5. *World Almanac and Book of Facts, 1992* (Microsoft CD-ROM edition).

6. See Ira Sharkansky, *The Political Economy of Israel* (New Brunswick, N.J.: Transaction Books, 1987).

7. For discussions of these issues, see *Israel Law Review* 23, nos. 2–3 (spring–summer 1989), and Menachem Hofnung, *Israel—State Security Against the Rule of Law 1948–1991* (Jerusalem: Nevo Publisher, 1991) (in Hebrew).

8. Meron Benvenisti, *The West Bank Data Project: A Survey of Israel's Policies* (Washington, D.C.: American Enterprise Institute for Policy Research, 1984), 34; Benvenisti, *The Sling and the Club: Territories, Jews and Arabs* (Jerusalem: Keter Publishing House, 1988) (in Hebrew); Benvenisti, *The Shepherds' War: Collected Essays (1981–1989)* (Jerusalem: Jerusalem Post, 1989); Yeshayahu Leibowitz, *On Just About Everything: Talks with Michael Shashar* (Jerusalem: Keter Publishing House, 1988) (in Hebrew); Yehoshafat Harkabi,

The Bar Kokhba Syndrome: Risk and Realism in International Relations, trans. Max D. Ticktin and ed. David Altshuler (Chappaqua, N.Y.: Rossel Books, 1983); Harkabi, *Israel's Fateful Hour,* trans. Lenn Schramm (New York: Harper & Row, 1988); Amos Oz, *A Journey in Israel: Autumn 1982* (Tel Aviv: Am Oved, 1986) (in Hebrew).

9. *Ha'Aretz,* 15 July 1996, p. 1 (in Hebrew).

10. *Statistical Abstract of Israel, 1992* (Jerusalem: Central Bureau of Statistics, 1992), chap. 2.

11. Definitions of urban vary with the measurement. The percentages of urban population in the twenty-two countries are as follows: Australia, 85 percent; Austria, 62 percent; Belgium, 76 percent; Canada, 76 percent; Denmark, 86 percent; Finland, 61 percent; France, 77 percent; Germany, 86 percent; Greece, 58 percent; Ireland, 57 percent; Israel, 89 percent; Italy, 67 percent; Japan, 77 percent; New Zealand, 84 percent; the Netherlands, 88 percent; Norway, 80 percent; Portugal, 30 percent; Spain, 75 percent; Sweden, 85 percent; Switzerland, 60 percent; United Kingdom, 93 percent; United States, 76 percent. *World Almanac and Book of Facts, 1992* (Microsoft CD-ROM edition).

12. *Statistical Abstract of the United States, 1993* (Washington, D.C.: U.S. Government Printing Office, 1993), chap. 1 (CD-ROM edition).

13. Harold D. Lasswell, *Who Gets What, When, How?* (New York: McGraw-Hill, 1936).

14. David Dery, *Problem Definition in Policy Analysis* (Lawrence: University of Kansas Press, 1984).

15. David A. Stockman, *The Triumph of Politics: The Inside Story of the Reagan Administration* (New York: Avon, 1987).

16. James Q. Wilson, "Why Reagan Won and Stockman Lost," *Commentary* 82, no. 2 (August 1986): 17–21. For a collection of at least partly positive views on the Reagan administration, see Charles O. Jones, ed., *The Reagan Legacy: Promise and Performance* (Chatham, N.J.: Chatham House, 1988).

17. Seymour M. Hersh, *The Price of Power: Kissinger in the Nixon White House* (New York: Summit Books, 1983).

18. Ze'ev Schiff and Ehud Ya'ari, *Israel's Lebanon War,* ed. and trans. Ina Friedman (New York: Simon and Schuster, 1984).

19. Graham T. Allison, *Essence of Decision: Explaining the Cuban Missile Crisis* (Boston: Little, Brown and Company, 1971).

20. Prominent examples of rational advocacy are provided by Yehezkel Dror, *Public Policymaking Reexamined* (San Francisco: Chandler Publishing Company, 1968); Dror, *Policymaking Under Adversity* (New Brunswick, N.J.: Transaction Books, 1986); and E.S. Quade and Grace M. Carter, *Analysis for Public Decisions* (New York: North-Holland, 1989).

21. Geoffrey Vickers, "Econology, Planning and the American Dream," in *Value Systems and Social Process* (Harmondsworth: Penguin Books, 1970), 48–68. A classic expression of a skeptical view of rationality by a social scientist appears in Charles E. Lindblom, *The Policy-making Process* (Englewood Cliffs, N.J.: Prentice-Hall, 1968). See also Deborah A. Stone, *Policy Paradox and Political Reason* (Glenview, Ill.: Scott, Foresman, 1988). For a critique of the

Grace Commission's recent rational perspective on government reform, see George W. Downs and Patrick D. Larkey, *The Search for Government Efficiency: From Hubris to Helplessness* (Philadelphia: Temple University Press, 1986).

22. A classic expression of the problem appears in Thomas S. Kuhn, *The Structure of Scientific Revolutions* (Chicago: University of Chicago Press, 1970).

23. Irving L. Janis, *Groupthink: Psychological Studies of Policy Decisions and Fiascoes* (Boston: Houghton Mifflin Company, 1983). See also Paul Hart, *Groupthink in Government: A Study of Small Groups and Policy Failure* (Baltimore: Johns Hopkins University Press, 1994).

24. Ze'ev Schiff and Ehud Ya'ari, *Intifada* (Tel Aviv: Schocken Books, 1990), chap. 1(in Hebrew).

25. Robert A. Caro, *The Power Broker: Robert Moses and the Fall of New York City* (New York: Knopf, 1974).

26. Judith E. Gruber, *Controlling Bureaucracies: Dilemmas in Democratic Governance* (Berkeley: University of California Press, 1987).

27. Richard E. Neustadt and Ernest R. May, *Thinking in Time: The Uses of History for Decision Makers* (New York: Free Press, 1986), 13.

28. Michael Lipsky, *Street Level Bureaucracy: Dilemmas of the Individual in Public Services* (New York: Russell Sage Foundation, 1980); Bryan D. Jones, *Governing Buildings and Building Government: A New Perspective on the Old Party* (University: University of Alabama Press, 1985).

29. See, for example, Charles Noble, *Liberalism at Work: The Rise and Fall of OSHA* (Philadelphia: Temple University Press, 1986). For an overtly reformist book that began a virtual reform industry, see Ralph Nader, *Unsafe at Any Speed* (New York: Grossman, 1972).

30. Martha Derthick and Paul J. Quirk, *The Politics of Deregulation* (Washington, D.C.: Brookings Institution, 1985).

31. V. Kerry Smith, *Environmental Policy Under Reagan's Executive Order: The Role of Cost-Benefit Analysis* (Chapel Hill: University of North Carolina Press, 1984).

32. For an analysis of a major policy innovation that managed to pass all the hurdles usually erected by policy gridlock, see Jeffrey H. Birnbaum and Alan S. Murray, *Showdown at Gucci Gulch: Lawmakers, Lobbyists, and the Unlikely Triumph of Tax Reform* (New York: Random House, 1987). For a consideration of a major reform in the structure of policy making, see James L. Sundquist, *Constitutional Reform and Effective Government* (Washington, D.C.: Brookings Institution, 1985). For a recent study of local government structures that can stack the deck in favor of or against certain interests or policies, see Susan Welch and Timothy Bledsoe, *Urban Reform and Its Consequences: A Study in Representation* (Chicago: University of Chicago Press, 1988).

33. See, for example, Brian J. Cook, *Bureaucratic Politics and Regulatory Reform: The EPA and Emissions Trading* (New York: Greenwood Press, 1988).

34. See Charles H. Moore and Patricia A. Hoban-Moore, "Some Lessons From Reagan's HUD: Housing Policy and Public Service," *PS: Political Science and Politics* 23 (March 1990): 13–18.

35. Neustadt and May, *Thinking in Time.*

36. Barbara W. Tuchman, *The March of Folly: From Troy to Vietnam* (New York: Ballantine Books, 1984).

37. Gary Sick, *All Fall Down: America's Tragic Encounter with Iran* (New York: Penguin Books, 1986), esp. chap. 2.

38. Thomas Brown, *JFK: History of an Image* (Bloomington: University of Indiana Press, 1988).

39. For a fanciful effort to define the improbability of successful project implementation, see Jeffrey L. Pressman and Aaron Wildavsky, *Implementation* (Berkeley: University of California Press, 1973).

40. Henry J. Aaron, Thomas E. Mann, and Timothy Taylor, eds., *Values and Public Policy* (Washington, D.C.: Brookings Institution, 1994); Helen Ingram and Steven Rathgeb Smith, eds., *Public Policy for Democracy* (Washington, D.C.: Brookings Institution, 1993); Charles Piller, *The Fail-safe Society: Community Defiance and the End of Technological Optimism* (New York: Basic Books, 1991); Luther J. Carter, *Nuclear Imperatives and Public Trust: Dealing with Radioactive Waste* (Washington, D.C.: Resources for the Future, 1987); Theodore Lowi, *The End of Liberalism* (New York: Norton, 1979).

41. For examinations of the definition of public problems, see Stone, *Policy Paradox and Political Reason;* Charles E. Lindblom and David K. Cohen, *Usable Knowledge: Social Science and Social Problem Solving* (New Haven: Yale University Press, 1979); David Dery, *Data and Policy Change* (Boston: Kluwer Academic Publishers, 1990); Dery, *Problem Definition.*

Chapter 2. Simple Problems, Complex Problems, and Insoluble Problems

1. See, for example, Erich Goode, *Drugs in American Society* (New York: McGraw-Hill, 1993).

2. *Statistical Abstract of the United States, 1993* (Washington, D.C.: U.S. Government Printing Office, 1993), table 208; *Jerusalem Post,* 31 March 1995, p. 10.

3. *Oxford English Dictionary* (London: Oxford University Press, 1933).

4. *Webster's New Collegiate Dictionary* (Springfield, Mass.: G. C. Merriam Co., 1977).

5. See, for example, *Webster's New Collegiate Dictionary.*

6. A "dilemma of democracy" is said to reflect the weaknesses built into polities that seem destined to offer services beyond their ability to finance them or administer them well. See Morris Janowitz, *Social Control of the Welfare State* (New York: Elsevier, 1976); and Michael Crozier, Samuel P. Huntington, and Joji Watanuki, *The Crisis of Democracy: Report on the Governability of Democracies to the Trilateral Commission* (New York: New York University Press, 1975).

7. V. O. Key, Jr., "The Lack of a Budgetary Theory," *American Political Science Review* 34 (December 1940): 1137–44.

8. Henry Teune, "A Logic of Comparative Policy Analysis," in Douglas E. Ashford, ed., *Comparing Public Policies: New Concepts and Methods* (Beverly Hills, 1978), 43–55.

9. See Ira Sharkansky, *The Routines of Politics* (New York: Van Nostrand, 1970).

10. My thanks to Stefan M. Sharkansky for pressing on me the significance of paradoxes.

11. See, for example, Deborah A. Stone, *Policy Paradox and Political Reason* (Glenview, Ill.: Scott, Foresman and Company, 1988), 1–4, and Donald F. Kettl, *Government by Proxy: (Mis?)Managing Federal Programs* (Washington, D.C.: CQ Press, 1988), chap. 1.

12. Steven J. Brams, *Paradoxes in Politics: An Introduction to the Nonobvious in Political Science* (New York: Free Press, 1976).

13. Charles W. Anderson, "The Logic of Public Problems: Evaluation in Comparative Policy Research," in Ashford, ed., *Comparing Public Policies*, 19–41.

14. On policy making for the disabled, see Robert A. Katzmann, *Institutional Disability: The Saga of Transportation Policy for the Disabled* (Washington, D.C.: Brookings Institution, 1986).

15. Herbert Jacob, *The Frustration of Policy: Responses to Crime by American Cities* (Boston: Little, Brown, 1984). See also Kevin N. Wright, *The Great American Crime Myth* (Westport, Conn.: Greenwood Press, 1985). Jacob's proposal would make the treatment of crime resemble no-fault accident insurance. Rather than bother courts with the elusive and expensive task of deciding who was at fault and who should pay, insurance companies would simply award compensation based on set tariffs.

16. See David Dery, *Problem Definition in Policy Analysis* (Lawrence, KS: University of Kansas Press, 1984).

17. Kristen Luker, *Abortion and the Politics of Motherhood* (Berkeley: University of California Press, 1984).

18. Gilbert Y. Steiner, *Constitutional Inequality: The Political Fortunes of the Equal Rights Amendment* (Washington, D.C.: Brookings Institution, 1985).

19. Except to honor another commandment, as in a breach of the Sabbath to save a human life.

20. George V. Coelho, David A. Hamburg, and John E. Adams, eds., *Coping and Adaptation* (New York: Basic Books, 1974).

21. See Ira Sharkansky, "Coping Strategies of Engagement and Avoidance: The Case of Jerusalem," *Policy and Politics* 23 (April 1995): 91–102.

22. Herbert Simon, *Administrative Behavior* (New York: Free Press, 1976).

23. Jack T. Tapp, "Multisystems Holistic Model of Health, Stress and Coping," in Tiffany M. Field, Philip M. McCabe and Neil Schneiderman, eds., *Stress and Coping* (Hillsdale, N.J.: Lawrence Erlbaum Associates, 1985), 285–304. Some writers perceive engagement coping as leading to more effective adaptations to crisis situations. See Rudolf H. Moos and Jeanne A. Schaefer, "Life Transitions and Crises: A Conceptual Overview," in Moos and Schaefer, eds., *Coping with Life Crises: An Integrated Approach* (New York: Plenum Press, 1986), 3–28. Other researchers make the point that the literature has yet to confirm any strong linkage between types of coping and the outcomes of stressful situations. See Susan Folkman, "Personal Control and Stress and Coping Processes: A Theoretical Analysis," *Journal of Personality and Social Psycholo-*

gy 46 (1984): 839–52.

24. William E. Connolly, *Politics and Ambiguity* (Madison: University of Wisconsin Press, 1987).

Chapter 3. Israeli Government and Politics

1. In 1990 Israel was the leader among a group of forty-three highly and moderately developed countries in percentage of GDP accounted for by government expenditures. Selected percentages were as follows: Israel, 30.3 percent; Sweden, 27.2 percent; Denmark, 25.2 percent; United States, 21.7 percent; Japan, 9.1 percent. See *International Financial Statistics* (Washington, D.C.: International Monetary Fund, 1992). See also Ira Sharkansky, *The Political Economy of Israel* (New Brunswick, N.J.: Transaction Books, 1987).

2. For an argument that regionalism is growing in Israel, see Y. Gradus, "The Emergence of Regionalism in a Centralized System: The Case of Israel," *Environment and Planning D: Society and Space* 2(1984): 87–100.

3. Ze'ev Sternhell, *Nation Building or a New Society? The Zionist Labor Movement (1904–1940) and the Origins of Israel* (Tel Aviv: Am Oved, 1995) (in Hebrew).

4. *Jerusalem Post*, 25 June 1993, p. 5.

5. *Audit Report on the Provision of Support to Institutions by Local Authorities* (Jerusalem: State Comptroller, 1991) (in Hebrew).

6. Yael Yishai, *Interest Groups in Israel* (Tel Aviv: Am Oved, 1987) (in Hebrew); Marcia Drezon-Tepler, *Interest Groups and Political Change in Israel* (Albany: State University of New York Press, 1990).

7. Sternhell, *Nation Building*.

8. *Jerusalem Post*, 26 November 1993, p. 4A.

9. Michael Shalev, *Labour and the Political Economy in Israel* (New York: Oxford University Press, 1992), 245–46.

10. Dan Horowitz and Moshe Lissak, *Trouble in Utopia: The Overburdened Polity of Israel* (Albany: State University of New York Press, 1989), 83ff.

11. Timothy M. Sneeding, Michael O'Higgins, and Lee Rainwater, eds., *Poverty, Inequality and Income Distribution in Comparative Perspective: The Luxembourg Income Study (LIS)* (New York: Harvester Wheatsheaf, 1993).

12. The ratios of actual to predicted GINI values for the Israeli data are as follows: household income, .83; proportion of total income in families in the lowest 20 percent of income, 1.11; proportion of total income in families in the highest 20 percent of income, .85; proportion of total income in families in the highest 10 percent of income, .73.

13. Sneeding, O'Higgins, and Rainwater, eds., *Poverty, Inequality and Income Distribution*.

14. *Statistical Abstract of the United States, 1993* (Washington, D.C.: U.S. Government Printing Office, 1993), table 1432. The countries included in this comparison were Australia, Canada, Denmark, Finland, France, Italy, Japan, the Netherlands, Norway, Spain, Sweden, Switzerland, the United Kingdom, the United States, and West Germany.

15. See, for example, Martin Rein, Goesta Esping-Andersen, and Lee Rainwater, eds., *Stagnation and Renewal in Social Policy: The Rise and Fall of Policy*

Regimes (Armonk, N.Y.: M. E. Sharpe, 1987).

16. Denny Braun, *The Rich Get Richer: The Rise of Inequality in the United States and the World* (Chicago: Nelson-Hall, 1991), 186.

17. *Statistical Abstract of the United States, 1993*, table 735.

18. *Statistical Abstract of Israel* (Jerusalem: Central Bureau of Statistics, 1987 and 1993).

19. *Statistical Abstract of the United States, 1993*, table 750. Israeli data appear in the various issues of the *Statistical Abstract of Israel*.

20. *Jerusalem Post*, 8 November 1993, p. 1; 29 December 1994, p. 6; 24 November 1995, p. 10.

21. *Jerusalem Post*, 2 August 1995, p. 1.

22. *Jerusalem Post*, 24 November 1995, p. 10.

23. *Statistical Abstract of the United States, 1993*, table 1396; *Statistical Abstract of Israel* (1975), table 29.8; (1992), table 18.25. As in other fields of policy analysis, policy advocates argue for one or another conception or indicator. The data employed here come from reliable public sources that employ widely used indicators.

24. *Jerusalem Post*, 2 June 1995, p. 11.

25. *Ha'aretz*, 1 January 1996, p. 7(in Hebrew).

26. This story was told to the author.

27. David Dery and Binat Schwarz-Milner, *Who Governs Local Government?* (Jerusalem: Israeli Institute of Democracy, 1994) (in Hebrew).

28. Daniel J. Elazar and Chaim Kalchheim, eds., *Local Government in Israel* (Lanham, Md.: University Press of America, 1988).

29. Paul E. Peterson, *City Limits* (Chicago: University of Chicago Press, 1981); Lawrence J.R. Herson and John M. Bolland, *The Urban Web: Politics, Policy, and Theory* (Chicago: Nelson-Hall, 1990); Andrew Kirby, *Power/Resistance: Local Politics and the Chaotic State* (Bloomington: Indiana University Press, 1993).

30. The 81 percent figure encompasses the populations of the Jerusalem, Tel Aviv, Central, and Haifa districts, and of the Ashkelon and Akko subdistricts, as reported in the *Statistical Abstract of Israel, 1992*.

31. *Israel 2020: A Master Plan for Israel in the Twenty-first Century* (Haifa: Technion–Israel Institute of Technology, 1993) (in Hebrew); Baruch A. Kipnis, "Metropolitan Processes: Their Impact on Regional Development Strategies Along Israel's Urbanized Coastal Plain," *Journal of Agricultural and Planning Research* 1 (1984): 191–207; E. Razin, "Metropolitan Reform in the Tel Aviv Metropolis: Metropolitan Government or Metropolitan Cooperation?" *Environment and Planning C: Government and Policy* 14 (1996): 39–54.

32. Gradus, "The Emergence of Regionalism."

33. Erik Cohen, "The City in the Zionist Ideology" (Jerusalem: Hebrew University Institute of Urban and Regional Studies, 1970).

34. Howard F. Vos, *Ezra, Nehemiah, and Esther* (Grand Rapids: Zondervan Publishing House, 1987).

35. Chaim Kalchheim, "The Division of Functions and the Interrelationships Between Local and State Authorities," in Elazar and Kalchheim, eds., *Local Government*, 41–82; Frederick A. Lazin, *Policy Implementation and*

Social Welfare: Israel and the United States (New Brunswick, N.J.: Transaction Books, 1986).

36. On the character and techniques of Israel's civil service, see Ya'acov Reuveni, *Public Administration in Israel: The Government System in Israel and Its Development During the Years 1948–73* (Ramat Gan: Massada, 1974) (in Hebrew). The incidence of politically motivated appointments varies with the indicators and the time periods employed. Details appear in Ira Sharkansky, "Israeli Civil Service Positions Open to Political Appointments," *International Journal of Public Administration* 12, no. 5 (1989), 731–48. For further implications of the politicization of Israel's public service, see David Dery, *Political Appointments in Israel* (Jerusalem: Israel Democracy Institute, 1993) (in Hebrew).

37. Kalchheim, "The Division of Functions."

38. Kalchheim, "The Division of Functions."

39. Elazar and Kalchheim, *Local Government.*

40. *Audit Report.*

41. Ira Sharkansky, *What Makes Israel Tick? How Domestic Policy-Makers Cope with Constraints* (Chicago: Nelson-Hall, 1985).

42. Kalchheim, "The Division of Functions"; Lazin, *Policy Implementation.*

43. Sharkansky, *What Makes Israel Tick?*, chap. 6.

44. See, for example, Arend Lijphart, *Democracies: Patterns of Majoritarian and Consensus Government in Twenty-one Countries* (New Haven: Yale University Press, 1984); G. Bingham Powell, Jr., *Contemporary Democracies: Participation, Stability, and Violence* (Cambridge: Harvard University Press, 1982); and Peter Y. Medding, *The Founding of Israeli Democracy 1948–1967* (New York: Oxford University Press, 1990). This section borrows heavily from Ira Sharkansky, *Israel and Its Bible: A Political Analysis* (New York: Garland, 1996).

45. The United Kingdom, Finland, Sweden, Norway, Denmark, Iceland, Switzerland, Greece, Australia, and New Zealand all include a cross in their flag.

46. Not counting the non-Jews of the occupied territories outside East Jerusalem.

47. See Yehoshafat Harkabi, *The Bar Kokhba Syndrome: Risk and Realism in International Relations*, trans. Max D. Ticktin and ed. David Altshuler (Chappaqua, N.Y.: Rossel Books, 1983), and Harkabi, *Israel's Fateful Hour*, trans. Lenn Schramm (New York: Harper & Row, 1988).

48. Meron Benvenisti, *The West Bank Data Project: A Survey of Israel's Policies* (Washington, D.C.: American Enterprise Institute for Policy Research, 1984), 34; Benvenisti, *The Sling and the Club: Territories, Jews and Arabs* (Jerusalem: Keter Publishing House, 1988) (in Hebrew); Benvenisti, *The Shepherds' War: Collected Essays (1981–1989)* (Jerusalem: Jerusalem Post, 1989).

49. Yeshayahu Leibowitz, *On Just About Everything: Talks with Michael Shashar* (Jerusalem: Keter Publishing House, 1988) (in Hebrew).

50. A. Friedberg, et al., eds., *State Audit and Accountability* (Jerusalem: State Comptroller, 1991); *Report on the Results of Expenditure Audit of Political Groups for the Period of the Election to the 13th Knesset: 1.1.92 to 31.7.92*

(Jerusalem: State Comptroller, 1993) (in Hebrew).

51. Gadi Wolfsfeld, *The Politics of Provocation* (Albany: State University of New York Press, 1988).

52. Nachman Ben-Yehuda, *Political Assassinations by Jews: A Rhetorical Device for Justice* (Albany: State University of New York Press, 1993). Ben-Yehuda offers an extensive review of political assassinations by Jews and concedes that a lack of reliable comparative data precludes anything stronger than a surmise about their relative incidence.

53. Gregg Barak, "Toward a Criminology of State Criminality," in Barak, ed., *Crimes by the Capitalist State: An Introduction to State Criminality* (Albany: State University of New York Press, 1991), 3–16; Daniel E. Georges-Abeyie, "Piracy, Air Piracy, and Recurrent U.S. and Israeli Civilian Aircraft Interceptions," in Barak, ed., *Crimes*, 129–44; Avner Yaniv, ed., *National Security and Democracy in Israel* (Boulder, Colo.: Lynne Rienner Publishers, 1993); Horowitz and Lissak, *Trouble in Utopia*; *Israel Law Review* 23, nos. 2–3 (spring–summer 1989).

54. William V. O'Brien, *Law and Morality in Israel's War with the PLO* (New York: Routledge, 1991).

55. Ezra Mendelsohn, *On Modern Jewish Politics* (New York: Oxford University Press, 1993); Jonathan Frankel, *Prophecy and Politics: Socialism, Nationalism, and the Russian Jews, 1862–1917* (Cambridge: Cambridge University Press, 1981); Zvi Gitelman, ed., *The Quest for Utopia: Jewish Political Ideas and Institutions Through the Ages* (Armonk, N.Y.: M.E. Sharpe, 1992); Eli Lederhandler, *The Road to Modern Jewish Politics: Political Tradition and Political Reconstruction in the Jewish Community of Tsarist Russia* (New York: Oxford University Press, 1989).

56. Michael Keren, *Ben-Gurion and the Intellectuals: Power, Knowledge, and Charisma* (Dekalb: Northern Illinois University Press, 1983).

57. This section relies on Sharkansky, *Israel and Its Bible*.

58. Martin Buber, "The Man of Today and the Jewish Bible," and "The Faith of Judaism," in *Israel and the World: Essays in a Time of Crisis* (New York: Schocken Books, 1963); Gershom Scholem, *Sabbatai Sevi: The Mystical Messiah*, trans. R. J. Zwi Werblowsky (Princeton: Princeton University Press, 1973); Richard Elliott Friedman, *Who Wrote the Bible?* (New York: Harper and Row, 1987); Norman K. Gottwald, *The Tribes of Yahweh: A Sociology of the Religion of Liberated Israel, 1250–1050 BCE* (Maryknoll, N.Y.: Orbis Books, 1979); Gottwald, *The Hebrew Bible: A Socio-Literary Introduction* (Philadelphia: Fortress Press, 1985); Aaron Wildavsky, *The Nursing Father: Moses as a Political Leader* (University, AL: University of Alabama Press, 1984). Other recent works examining politics in the Hebrew Bible include Steven J. Brams, *Superior Beings: If They Exist, How Would We Know?* (New York: Springer-Verlag, 1983); Michael Walzer, *Exodus and Revolution* (New York: Basic Books, 1985); Stuart A. Cohen, *The Three Crowns: Structures of Communal Politics in Early Rabbinic Jewry* (Cambridge: Cambridge University Press, 1990); H. Mark Roelofs, "Hebraic-Biblical Political Thinking," *Polity* 20, no. 4 (summer 1988): 572–97; and Roelofs, "Liberation Theology: The Recovery of Biblical Radicalism," *American Political Science Review* 82 (June 1988): 549–66.

59. Daniel J. Elazar and Stuart A. Cohen, *The Jewish Polity: Jewish Political Organization from Biblical Times to the Present* (Bloomington: Indiana University Press, 1985); Elazar, "The Book of Joshua as a Political Classic," *Jewish Political Studies Review* 1, nos. 1–2 (1989): 93–150.

60. Wildavsky, *The Nursing Father*; Walzer, *Exodus*.

61. Deuteronomy 17:14–20.

62. Judges 21:25.

63. 1 Samuel 8:10–18.

64. 1 Samuel 25.

65. 1 Samuel 27–29.

66. Robert Davidson, *The Courage to Doubt: Exploring An Old Testament Theme* (London: SCM Press, 1983).

67. William Safire, *The First Dissident: The Book of Job in Today's Politics* (New York: Random House, 1992); David Penchansky, *The Betrayal of God: Ideological Conflict in Job* (Louisville, KY: Westminster/John Knox Press, 1990).

68. Ecclesiastes 5:8.

69. 1 Samuel 2:12–17.

70. Proverbs 24:23–25.

71. Ecclesiastes 5:8. See Davidson, *The Courage to Doubt*, 191–92.

72. Jeremiah 38.

Chapter 4. The Drama and Routine of Immigration

1. Robert Lacey, *Little Man: Meyer Lansky and the Gangster Life* (Boston: Little, Brown, 1991).

2. Tamar Horowitz, ed., *The Soviet Man in an Open Society* (Lanham, Md.: University Press Of America, 1989); Ruth Karola Westheimer, *Surviving Salvation: The Ethiopian Jewish Family in Transition* (New York: New York University Press, 1992); Zvi Gitelman, *Becoming Israelis: Political Resocialization of Soviet and American Immigrants* (New York: Praeger, 1982).

3. *Kal Ha'ir*, 25 October 1991 (in Hebrew).

4. On earlier social protests in Jerusalem, see Shlomo Hasson, *Urban Social Movements in Jerusalem: The Protest of the Second Generation* (Albany: State University of New York Press, 1993).

5. Charles Piller, *The Fail-safe Society: Community Defiance and the End of Technological Optimism* (New York: Basic Books, 1991).

6. *Kal Ha'ir*, 17 May 1991 (in Hebrew).

7. *Kal Ha'ir*, 31 May 1991 (in Hebrew).

8. *Kal Ha'ir*, 7 June 1991 (in Hebrew).

9. *Kal Ha'ir*, 20 September 1991 (in Hebrew).

10. *Kal Ha'ir*, 30 August 1991 (in Hebrew).

11. *Kal Ha'ir*, 20 September 1991 (in Hebrew).

12. *Ma'ariv*, 8 April 1992 (in Hebrew).

13. *Kal Ha'ir*, 17 April 1992 (in Hebrew).

14. Exodus 16:2–8; Numbers 11:5.

15. *Kal Ha'ir*, 1 November 1991 (in Hebrew).

16. *Jerusalem Post*, 14 June 1994, p. 2.

17. For the author's experiences as an immigrant, see "How to Cope with the Bureaucracy," *Jerusalem Quarterly,* February 1978, 80–93; "Professor Becomes Army Recruit," *Jerusalem Quarterly* 24 (summer 1982), 3–12.

18. *Jerusalem Post,* 7 February 1992, p. 9.

19. *Jerusalem Post,* 26 June 1992, p. 7.

20. *Jerusalem Post,* 13 December 1994, p. 3.

21. *Jerusalem Post,* 26 May 1991, p. 12.

22. Paul Johnson, *A History of Christianity* (New York: Atheneum, 1976), 11.

23. A.B. Yehoshua, "The Golah as a Neurotic Solution," *Forum: On the Jewish People, Zionism and Israel* 35 (spring–summer 1979): 17–36.

24. Norman F. Cantor, *The Sacred Chain: The History of the Jews* (New York: Harper Collins, 1994).

25. Zion Ravi, "Emigration from Israel, 1948–84," *Ha'aretz,* 5–6 January 1986 (in Hebrew), quoted in Ravi, "Avoiding the Irresistible: Should the Israeli Government Combat Jewish Emigration?" *Jerusalem Quarterly* 41 (winter 1987): 95–111.

26. *Jerusalem Post Magazine,* 4 March 1994, p. 6.

27. *Jerusalem Post,* 10 August 1994, p. 6.

Chapter 5. Bringing Peace to the Middle East

1. Karl von Clausewitz, *On War* (London: Penguin Books, 1968 [1833]). For the quotation attributed to Mao Tse-tung, see *Bartlett's Familiar Quotations* (Little, Brown, 1980; Microsoft Bookshelf 1992 edition).

2. See, in particular, Gershon R. Kieval, *Party Politics in Israel and the Occupied Territories* (Westport, Conn.: Greenwood Press, 1983).

3. There are many credible surveys of the Arab-Israeli disputes, and new publications continue to appear. A reader might begin by consulting the following books, which represent different emphases and approaches: Avi Shlaim, *Collusion Across the Jordan: King Abdullah, the Zionist Movement, and the Partition of Palestine* (New York: Columbia University Press, 1988); Robert F. Hunter, *The Palestinian Uprising: A War by Other Means* (Berkeley: University of California Press, 1993); Patrick Seale, *Asad: The Struggle for the Middle East* (Berkeley: University of California Press, 1988); Conor Cruise O'Brien, *The Siege: The Saga of Israel and Zionism* (New York: Simon and Schuster, 1987).

4. That is, the area on the west bank of the Jordan River. Also at issue is Gaza, for which the terminological options have been less contentious.

5. Shlomo Gazit, *The Carrot and the Stick: The Israeli Government in Yehuda and Shomron* (Tel Aviv: Zmora, Bitan, 1985), 136 (in Hebrew).

6. Rafik Halabi, *The West Bank Story: An Israeli Arab's View of Both Sides of a Tangled Conflict,* trans. Ina Friedman (New York: Harcourt Brace Jovanovich, 1981).

7. *Jerusalem Post,* 19 December 1993, p. 2.

8. The totals were as follows: Mapam, three; Ratz, five: Shinui, two.

9. The totals were as follows: National Religious Party, five; Tahiya, three; Tsomet, two.

10. *Ha'aretz,* 25 July 1996, p. 3 (in Hebrew).

11. *Ha'aretz*, 29 July 1996, p. 3 (in Hebrew).

12. This section relies on Uriel Dann, *King Hussein and the Challenge of Arab Radicalism: Jordan, 1955–1967* (New York: Oxford University Press, 1989); Clinton Bailey, *Jordan's Palestinian Challenge 1948–1983: A Political History* (Boulder, Colo.: Westview Press, 1984); Arthur R. Day, *East Bank/West Bank: Jordan and the Prospects for Peace* (New York: Council on Foreign Relations, 1986); Robert B. Satloff, *Troubles on the East Bank: Challenges to the Domestic Stability of Jordan* (New York: Praeger, 1986); Uri Bar-Joseph, *The Best of Enemies: Israel and Transjordan in the War of 1948* (London: Frank Cass, 1987); and Shlaim, *Collusion Across the Jordan*.

13. Meron Benvenisti, *Jerusalem: The Torn City* (Minneapolis: University of Minnesota Press, 1976); Uzi Benziman, "Israeli Policy in East Jerusalem After Reunification," in Joel L. Kraemer, ed., *Jerusalem: Problems and Prospects* (New York: Praeger, 1980), 100–30; Daniel Rubinstein, "The Jerusalem Municipality Under the Ottomans, British, and Jordanians," in Kraemer, ed., *Jerusalem*, 72–99.

14. Gerald Caplan and Ruth B. Caplan, *Arab and Jew in Jerusalem: Explorations in Community Mental Health* (Cambridge: Harvard University Press, 1980), chap. 5.

15. Teddy Kollek and Amos Kollek, *For Jerusalem: A Life* (New York: Random House, 1978), chap. 14.

16. Itamar Rabinovitch, *The War for Lebanon: 1970–1985* (Ithaca: Cornell University Press, 1984), esp. chap. 1.

17. This section relies on Rabinovitch, *War for Lebanon*, chs. 2–4.

18. Richard A. Gabriel, *Operation Peace for Galilee: The Israeli-PLO War in Lebanon* (New York: Hill and Wang, 1984), 216.

19. *Annual Report 29* (Jerusalem: State Comptroller, 1978), 700–09.

20. Yoram Peri, *Between Battles and Ballots: Israeli Military in Politics* (Cambridge: Cambridge University Press, 1983).

21. Gabriel, *Operation Peace for Galilee*, 21.

22. Shai Feldman and Heda Rechnitz-Kijner, *Deception, Consensus and War: Israel in Lebanon* (Tel-Aviv University: Jaffee Center for Strategic Studies, 1984), 3.

23. Ze'ev Schiff and Ehud Ya'ari, *Israel's Lebanon War*, ed. and trans. Ina Friedman (New York: Simon and Schuster, 1984).

24. Zvi Lanir, "Political Aims and Military Objectives—Some Observations on the Israeli Experience," in Saul Cohen, ed., *Israeli Security Planning in the 1980's* (New York: Praeger, 1984), 14–49.

25. Feldman and Rechnitz-Kijner, *Deception, Consensus and War*.

26. *Jerusalem Post*, 12 December 1994, p. 6; *Ha'aretz*, 19 June 1995, p. 2 (in Hebrew).

27. David Grossman, *The Yellow Wind*, trans. Haim Watzman (London: Jonathan Cape, 1988).

28. Shlaim, *Collusion Across the Jordan*; Bar-Joseph, *The Best of Enemies*. For a detailed review of the Israeli-Palestinian conflict over the years, see Deborah J. Gerner, *One Land, Two Peoples: The Conflict over Palestine* (Boulder, Colo.: Westview Press, 1991). For a critique of Israeli revisionist historians,

including Shlaim, see Efraim Karsh, "Rewriting Israel's History," *Middle East Quarterly*, June 1996, 19–29.

29. For some of the problems, see Joan Peters, *From Time Immemorial* (New York: Harper & Row, 1984).

30. As in other issues in the Arab-Israeli disputes, the literature here is large and contentious. A reader might begin with Sammy Smooha, *Arabs and Jews in Israel: Conflicting and Shared Attitudes in a Divided Society* (Boulder, Colo.: Westview Press, 1989).

31. *Statistical Abstract of Israel, 1990* (Jerusalem: Central Bureau of Statistics, 1990), chs. 11, 22.

32. Hillel Frisch, "From Armed Struggle over State Borders to Political Mobilization and Intifada within It: The Transformation of PLO Strategy in the Territories," *Plural Societies* 19, nos. 2–3 (March 1990): 92–115.

33. *Ha'aretz*, 18 July 1996, p. 7 (in Hebrew).

34. Seale, *Asad.*

35. L. Carl Brown, *International Politics and the Middle East: Old Rules, Dangerous Game* (Princeton: Princeton University Press, 1984).

36. Peters, *From Time Immemorial*, 253 ff.

37. Aharon Ben-Ami, *Social Change in a Hostile Environment: The Crusader Kingdom of Jerusalem* (Princeton: Princeton University Press, 1969). For a history that puts the emphasis on the sanctity of holy places, see Jean Richard, *The Latin Kingdom of Jerusalem*, trans. Janet Shirly (Amsterdam: North Holland Publishing Company, 1979).

38. Norman Rich, *Why the Crimean War? A Cautionary Tale* (Hanover, NH: University Press of New England, 1985); Brison D. Gooch, ed., *The Origins of the Crimean War* (Lexington, Mass.: D.C. Heath, 1969).

39. *Jerusalem Post*, 24 December 1993, p. 4B; *Ha'aretz*, 9 April 1995, p. 4 (in Hebrew).

Chapter 6. The Difficult Problems of Jerusalem

1. This chapter draws heavily on Ira Sharkansky, *Governing Jerusalem: Again on the World's Agenda* (Detroit: Wayne State University Press, 1996).

2. 2 Samuel 6.

3. Lamentations 1:1.

4. Saul B. Cohen, *Jerusalem: Bridging the Four Walls—A Geopolitical Perspective* (New York: Herzl Press, 1977), 23.

5. Ronald Segal, *Whose Jerusalem? The Conflicts of Israel* (London: Jonathan Cape, 1973), 136.

6. F.E. Peters, *Jerusalem: The Holy City in the Eyes of Chroniclers, Visitors, Pilgrims, and Prophets from the Days of Abraham to the Beginnings of Modern Times* (Princeton: Princeton University Press, 1985), 285–86.

7. Peters, *Jerusalem*, 521.

8. *Kal Ha'ir*, 7 February 1992 (in Hebrew).

9. Daphne Tsimhoni, "Continuity and Change in Communal Autonomy: The Christian Communal Organizations in Jerusalem, 1948–1980," *Middle East Studies* 22 (July 1986): 398–417.

10. Islamic Council of Europe, *Jerusalem: The Key to World Peace* (London:

Islamic Council of Europe, 1980), vii.

11. M. A. Aamiry, *Jerusalem: Arab Origin and Heritage* (London: Longman, 1978). The quotations are from the preface and pp. 1–12.

12. Cohen, *Jerusalem.*

13. For various views on the Jewish-Palestinian conflict as it applies to Jerusalem, see Henry Near, ed. *The Seventh Day (London: Andre Deutsch, 1970); Segal, Whose Jerusalem?;* Cohen, *Jerusalem;* Meron Benvenisti, *Jerusalem: The Torn City* (Minneapolis: University of Minnesota Press, 1976); Benvenisti, *The Shepherds' War: Collected Essays (1981–1989)* (Jerusalem: *Jerusalem Post,* 1989); Benvenisti, *The West Bank Data Project: A Survey of Israel's Policies* (Washington, D.C.: American Enterprise Institute for Policy Research, 1984); Benvenisti, *The Sling and the Club: Territories, Jews and Arabs* (Jerusalem: Keter Publishing House, 1988) (in Hebrew); Avner Yaniv, ed., *National Security and Democracy in Israel* (Boulder, Colo.: Lynne Rienner Publishers, 1993); Michael Shalev, *Labour and the Political Economy in Israel* (New York: Oxford University Press, 1992); Baruch Kimmerling, ed., *The Israeli State and Society: Boundaries and Frontiers* (Albany: State University of New York Press, 1989); Michael Romann and Alex Weingrod, *Living Together Separately: Arabs and Jews in Contemporary Jerusalem* (Princeton: Princeton University Press, 1991); Aamiry, *Jerusalem;* Islamic Council of Europe, *Jerusalem;* Walid Khalidi, *From Haven to Conquest: Readings in Zionism and the Palestine Problem Until 1948* (Beirut: Institute for Palestine Studies, 1971); George T. Abed, "The Economic Viability of a Palestinian State," *Journal of Palestine Studies* 19, no. 2 (winter 1990): 3–28; Edward W. Said, "Reflections on Twenty Years of Palestinian History," *Journal of Palestine Studies* 20, no. 4 (summer 1991): 5–22; and Elia Zureik, "Prospects of the Palestinians in Israel—I," *Journal of Palestine Studies* 22, no. 2 (winter 1993): 90–109.

14. For the higher estimate, which was from the Interior Ministry, see *Kal Ha'ir,* 17 January 1992 (in Hebrew). The lower estimate was provided by a senior Jerusalem municipal official.

15. In 1990 Israeli statisticians admitted to difficulties in updating their surveys of the occupied territories since the beginning of the intifada. See *Statistical Abstract of Israel, 1990* (Jerusalem: Central Bureau of Statistics, 1990), 705, 730.

16. Israel Kimhi, Shalom Reichman, and Joseph Schweid, "Arab Settlement in the Metropolitan Area of Jerusalem" (Jerusalem: Jerusalem Institute for Israel Studies, 1986) (in Hebrew); Kimhi, Reichman, and Schweid, "The Metropolitan Area of Jerusalem" (Jerusalem: Jerusalem Institute for Israel Studies, 1984); *Ha'aretz,* 18 July 1992 (in Hebrew).

17. Abraham Ashkenasi, "Israeli Policies and Palestinian Fragmentation: Political and Social Impacts in Israel and Jerusalem" (Jerusalem: Hebrew University Leonard Davis Institute, 1988); Ashkenasi, "Opinion Trends Among Jerusalem Palestinians" (Jerusalem: Hebrew University Leonard Davis Institute, 1990).

18. Romann and Weingrod, *Living Together Separately.*

19. Some residents of the Christian Quarter are not Palestinians but clerics assigned to Jerusalem by overseas churches.

20. The numbers appear in Romann and Weingrod, *Living Together Separately,* 207; Terrence Prittie, *Whose Jerusalem?* (London: Frederick Muller, 1981); and Ashkenasi, "Israeli Policies and Palestinian Fragmentation."

21. Benvenisti, *Jerusalem,* vii.

22. Daniel J. Elazar and Chaim Kalchheim, eds., *Local Government in Israel* (Lanham, Md.: University Press of America, 1988).

23. Benvenisti, *Jerusalem;* Gerald Caplan and Ruth B. Caplan, *Arab and Jew in Jerusalem: Explorations in Community Mental Health* (Cambridge: Harvard University Press, 1980).

24. *Kal Ha'ir,* 23 February 1996, p. 23 (in Hebrew).

25. David Biale, *Power and Powerlessness in Jewish History* (New York: Schocken Books, 1987).

26. Moshe Amirav, "Jerusalem: The Open-City Solution," *Jerusalem Post,* 4 February 1990, p. 4; Amirav, "Toward Coexisting in the Capital," *Jerusalem Post,* 18 October 1990, p. 4.

27. Ashkenasi, "Opinion Trends Among Jerusalem Palestinians."

28. Martha Crenshaw, ed., *Terrorism, Legitimacy, and Power: The Consequences of Political Violence* (Middletown, Conn.: Wesleyan University Press, 1983); Brian A. Crozier, *A Theory of Conflict* (London: Hamish Hamilton, 1974).

29. Robert F. Hunter, *The Palestinian Uprising: A War by Other Means* (Berkeley: University of California Press, 1993); *Jerusalem Post,* 19 December 1993, p. 2.

30. *Statistical Abstract of Israel, 1992* (Jerusalem: Central Bureau of Statistics, 1993), table 21.14; *Statistical Abstract of the United States, 1993* (Washington, D.C.: U.S. Government Printing Office, 1994), tables 300, 303.

31. *Statistical Yearbook of Jerusalem, 1991* (Municipality of Jerusalem and Jerusalem Institute for Israel Studies, 1993; CD-ROM edition), chap. 13.

32. Mark Twain, *The Innocents Abroad* (London, 1869), 295, quoted in Yehoshua Ben-Arieh, *Jerusalem in the 19th Century: The Old City* (New York: St. Martin's Press, 1984), 57.

33. Quoted in D. H. K. Amiran, "The Development of Jerusalem, 1860–1979," in David H. K. Amiran, Arie Shachar, and Israel Kimhi, eds., *Urban Geography of Jerusalem: A Companion Volume to the Atlas of Jerusalem* (Jerusalem: Massada Press, 1973), 26.

34. Ben-Arieh, *Jerusalem,* 94.

35. David Grossman, *Present Absentees* (Tel Aviv: Kibbutz Meuchad, 1992), esp. 111 (in Hebrew).

36. *Foreign Broadcast Information Service:* FBIS-NES-93-217, p. 47.

37. U. O. Schmelz, "Jerusalem's Arab Population Since the Mandatory Period (1918–1990)," in Aharon Layish, ed., *The Arabs in Jerusalem: From the Late Ottoman Period to the Beginning of the 1990's—Religious, Social and Cultural Distinctiveness* (Jerusalem: Magnes Press, 1992), 6–42 (in Hebrew).

Chapter 7. Insoluble Religious Disputes Among the Jews

1. This chapter draws heavily on Ira Sharkansky, *Rituals of Conflict: Reli-*

gion, Politics, and Public Policy in Israel (Boulder, Colo.: Lynne Rienner Publishers, 1996).

2. See, for example, Victor Tcherikover, *Hellenistic Civilization and the Jews* (New York: Atheneum, 1959). The First Book of Maccabees portrays the onset of the Maccabean revolt against the Greeks as an attack on Hellenized Jews. Josephus's *The Jewish War* describes the conflict between Jewish Zealots and Romanized Jews that preceded and continued into the period of the rebellion against the Romans in 66–73 C.E.

3. Jacob Neusner, *Death and Birth of Judaism: The Impact of Christianity, Secularism, and the Holocaust on Jewish Faith* (New York: Basic Books, 1987).

4. Jacob Neusner, "Judaism in America: The Social Crisis of Freedom," in Calvin Goldscheider and Jacob Neusner, eds., *Social Foundations of Judaism* (Englewood Cliffs, N.J.: Prentice Hall, 1990), 130–33.

5. Ehud Sprinzak, *The Ascendance of Israel's Radical Right* (New York: Oxford University Press, 1991).

6. For the author's parsing of this and alternative definitions of public policy, see Ira Sharkansky, ed., *Policy Analysis in Political Science* (Chicago: Markham Publishing Company, 1970), chap. 1. For other approaches, see B. Guy Peters, *American Public Policy: Promise and Performance* (Chatham, N.J.: Chatham House, 1993), chap. 1.

7. Murray Edelman, *The Symbolic Uses of Politics* (Urbana: University of Illinois Press, 1964). On the problems involved in classifying issues related to policy disputes, see Deborah A. Stone, *Policy Paradox and Political Reason* (Glenview, Ill.: Scott, Foresman and Company, 1988); Charles E. Lindblom and David K. Cohen, *Usable Knowledge: Social Science and Social Problem Solving* (New Haven: Yale University Press, 1979); and David Dery, *Data and Policy Change* (Boston: Kluwer Academic Publishers, 1990).

8. On the competing allegations about the contribution of Jerusalem's holy sites to that war, see Norman Rich, *Why the Crimean War? A Cautionary Tale* (Hanover, NH: University Press of New England, 1985), and Brison D. Gooch, ed., *The Origins of the Crimean War* (Lexington, Mass.: D.C. Heath, 1969).

9. *Ha'aretz*, 11 August 1996, p. 5 (in Hebrew).

10. *Jerusalem Post*, 21 December 1993, p. 2.

11. *Jerusalem Post*, 24 December 1993, p. 4B.

12. *Jerusalem Post*, 18 May 1990, p. 7.

13. *Ha'aretz*, 9 April 1995, p. 4 (in Hebrew).

14. *Jerusalem Post*, 7 January 1994, p. 4B. For a discussion of nuances among categories of Israeli Jews, see Eliezer Don-Yehiya, "Does Place Make a Difference? Jewish Orthodoxy in Israel and the Diaspora," in Chaim I. Waxman, ed., *Israel as a Religious Reality* (Northvale, N.J.: Jason Aronson, 1994), 43–74.

15. *Jerusalem Statistical Data* (Jerusalem Municipality and the Jerusalem Institute for Israel Studies, 1983), 176; *Statistical Yearbook of Jerusalem, 1992* (Jerusalem: Municipality of Jerusalem and Jerusalem Institute for Israel Studies, 1994), 257.

16. *Ha'Aretz*, 7 March 1995, pp. 8–9 (in Hebrew).

17. Song of Songs 7:5–8. A report on the different responses of the rabbinical members of the Knesset appears in *Ma'ariv*, 21 November 1990 (in Hebrew).

18. 2 Samuel 1:26.

19. *Ha'aretz*, 15 December 1994 (in Hebrew).

20. See 2 Samuel 12:9. For a summary of the rabbinical writings, see Yehuda Kil, *The Book of Samuel: Second Samuel* (Jerusalem: Mossad Harav Kook, 1981), 420 ff. (in Hebrew).

21. *Jerusalem Post*, 10 May 1993, p. 2.

22. *Jerusalem Post*, 3 December 1993, p. 1.

23. *Jerusalem Post*, 12 November 1993, p. 2.

24. *Jerusalem Post*, 27 January 1993, p. 1.

25. *Jerusalem Post*, 9 December 1993, p. 14.

26. *Jerusalem Post*, 17 July 1992, p. 1B.

27. *Jerusalem Post*, 8 February 1993, p. 2.

28. *Jerusalem Post*, 5 February 1993, p. 1.

29. *Jerusalem Post*, 5 February 1993, p. 1.

30. *Jerusalem Post*, 8 February 1993, p. 2.

31. *Ha'aretz*, 19 April 1995, p. 6 (in Hebrew).

32. See Ira Sharkansky, *What Makes Israel Tick? How Domestic Policymakers Cope with Constraints* (Chicago: Nelson Hall, 1985), chap. 4.

33. John C. Green, "The Christian Right and the 1994 Elections: A View from the States." *PS: Political Scence & Politics* 27 (March 1995): 5–8.

34. *Jerusalem Post*, 16 January 1992, p. 1.

35. *Ha'aretz*, 14 April 1995, p. 6 (in Hebrew).

36. David C. Leege and Lyman A. Kellstedt, eds., *Rediscovering the Religious Factor in American Politics* (Armonk, N.Y.: M. E. Sharpe, 1993); Kenneth D. Wald, *Religion and Politics in the United States* (Washington, D.C.: CQ Press, 1992); Stephen D. Johnson and Joseph B. Tamney, eds., *The Political Role of Religion in the United States* (Boulder, Colo.: Westview Press, 1986); Robert Wuthnow, *The Restructuring of American Religion* (Princeton: Princeton University Press, 1988); R. Laurence Moore, *Selling God: American Religion in the Marketplace of Culture* (New York: Oxford University Press, 1994); Michael J. Lacey, ed., *Religion and Twentieth-Century American Intellectual Life* (New York: Cambridge University Press, 1989).

37. Robert A. Campbell and James E. Curtis, "Religious Involvement Across Societies: Analysis for Alternative Measures in National Surveys," *Journal for the Scientific Study of Religion* 33, no. 3 (1994): 215–29.

38. Allen D. Hertzke, *Representing God in Washington: The Role of Religious Lobbies in the American Polity* (Knoxville: University of Tennessee Press, 1988); Leege and Kellstedt, eds., *Rediscovering the Religious Factor in American Politics.*

39. Sprinzak, *Ascendance of Israel's Radical Right.*

40. *Kal Ha'ir*, 12 July 1996, p. 1 (in Hebrew).

Chapter 8. Another Look at Problems, Routines, and Coping Mechanisms

1. For example, Thomas S. Kuhn, *The Structure of Scientific Revolutions* (Chicago: University of Chicago Press, 1970), and Michel Foucault, *Discipline and Punish: The Birth of the Prison,* trans. Alan Sheridan (New York: Vintage

Books, 1979).

2. Michael Lipsky, *Street-Level Bureaucracy: Dilemmas of the Individual in Public Services* (New York: Russell Sage Foundation, 1980).

3. *Oxford English Dictionary.*

4. *Macbeth*, act 5.

Bibliography

Aamiry, M. A. *Jerusalem: Arab Origin and Heritage*. London: Longman, 1978.

Aaron, Henry J., Thomas E. Mann, and Timothy Taylor, eds. *Values and Public Policy*. Washington, D.C.: Brookings Institution, 1994.

Abed, George T. "The Economic Viability of a Palestinian State." *Journal of Palestine Studies* 19, no. 2 (winter 1990): 3–28.

Allison, Graham T. *Essence of Decision: Explaining the Cuban Missile Crisis*. Boston: Little, Brown and Company, 1971.

Amiran, D. H. K. "The Development of Jerusalem, 1860–1979." In David H. K. Amiran, Arie Shachar, and Israel Kimhi, eds., *Urban Geography of Jerusalem: A Companion Volume to the Atlas of Jerusalem* (Jerusalem: Massada Press, 1973).

Anderson, Charles W. "The Logic of Public Problems: Evaluation in Comparative Policy Research." In Ashford, ed., *Comparing Public Policies*, 19–41.

Ashford, Douglas E., ed. *Comparing Public Policies: New Concepts and Methods*. Beverly Hills, 1978.

Ashkenasi, Abraham. "Israeli Policies and Palestinian Fragmentation: Political and Social Impacts in Israel and Jerusalem." Jerusalem: Hebrew University Leonard Davis Institute, 1988.

———. "Opinion Trends Among Jerusalem Palestinians." Jerusalem: Hebrew University Leonard Davis Institute, 1990.

Bailey, Clinton. *Jordan's Palestinian Challenge 1948–1983: A Political History*. Boulder, Colo.: Westview Press, 1984.

Barak, Gregg. "Toward a Criminology of State Criminality." In Barak, ed., *Crimes by the Capitalist State: An Introduction to State Criminality* (Albany: State University of New York Press, 1991), 3–16.

Bar-Joseph, Uri. *The Best of Enemies: Israel and Transjordan in the War of 1948*. London: Frank Cass, 1987.

Ben-Ami, Aharon. *Social Change in a Hostile Environment: The Crusader Kingdom of Jerusalem*. Princeton: Princeton University Press, 1969.

Ben-Arieh, Yehoshua. *Jerusalem in the Nineteenth Century: The Old City*. New York: St. Martin's Press, 1984.

Benvenisti, Meron. *Jerusalem: The Torn City*. Minneapolis: University of Minnesota Press, 1976.

———. *The Shepherds' War: Collected Essays (1981–1989)*. Jerusalem: *Jerusalem Post*, 1989.

———. *The Sling and the Club: Territories, Jews and Arabs*. Jerusalem: Keter, 1988. In Hebrew.

———. *The West Bank Data Project: A Survey of Israel's Policies*. Washington, D.C.: American Enterprise Institute for Policy Research, 1984.

Ben-Yehuda, Nachman. *Political Assassinations by Jews: A Rhetorical Device for Justice*. Albany: State University of New York Press, 1993.

Benziman, Uzi. "Israeli Policy in East Jerusalem After Reunification." In Kraemer, ed., *Jerusalem*, 100–30.

Biale, David. *Power and Powerlessness in Jewish History*. New York: Schocken Books, 1987.

Birnbaum, Jeffrey H., and Alan S. Murray. *Showdown at Gucci Gulch: Lawmakers, Lobbyists, and the Unlikely Triumph of Tax Reform*. New York: Random House, 1987.

Brams, Steven J. *Paradoxes in Politics: An Introduction to the Nonobvious in Political Science*. New York: Free Press, 1976.

———. *Superior Beings: If They Exist, How Would We Know?* New York: Springer-Verlag, 1983.

Braun, Denny. *The Rich Get Richer: The Rise of Income Inequality in the United States and the World*. Chicago: Nelson-Hall, 1991.

Brown, L. Carl. *International Politics and the Middle East: Old Rules, Dangerous Game*. Princeton: Princeton University Press, 1984.

Brown, Thomas. *JFK: History of an Image*. Bloomington: University of Indiana Press, 1988.

Buber, Martin. *Israel and the World: Essays in a Time of Crisis*. New York: Schocken Books, 1963.

Busson, Terry, and Philip Coulter, eds. *Policy Evaluation for Local Government*. Westport, Conn.: Greenwood Press, 1987.

Campbell, Robert A., and James E. Curtis. "Religious Involvement Across Societies: Analysis for Alternative Measures in National Surveys." *Journal for the Scientific Study of Religion* 33, no. 3 (1994): 215–29.

Cantor, Norman F. *The Sacred Chain: The History of the Jews*. New York: Harper Collins, 1994.

Caplan, Gerald, and Ruth B. Caplan. *Arab and Jew in Jerusalem: Explorations in Community Mental Health*. Cambridge: Harvard University Press, 1980.

Caro, Robert A. *The Power Broker: Robert Moses and the Fall of New York City*. New York: Knopf, 1974.

Carter, Luther J. *Nuclear Imperatives and Public Trust: Dealing with Radioactive Waste*. Washington, D.C.: Resources for the Future, 1987.

Chelimsky, Eleanor. *Program Evaluation: Patterns and Directions*. Washington, D.C.: American Society for Public Administration, 1985.

Clausewitz, Karl von. *On War*. London: Penguin Books, 1968 [1833].

Coelho, George V., David A. Hamburg, and John E. Adams, eds., *Coping and Adaptation*. New York: Basic Books, 1974.

Cohen, Erik. "The City in the Zionist Ideology." Jerusalem: Hebrew University Institute of Urban and Regional Studies, 1970.

Cohen, Saul B. *Jerusalem: Bridging the Four Walls—A Geopolitical Perspective*. New York: Herzl Press, 1977.

Cohen, Stuart A. *The Three Crowns: Structures of Communal Politics in Early Rabbinic Jewry.* Cambridge: Cambridge University Press, 1990.

Connolly, William E. *Politics and Ambiguity.* Madison: University of Wisconsin Press, 1987.

Cook, Brian J. *Bureaucratic Politics and Regulatory Reform: The EPA and Emissions Trading.* New York: Greenwood Press, 1988.

Crenshaw, Martha, ed. *Terrorism, Legitimacy, and Power: The Consequences of Political Violence.* Middletown, Conn.: Wesleyan University Press, 1983.

Crozier, Brian A. *Theory of Conflict.* London: Hamish Hamilton, 1974.

Crozier, Michael, Samuel P. Huntington, and Joji Watanuki. *The Crisis of Democracy: Report on the Governability of Democracies to the Trilateral Commission.* New York: New York University Press, 1975.

Dann, Uriel. *King Hussein and the Challenge of Arab Radicalism: Jordan, 1955–1967.* New York: Oxford University Press, 1989.

Davidson, Robert. *The Courage to Doubt: Exploring an Old Testament Theme.* London: SCM Press, 1983.

Day, Arthur R. *East Bank/West Bank: Jordan and the Prospects for Peace.* New York: Council on Foreign Relations, 1986.

Derthick, Martha, and Paul J. Quirk. *The Politics of Deregulation.* Washington, D.C.: Brookings Institution, 1985.

Dery, David. *Data and Policy Change.* Boston: Kluwer Academic Publishers, 1990.

———. *Political Appointments in Israel.* Jerusalem: Israel Democracy Institute, 1993. In Hebrew.

———. *Problem Definition in Policy Analysis.* Lawrence: University of Kansas Press, 1984.

Dery, David, and Binat Schwarz-Milner. *Who Governs Local Government?* Jerusalem: Israeli Institute of Democracy, 1994. In Hebrew.

Don-Yehiya, Eliezer. "Does Place Make a Difference? Jewish Orthodoxy in Israel and the Diaspora." In Chaim I. Waxman, ed., *Israel as a Religious Reality* (Northvale, N.J.: Jason Aronson, 1994), 43–74.

Downs, George W., and Patrick D. Larkey. *The Search for Government Efficiency: From Hubris to Helplessness.* Philadelphia: Temple University Press, 1986.

Drezon-Tepler, Marcia. *Interest Groups and Political Change in Israel.* Albany: State University of New York Press, 1990.

Dror, Yehezkel. *Policymaking Under Adversity.* New Brunswick, N.J.: Transaction Books, 1986.

———. *Public Policymaking Reexamined.* San Francisco: Chandler, 1968.

Edelman, Murray. *The Symbolic Uses of Politics.* Urbana: University of Illinois Press, 1964.

Elazar, Daniel J. "The Book of Joshua as a Political Classic." *Jewish Political Studies Review* 1, nos. 1–2 (1989): 93–150.

Elazar, Daniel J., and Stuart A. Cohen. *The Jewish Polity: Jewish Political Organization from Biblical Times to the Present.* Bloomington: Indiana University Press, 1985.

Elazar, Daniel J., and Chaim Kalchheim, eds. *Local Government in Israel.* Lanham, Md.: University Press of America, 1988.

Feldman, Shai, and Heda Rechnitz-Kijner. *Deception, Consensus and War:*

Israel in Lebanon. Tel Aviv: Tel Aviv University Jaffee Center for Strategic Studies, 1984.

Folkman, Susan. "Personal Control and Stress and Coping Processes: A Theoretical Analysis." *Journal of Personality and Social Psychology* 46 (1984): 839–52.

Foucault, Michel. *Discipline and Punish: The Birth of the Prison*. Translated by Alan Sheridan. New York: Vintage Books, 1979.

Frankel, Jonathan. *Prophecy and Politics: Socialism, Nationalism, and the Russian Jews, 1862–1917*. Cambridge: Cambridge University Press, 1981.

Friedberg, A., et al., eds. *State Audit and Accountability*. Jerusalem: State Comptroller, 1991.

Friedman, Richard Elliott. *Who Wrote the Bible?* New York: Harper and Row, 1987.

Frisch, Hillel. "From Armed Struggle over State Borders to Political Mobilization and Intifada Within It: The Transformation of PLO Strategy in the Territories." *Plural Societies* 19, nos. 2–3 (March 1990): 92–115.

Gabriel, Richard A. *Operation Peace for Galilee: The Israeli-PLO War in Lebanon*. New York: Hill and Wang, 1984.

Gazit, Shlomo. *The Carrot and the Stick: The Israeli Government in Yehuda and Shomron*. Tel Aviv: Zmora, Bitan, 1985. In Hebrew.

Georges-Abeyie, Daniel E. "Piracy, Air Piracy, and Recurrent U.S. and Israeli Civilian Aircraft Interceptions." In Barak, ed., *Crimes by the Capitalist State*, 129–44.

Gerner, Deborah J. *One Land, Two Peoples: The Conflict over Palestine*. Boulder, Colo.: Westview Press, 1991.

Gitelman, Zvi. *Becoming Israelis: Political Resocialization of Soviet and American Immigrants*. New York: Praeger, 1982.

Gitelman, Zvi, ed. *The Quest for Utopia: Jewish Political Ideas and Institutions Through the Ages*. Armonk, N.Y.: M. E. Sharpe, 1992.

Gooch, Brison D., ed. *The Origins of the Crimean War*. Lexington, Mass.: D.C. Heath, 1969.

Goode, Erich. *Drugs in American Society*. New York: McGraw-Hill, 1993.

Gottwald, Norman K. *The Hebrew Bible: A Socio-Literary Introduction*. Philadelphia: Fortress Press, 1985.

———. *The Tribes of Yahweh: A Sociology of the Religion of Liberated Israel, 1250–1050 BCE*. Maryknoll, N.Y.: Orbis Books, 1979.

Gradus, Y. "The Emergence of Regionalism in a Centralized System: The Case of Israel." *Environment and Planning D: Society and Space* 2 (1984): 87–100.

Green, John C. "The Christian Right and the 1994 Elections: A View from the States." *PS: Political Scence & Politics* 27 (March 1995): 5–8.

Grossman, David. *Present Absentees*. Tel Aviv: Kibbutz Meuchad, 1992. In Hebrew.

———. *The Yellow Wind*. Translated by Haim Watzman. London: Jonathan Cape, 1988.

Gruber, Judith E. *Controlling Bureaucracies: Dilemmas in Democratic Governance*. Berkeley: University of California Press, 1987.

Halabi, Rafik. *The West Bank Story: An Israeli Arab's View of Both Sides of a Tangled Conflict*. Translated by Ina Friedman. New York: Harcourt Brace Jovanovich, 1981.

Harkabi, Yehoshafat. *The Bar Kokhba Syndrome: Risk and Realism in International Relations*. Translated by Max D. Ticktin and edited by David Altshuler. Chappaqua, N.Y.: Rossel Books, 1983.

———. *Israel's Fateful Hour*. Translated by Lenn Schramm. New York: Harper & Row, 1988.

Hart, Paul. *Groupthink in Government: A Study of Small Groups and Policy Failure*. Baltimore: Johns Hopkins University Press, 1994.

Hasson, Shlomo. *Urban Social Movements in Jerusalem: The Protest of the Second Generation*. Albany: State University of New York Press, 1993.

Hawkesworth, M. E. *Theoretical Issues in Policy Analysis*. Albany: State University of New York Press, 1988.

Hersh, Seymour M. *The Price of Power: Kissinger in the Nixon White House*. New York: Summit Books, 1983.

Herson, Lawrence J. R., and John M. Bolland. *The Urban Web: Politics, Policy, and Theory*. Chicago: Nelson-Hall, 1990.

Hertzke, Allen D. *Representing God in Washington: The Role of Religious Lobbies in the American Polity*. Knoxville: University of Tennessee Press, 1988.

Hofnung, Menachem. *Israel—State Security Against the Rule of Law 1948–1991*. Jerusalem: Nevo Publisher, 1991. In Hebrew.

Horowitz, Dan, and Moshe Lissak. *Trouble in Utopia: The Overburdened Polity of Israel*. Albany: State University of New York Press, 1989.

Horowitz, Tamar, ed. *The Soviet Man in an Open Society*. Lanham, Md.: University Press Of America, 1989.

Hunter, Robert F. *The Palestinian Uprising: A War by Other Means*. Berkeley: University of California Press, 1993.

Ingram, Helen, and Steven Rathgeb Smith, eds. *Public Policy for Democracy*. Washington, D.C.: Brookings Institution, 1993.

Islamic Council of Europe. *Jerusalem: The Key to World Peace*. London: Islamic Council of Europe, 1980.

Israel 2020: A Master Plan for Israel in the Twenty-first Century. Haifa: Technion–Israel Institute of Technology, 1993. In Hebrew.

Jacob, Herbert. *The Frustration of Policy: Responses to Crime by American Cities*. Boston: Little, Brown, 1984.

Janis, Irving L. *Groupthink: Psychological Studies of Policy Decisions and Fiascoes*. Boston: Houghton Mifflin Company, 1983.

Janowitz, Morris. *Social Control of the Welfare State*. New York: Elsevier, 1976.

Johnson, Paul. *A History of Christianity*. New York: Atheneum, 1976.

Johnson, Stephen D., and Joseph B. Tamney, eds. *The Political Role of Religion in the United States*. Boulder, Colo.: Westview Press, 1986.

Jones, Bryan D. *Governing Buildings and Building Government: A New Perspective on the Old Party*. University, AL: University of Alabama Press, 1985.

Jones, Charles O., ed. *The Reagan Legacy: Promise and Performance*. Chatham, N.J.: Chatham House, 1988.

Kalchheim, Chaim. "The Division of Functions and the Interrelationships Between Local and State Authorities." In Elazar and Kalchheim, eds., *Local Government in Israel*, 41–82.

Karsh, Efraim. "Rewriting Israel's History." *Middle East Quarterly*, June 1996, 19–29.

Katzmann, Robert A. *Institutional Disability: The Saga of Transportation Policy for the Disabled.* Washington, D.C.: Brookings Institution, 1986.

Keren, Michael. *Ben-Gurion and the Intellectuals: Power, Knowledge, and Charisma.* Dekalb: Northern Illinois University Press, 1983.

Kettl, Donald F. *Government by Proxy: (Mis?)Managing Federal Programs.* Washington, D.C.: CQ Press, 1988.

Key, V. O., Jr. "The Lack of a Budgetary Theory." *American Political Science Review* 34 (December 1940): 1137–44.

Khalidi, Walid. *From Haven to Conquest: Readings in Zionism and the Palestine Problem Until 1948.* Beirut: Institute for Palestine Studies, 1971.

Kieval, Gershon R. *Party Politics in Israel and the Occupied Territories.* Westport, Conn.: Greenwood Press, 1983.

Kil, Yehuda. *The Book of Samuel: Second Samuel.* Jerusalem: Mossad Harav Kook, 1981. In Hebrew.

Kimhi, Israel, Shalom Reichman, and Joseph Schweid. "Arab Settlement in the Metropolitan Area of Jerusalem." Jerusalem: Jerusalem Institute for Israel Studies, 1986. In Hebrew.

———. "The Metropolitan Area of Jerusalem." Jerusalem: Jerusalem Institute for Israel Studies, 1984. In Hebrew.

Kimmerling, Baruch, ed. *The Israeli State and Society: Boundaries and Frontiers.* Albany: State University of New York Press, 1989.

King, Gary, Robert O. Keohane, and Sidney Verba. *Designing Social Inquiry: Scientific Inference in Qualitative Research.* Princeton: Princeton University Press, 1994.

Kipnis, Baruch A. "Metropolitan Processes: Their Impact on Regional Development Strategies Along Israel's Urbanized Coastal Plain." *Journal of Agricultural and Planning Research* 1(1984): 191–207.

Kirby, Andrew. *Power/Resistance: Local Politics and the Chaotic State.* Bloomington: Indiana University Press, 1993.

Kollek, Teddy, and Amos Kollek. *For Jerusalem: A Life.* New York: Random House, 1978.

Kraemer, Joel L., ed. *Jerusalem: Problems and Prospects.* New York: Praeger, 1980.

Kuhn, Thomas S. *The Structure of Scientific Revolutions.* Chicago: University of Chicago Press, 1970.

Lacey, Michael J., ed. *Religion and Twentieth-Century American Intellectual Life.* New York: Cambridge University Press, 1989.

Lacey, Robert. *Little Man: Meyer Lansky and the Gangster Life.* Boston: Little, Brown, 1991.

Lanir, Zvi. "Political Aims and Military Objectives—Some Observations on the Israeli Experience." In Saul Cohen, ed., *Israeli Security Planning in the 1980's* (New York: Praeger, 1984), 14–49.

Lasswell, Harold D. *Who Gets What, When, How?* New York: McGraw-Hill, 1936.

Lazin, Frederick A. *Policy Implementation and Social Welfare: Israel and the United States.* New Brunswick, N.J.: Transaction Books, 1986.

Lederhandler, Eli. *The Road to Modern Jewish Politics: Political Tradition and Political Reconstruction in the Jewish Community of Tsarist Russia.* New York: Oxford University Press, 1989.

Leege, David C., and Lyman A. Kellstedt, eds. *Rediscovering the Religious Factor in American Politics.* Armonk, N.Y.: M. E. Sharpe, 1993.

Lehman-Wilzig, Sam. *Stiff-necked People, Bottle-necked System: The Evolution and Roots of Israeli Public Protest, 1949–1986.* Bloomington: Indiana University Press, 1991.

Leibowitz, Yeshayahu. *On Just About Everything: Talks with Michael Shashar.* Jerusalem: Keter, 1988. In Hebrew.

Lijphart, Arend. *Democracies: Patterns of Majoritarian and Consensus Government in Twenty-one Countries.* New Haven: Yale University Press, 1984.

Lindblom, Charles E. *The Policy-making Process.* Englewood Cliffs, N.J.: Prentice-Hall, 1968.

Lindblom, Charles E., and David K. Cohen. *Usable Knowledge: Social Science and Social Problem Solving.* New Haven: Yale University Press, 1979.

Lipsky, Michael. *Street-Level Bureaucracy: Dilemmas of the Individual in Public Services.* New York: Russell Sage Foundation, 1980.

Lowi, Theodore. *The End of Liberalism.* New York: Norton, 1979.

Luker, Kristen. *Abortion and the Politics of Motherhood.* Berkeley: University of California Press, 1984.

Medding, Peter Y. *The Founding of Israeli Democracy 1948–1967.* New York: Oxford University Press, 1990.

Mendelsohn, Ezra. *On Modern Jewish Politics.* New York: Oxford University Press, 1993.

Moore, Charles H., and Patricia A. Hoban-Moore. "Some Lessons From Reagan's HUD: Housing Policy and Public Service." *PS: Political Science and Politics* 23 (March 1990): 13–18.

Moore, R. Laurence. *Selling God: American Religion in the Marketplace of Culture.* New York: Oxford University Press, 1994.

Moos, Rudolf H., and Jeanne A. Schaefer. "Life Transitions and Crises: A Conceptual Overview." In Moos and Schaefer, eds., *Coping with Life Crises: An Integrated Approach* (New York: Plenum Press, 1986), 3–28.

Nader, Ralph. *Unsafe at Any Speed.* New York: Grossman, 1972.

Near, Henry, ed. *The Seventh Day.* London: Andre Deutsch, 1970.

Neusner, Jacob. *Death and Birth of Judaism: The Impact of Christianity, Secularism, and the Holocaust on Jewish Faith.* New York: Basic Books, 1987.

———. "Judaism in America: The Social Crisis of Freedom." In Calvin Goldscheider and Jacob Neusner, eds., *Social Foundations of Judaism* (Englewood Cliffs, N.J.: Prentice Hall, 1990), 130–33.

Neustadt, Richard E., and Ernest R. May. *Thinking in Time: The Uses of History for Decision Makers.* New York: Free Press, 1986.

Noble, Charles. *Liberalism at Work: The Rise and Fall of OSHA.* Philadelphia: Temple University Press, 1986.

O'Brien, Conor Cruise. *The Siege: The Saga of Israel and Zionism.* New York: Simon and Schuster, 1987.

O'Brien, William V. *Law and Morality in Israel's War with the PLO.* New York: Routledge, 1991.

Oz, Amos. *A Journey in Israel: Autumn 1982.* Tel Aviv: Am Oved, 1986. In Hebrew.

Penchansky, David. *The Betrayal of God: Ideological Conflict in Job.* Louisville, KY: Westminster/John Knox Press, 1990.

Peri, Yoram. *Between Battles and Ballots: Israeli Military in Politics*. Cambridge: Cambridge University Press, 1983.

Peters, B. Guy. *American Public Policy: Promise and Performance*. Chatham, N.J.: Chatham House, 1993.

Peters, F. E. *Jerusalem: The Holy City in the Eyes of Chroniclers, Visitors, Pilgrims, and Prophets from the Days of Abraham to the Beginnings of Modern Times*. Princeton: Princeton University Press, 1985.

Peters, Joan. *From Time Immemorial*. New York: Harper & Row, 1984.

Peterson, Paul E. *City Limits*. Chicago: University of Chicago Press, 1981.

Piller, Charles. *The Fail-safe Society: Community Defiance and the End of Technological Optimism*. New York: Basic Books, 1991.

Powell, G. Bingham, Jr. *Contemporary Democracies: Participation, Stability, and Violence*. Cambridge: Harvard University Press, 1982.

Pressman, Jeffrey L., and Aaron Wildavsky. *Implementation*. Berkeley: University of California Press, 1973.

Prittie, Terrence. *Whose Jerusalem?* London: Frederick Muller, 1981.

Quade, E. S., and Grace M. Carter. *Analysis for Public Decisions*. New York: North-Holland, 1989.

Rabinovitch, Itamar. *The War for Lebanon: 1970–1985*. Ithaca: Cornell University Press, 1984.

Ravi, Zion. "Emigration from Israel, 1948–84." *Ha'aretz*, 5–6 January 1986. In Hebrew.

Razin, E. "Metropolitan Reform in the Tel Aviv Metropolis: Metropolitan Government or Metropolitan Cooperation?" *Environment and Planning C: Government and Policy* 14 (1996): 39–54.

Regens, James L., and Robert W. Rycroft. *The Acid Rain Controversy*. Pittsburgh: University of Pittsburgh Press, 1988.

Rein, Martin Goesta Esping-Andersen, and Lee Rainwater, eds. *Stagnation and Renewal in Social Policy: The Rise and Fall of Policy Regimes*. Armonk, N.Y.: M. E. Sharpe, 1987.

Reuveni, Ya'acov. *Public Administration in Israel: The Government System in Israel and Its Development During the Years 1948–73*. Ramat Gan: Massada Press, 1974. In Hebrew.

Rich, Norman. *Why the Crimean War? A Cautionary Tale*. Hanover, N.H.: University Press of New England, 1985.

Richard, Jean. *The Latin Kingdom of Jerusalem*. Translated by Janet Shirly. Amsterdam: North Holland, 1979.

Roelofs, H. Mark. "Hebraic-Biblical Political Thinking." *Polity* 20 (summer 1988): 572–97.

———. "Liberation Theology: The Recovery of Biblical Radicalism." *American Political Science Review* 82, no. 2 (June 1988): 549–66.

Romann, Michael, and Alex Weingrod. *Living Together Separately: Arabs and Jews in Contemporary Jerusalem*. Princeton: Princeton University Press, 1991.

Rubinstein, Daniel. "The Jerusalem Municipality Under the Ottomans, British, and Jordanians." In Kraemer, ed., *Jerusalem*, 72–99.

Safire, William. *The First Dissident: The Book of Job in Today's Politics*. New York: Random House, 1992.

Said, Edward W. "Reflections on Twenty Years of Palestinian History." *Journal of Palestine Studies* 20, no. 4 (summer 1991): 5–22.

Satloff, Robert B. *Troubles on the East Bank: Challenges to the Domestic Stability of Jordan.* New York: Praeger, 1986.

Schiff, Ze'ev, and Ehud Ya'ari. *Intifada.* Tel Aviv: Schocken Books, 1990. In Hebrew.

———. *Israel's Lebanon War.* Edited and translated by Ina Friedman. New York: Simon and Schuster, 1984.

Schmelz, U.O. "Jerusalem's Arab Population Since the Mandatory Period (1918–1990)." In Aharon Layish, ed., *The Arabs in Jerusalem: From the Late Ottoman Period to the Beginning of the 1990's—Religious, Social and Cultural Distinctiveness* (Jerusalem: Magnes Press, 1992), 6-42. In Hebrew.

Scholem, Gershom. *Sabbatei Sevi: The Mystical Messiah.* Translated by R. J. Zwi Werblowsky. Princeton: Princeton University Press, 1973.

Seale, Patrick. *Asad: The Struggle for the Middle East.* Berkeley: University of California Press, 1988.

Segal, Ronald. *Whose Jerusalem? The Conflicts of Israel.* London: Jonathan Cape, 1973.

Shalev, Michael. *Labour and the Political Economy in Israel.* New York: Oxford University Press, 1992.

Sharkansky, Ira. "Coping Strategies of Engagement and Avoidance: The Case of Jerusalem." *Policy and Politics* 23 (April 1995): 91–102.

———. *Governing Jerusalem: Again on the World's Agenda.* Detroit: Wayne State University Press, 1996.

———. *Israel and Its Bible.* New York: Garland, 1996.

———. "Israeli Civil Service Positions Open to Political Appointments." *International Journal of Public Administration* 12 (1989): 731–48.

———. *The Political Economy of Israel.* New Brunswick, N.J.: Transaction Books, 1987.

———. *Rituals of Conflict: Religion, Politics, and Public Policy in Israel.* Boulder, Colo.: Lynne Rienner Publishers, 1996.

———. *The Routines of Politics.* New York: Van Nostrand, 1970.

———. *What Makes Israel Tick? How Domestic Policy-makers Cope with Constraints.* Chicago: Nelson-Hall, 1985.

Sharkansky, Ira, ed. *Policy Analysis in Political Science.* Chicago: Markham, 1970.

Shlaim, Avi. *Collusion Across the Jordan: King Abdullah, the Zionist Movement, and the Partition of Palestine.* New York: Columbia University Press, 1988.

Sick, Gary. *All Fall Down: America's Tragic Encounter with Iran.* New York: Penguin Books, 1986.

Simon, Herbert. *Administrative Behavior.* New York: Free Press, 1976.

Smith, V. Kerry. *Environmental Policy Under Reagan's Executive Order: The Role of Cost-Benefit Analysis.* Chapel Hill: University of North Carolina Press, 1984.

Smooha, Sammy. *Arabs and Jews in Israel: Conflicting and Shared Attitudes in a Divided Society.* Boulder, Colo.: Westview Press, 1989.

Sneeding, Timothy M., Michael O'Higgins, and Lee Rainwater, eds. *Poverty,*

Inequality and Income Distribution in Comparative Perspective: The Luxembourg Income Study (LIS). New York: Harvester Wheatsheaf, 1993.

Sprinzak, Ehud. *The Ascendance of Israel's Radical Right*. New York: Oxford University Press, 1991.

Steiner, Gilbert Y. *Constitutional Inequality: The Political Fortunes of the Equal Rights Amendment*. Washington, D.C.: Brookings Institution, 1985.

Sternhell, Ze'ev. *Nation Building or a New Society? The Zionist Labor Movement (1904–1940) and the Origins of Israel*. Tel Aviv: Am Oved, 1995. In Hebrew.

Stockman, David A. *The Triumph of Politics: The Inside Story of the Reagan Administration*. New York: Avon, 1987.

Stone, Deborah A. *Policy Paradox and Political Reason*. Glenview, Ill.: Scott, Foresman and Company, 1988.

Sundquist, James L. *Constitutional Reform and Effective Government*. Washington, D.C.: Brookings Institution, 1985.

Tapp, Jack T. "Multisystems Holistic Model of Health, Stress and Coping." In Tiffany M. Field, Philip M. McCabe, and Neil Schneiderman, eds., *Stress and Coping* (Hillsdale, N.J.: Lawrence Erlbaum Associates, 1985), 285–304.

Tcherikover, Victor. *Hellenistic Civilization and the Jews*. New York: Atheneum, 1959.

Teune, Henry. "A Logic of Comparative Policy Analysis." In Ashford, ed., *Comparing Public Policies*, 43–55.

Tsimhoni, Daphne. "Continuity and Change in Communal Autonomy: The Christian Communal Organizations in Jerusalem, 1948–1980." *Middle East Studies* 22 (July 1986): 398–417.

Tuchman, Barbara W. *The March of Folly: From Troy to Vietnam*. New York: Ballantine Books, 1984.

Vickers, Geoffrey. *Value Systems and Social Process*. Harmondsworth: Penguin Books, 1970.

Vos, Howard F. *Ezra, Nehemiah, and Esther*. Grand Rapids, Mich.: Zondervan, 1987.

Wald, Kenneth D. *Religion and Politics in the United States*. Washington, D.C.: CQ Press, 1992.

Walzer, Michael. *Exodus and Revolution*. New York: Basic Books, 1985.

Welch, Susan, and Timothy Bledsoe. *Urban Reform and Its Consequences: A Study in Representation*. Chicago: University of Chicago Press, 1988.

Westheimer, Ruth Karola. *Surviving Salvation: The Ethiopian Jewish Family in Transition*. New York: New York University Press, 1992.

Wildavsky, Aaron. *The Nursing Father: Moses as a Political Leader*. University, AL: University of Alabama Press, 1984.

———. *Speaking Truth to Power: The Art and Craft of Policy Analysis*. Boston: Little, Brown, 1979.

Wilson, James Q. "Why Reagan Won and Stockman Lost." *Commentary* 82, no. 2 (August 1986): 17–21.

Wolfsfeld, Gadi. *The Politics of Provocation*. Albany: State University of New York Press, 1988.

Wright, Kevin N. *The Great American Crime Myth*. Westport, Conn.: Greenwood Press, 1985.

Wuthnow, Robert. *The Restructuring of American Religion.* Princeton: Princeton University Press, 1988.

Yaniv, Avner, ed. *National Security and Democracy in Israel.* Boulder, Colo.: Lynne Rienner Publishers, 1993.

Yehoshua, A.B. "The Golah as a Neurotic Solution." *Forum: On the Jewish People, Zionism and Israel* 35 (spring/summer 1979): 17–36.

Yishai, Yael. *Interest Groups in Israel.* Tel Aviv: Am Oved, 1987. In Hebrew.

Zureik, Elia. "Prospects of the Palestinians in Israel—I." *Journal of Palestine Studies* 22, no. 2 (winter 1993): 90–109.

Index